Foucault's Last Decade

Stuart Elden

polity

First published in 2016 by Polity Press

Polity Press
65 Bridge Street
Cambridge CB2 1UR, UK

Polity Press
350 Main Street
Malden, MA 02148, USA

ISBN-13: 978-0-7456-8391-1 (hardback)
ISBN-13: 978-0-7456-8392-8 (paperback)

A catalogue record for this book is available from the British Library.

Library of Congress Cataloging-in-Publication Data

Names: Elden, Stuart, 1971-
Title: Foucault's last decade / Stuart Elden.
Description: Malden, MA : Polity, April 2016. | Includes bibliographical references and index.
Identifiers: LCCN 2015032601 | ISBN 9780745683911 (hardback) | ISBN 9780745683928 (pbk.)
Subjects: LCSH: Foucault, Michel, 1926–1984.
Classification: LCC B2430.F724 E43 2016 | DDC 194–dc23 LC record available at http://lccn.loc.gov/2015032601

Typeset in 10.5 on 12 pt Sabon
by Toppan Best-set Premedia Limited
Printed and bound in Great Britain by Clays, Ltd, St Ives PLC.

For further information on Polity, visit our website: politybooks.com

Foucault's Last Decade

Contents

Acknowledgements

The initial impetus to work on Foucault's lecture courses came from Paul Bové, who asked me to write a review essay of *Les Anormaux* for the journal he edits, *boundary 2*, and then invited me to the University of Pittsburgh in 2001 where I spoke about «*Il faut défendre la société*». Over the next several years, I wrote talks about, reviews of, or articles on each of the lecture courses as they came out, some of which I published, with the aim of eventually reworking them and bringing them together into a book. The text you are now reading is a much amended and transformed version of that initial idea. I am grateful for the enthusiasm of friends for this project, especially Ben Anderson, Neil Brenner, Sharon Cowan, Jeremy Crampton, Mick Dillon, Sophie Fuggle, Ben Golder, Colin Gordon, Peter Gratton, Bernard Harcourt, Laurence Paul Hemming, Jean Hillier, Alex Jeffrey, Morris Kaplan, Mark Kelly, Léopold Lambert, Stephen Legg, Eduardo Mendieta, Catherine Mills, Adam David Morton, Clare O'Farrell, Chris Philo, Sverre Raffnsøe, Alison Ross, Stephen Shapiro, Alex Vasudevan, Nick Vaughan-Williams and Michael Watts. Eduardo carefully read the entire manuscript and made many useful comments. Many readers of my Progressive Geographies blog followed this project and I am grateful for their interest. Some resources produced during this work are available at www .progressivegeographies.com/resources/foucault-resources.

The department of Politics and International Studies and the Humanities Research Centre at University of Warwick helped with funds for archive visits. At Polity Press, Emma Hutchinson understood the project and saw the proposal through to contract; John

Thompson and Pascal Porcheron were supportive of its changing shape; and the reports from three anonymous readers helped to sharpen the overall argument as well as improve many points of detail. Susan Beer did an excellent job copy-editing the text, and Lisa Scholey compiled the index.

I have lectured on Foucault's work in a number of institutions over several years, and am grateful to audiences in Australia (University of Melbourne; Monash University; University of Sydney; University of Tasmania); Canada (Memorial University, Newfoundland); France (Abbaye d'Ardenne, Caen); Sweden (University of Stockholm); Italy (University of Palermo; Monash University, Prato Centre); United Kingdom (Aberystwyth University; Bath Royal Literary and Scientific Institution; Birkbeck University; Durham University; University of East London; King's College London; University of Lancaster; University of Leeds; University of Leicester; University of Manchester; Nottingham Contemporary Gallery; St Catherine's Foundation; Staffordshire University); and the United States of America (American Political Science Association conference, San Francisco; University of Arizona; University of California, Berkeley; University of Pittsburgh; Purchase College, State University of New York).

I am grateful to the staff at the British Library, the Institut Mémoires de l'édition contemporaine (IMEC), the Bancroft library at University of California, Berkeley, the Bibliothèque Nationale de France, Bibliothèque et Archives nationales du Québec, State Library of Victoria, and the libraries of the University of Warwick, Durham University, Columbia University, Cornell University, Monash University, University of Melbourne, and New York University. James Bernauer, Dario Biocca, Mark Blasius, Peter Brown, Jeremy Carrette, Arnold I. Davidson, Arturo Escobar, Keith Gandal, Colin Gordon, Bernard Harcourt, David Horn, David Levin, Sylvère Lotringer, Mark Maslan, Michael Meranze, James Miller, Joseph Pearson, Paul Rabinow, Jamin Raskin, Jonathan Simon and Jerry Wakefield kindly answered questions in person or by correspondence. Several of those already mentioned, plus Natalie B (@160B), Sebastian Budgen, Graham Burchell, Michael Eldred, Mikkel Ibsen, Yoav Kenny, Patricia Lopez, Jacob Lunding, Ted Stolze, Andrea Teti and Philippe Theophanidis helped with getting hold of texts or recordings. I am especially grateful to Daniel Defert for his kindness over the years and a lengthy conversation in Paris in April 2015.

Parts of Chapter 1 first appeared in 'The Constitution of the Normal: Monsters and Masturbation at the *Collège de France*', *boundary* 2, 28 (1), Spring 2001: 91–105. An earlier version of Chapter 2 appeared as 'The War of Races and the Constitution of the State: Foucault's «*Il faut défendre la société*» and the Politics of Calculation', *boundary* 2, 29 (1), Spring 2002: 125–51. Both are reprinted with permission of Duke University Press. Some of the overall argument was first presented as 'The Problem of Confession: The Productive Failure of Foucault's "History of Sexuality" ', *Journal for Cultural Research*, 9 (1), 2009: 23–41. Parts are reprinted by permission of Taylor and Francis.

As ever my greatest debt is to Susan for her love and support.

Abbreviations

To ease reference, key texts are referred to by abbreviations. For texts where one book is translated in a single book, such as the lecture courses, the French page number is given first, followed by the English after a slash. So PP 105/103 would refer to the lecture course *Le pouvoir psychiatrique*, p. 105 in the French text, and p. 103 in the English translation *Psychiatric Power*. I have frequently modified existing translations.

In the text, English titles are used for books available in translation; French for untranslated works or unpublished manuscripts, though an English translation of the title is provided the first time they are used.

A   *Les Anormaux: Cours au Collège de France (1974–5)*, eds. Valerio Marchetti and Antonella Salomoni, Paris: Seuil/Gallimard, 1999; trans. Graham Burchell as *Abnormal: Lectures at the Collège de France 1974–5*, London: Verso, 2003.

ABHS   'About the Beginning of the Hermeneutic of the Self: Two Lectures at Dartmouth', ed. Mark Blasius, *Political Theory*, 21 (2), 1993: 198–227.

BB   *Naissance de la biopolitique: Cours au Collège de France (1978–9)*, ed. Michel Senellart, Paris: Seuil/Gallimard, 2004; trans. Graham Burchell as *The Birth of Biopolitics: Lectures at the Collège de France 1978–9*, London: Palgrave, 2008.

C   Daniel Defert, 'Chronologie', in *Dits et écrits 1954–88*, eds. Daniel Defert and François Ewald, Paris: Gallimard, 4 vols., 1994, vol. I, pp. 13–64; trans. Timothy O'Leary in Christopher Falzon, Timothy O'Leary and Jana Sawicki (eds.) *A Companion to Foucault*, Oxford: Blackwell, 2013, pp. 11–83.

CMPP   'Considérations sur le marxisme, la phénoménologie et le pouvoir: Entretien avec Colin Gordon et Paul Patton', *Cités*, 52, 2012: 101–26; trans. as Michel Foucault, Colin Gordon, and Paul Patton, 'Considerations on Marxism, Phenomenology and Power. Interview with Michel Foucault; Recorded on April 3rd, 1978', *Foucault Studies*, 14, September 2012: 98–114.

CT   *Le courage de la vérité: Le gouvernement des soi et des autres II: Cours au Collège de France*, ed. Frédéric Gros, Paris: Gallimard/Seuil; trans. Graham Burchell as *The Courage of Truth (The Government of the Self and Others II): Lectures at the Collège de France 1983–4*, London: Palgrave, 2011.

DE   *Dits et écrits 1954–88*, eds. Daniel Defert and François Ewald, Paris: Gallimard, 4 vols., 1994 – with reference to volume number, and also includes text number for ease of reference to the two editions of this text and to bibliographies of English translations.[1] Thus 'DE#81 II, 99–104' means text 81, in vol. II, pp. 99–104.

DF   Arlette Farge and Michel Foucault, *Le désordre des familles: Lettres de cachet des Archives de la Bastille au XVIIIe siècle*, Paris: Julliard/Gallimard, 1982.

DP   *Surveiller et punir – Naissance de la prison*, Paris: Gallimard, 1975; trans. Alan Sheridan as *Discipline and Punish: The Birth of the Prison*, London: Penguin, 1976.

E   Roger-Pol Droit, *Michel Foucault, Entretiens*, Odile Jacob, Paris, 2004.

EW   *Essential Works*, eds. Paul Rabinow and James Faubion, trans. Robert Hurley and others, London: Allen Lane, 3 vols., 1997–2000.

FL   *Foucault Live: Interviews 1961–84*, ed. Sylvère Lotringer, New York: Semiotext[e], 1996.

GSO   *Le gouvernement de soi et des autres: Cours au Collège de France 1982–3*, ed. Frédéric Gros, Paris: Gallimard/Seuil; trans. Graham Burchell as *The Government of the Self and Others: Lectures at the Collège de France 1982–3*, London: Palgrave, 2010.

GL   *Du gouvernement des vivants: Cours au Collège de France 1979–80*, ed. Michel Senellart, Paris: Gallimard/Seuil, 2012; trans. Graham Burchell as *On the Government of the Living: Lectures at the Collège de France 1979–80*, London: Palgrave, 2014.

HB   *Herculine Barbin dite Alexina B*, Paris: Gallimard, 1978; trans. Richard McDougall as *Herculine Barbin: Being the Recently Discovered Memoirs of a Nineteenth Century Hermaphrodite*, New York: Pantheon, 1980.

HS I   *Histoire de la sexualité I: La Volonté de savoir*, Paris: Gallimard, 1976; trans. Robert Hurley as *The History of Sexuality I: The Will to Knowledge*, London: Penguin, 1978.

HS II   *Histoire de la sexualité II: L'Usage des plaisirs*, Paris: Gallimard, 1984; *The History of Sexuality Volume II: The Use of Pleasure*, trans. Robert Hurley, London: Penguin, 1985.

HS III *Histoire de la sexualité III: Le Souci de soi*, Paris: Gallimard, 1984; *The History of Sexuality Volume III: The Care of the Self*, trans. Robert Hurley, London: Penguin, 1986.

HSu   *L'Herméneutique du sujet: Cours au Collège de France (1981–2)*, ed. Frédéric Gros, Paris: Gallimard/Seuil, 2001; trans. Graham Burchell as *The Hermeneutics of the Subject: Lectures at the Collège de France*, London: Palgrave, 2005.

MG   Michel Foucault, Blandine Barret-Kriegel, Anne Thalamy, François Béguin and Bruno Fortier, *Les machines à guérir (aux origines de l'hôpital moderne)*, Bruxelles: Pierre Mardaga, revised edn 1979 (original edn, Paris: Institut de l'environnement, 1976).

OHS   *L'origine de l'herméneutique de soi: Conférences prononcées à Dartmouth College, 1980*, eds. Henri-Paul Fruchaud and Daniele Lorenzini, Paris: Vrin, 2013.

P/K   *Power/Knowledge: Selected Interviews and Other Writings 1972–7*, ed. Colin Gordon, Brighton: Harvester, 1980.

PP   *Le pouvoir psychiatrique: Cours au Collège de France (1973–4)*, ed. Jacques Lagrange, Paris: Seuil/Gallimard, 2003; trans. Graham Burchell as *Psychiatric Power: Lectures at the Collège de France 1973–4*, London: Palgrave, 2006.

PPC   *Politics, Philosophy, Culture: Interviews and Other Writings 1977–84*, ed. Lawrence D. Kritzman, London: Routledge, 1990.

QC   *Qu'est-ce que la critique? Suivi de la culture de soi*, eds. Henri-Paul Fruchaud and Daniele Lorenzini, Paris: Vrin, 2015.

RC   *Religion and Culture*, ed. Jeremy R. Carrette, London: Routledge, 1999.

SMBD   *«Il faut défendre la société»: Cours au Collège de France (1975–6)*, eds. Mauro Bertani and Alessandro Fontana, Paris: Seuil/Gallimard, 1997; trans. David Macey as '*Society Must Be Defended*', London: Allen Lane, 2003.

SP   *La société punitive: Cours au Collège de France (1972–3)*, ed. Bernard E. Harcourt, Paris: Gallimard/Seuil, 2013.

SKP   *Space, Knowledge and Power: Foucault and Geography*, eds. Jeremy W. Crampton and Stuart Elden, Aldershot: Ashgate, 2007.

STP   *Sécurité, Territoire, Population: Cours au Collège de France (1977–8)*, ed. Michel Senellart, Paris: Seuil/Gallimard, 2004; trans. Graham Burchell as *Security, Territory, Population: Lectures at the Collège de France 1977–8*, London: Palgrave, 2008.

SV   *Subjectivité et vérité: Cours au Collège de France, 1980–1*, ed. Frédéric Gros, Paris: Gallimard/Seuil.

WDTT   *Mal faire, dire vrai: Le function de l'aveu en justice*, eds. Fabienne Brion and Bernard E. Harcourt, Louvain-la-Neuve, Presses Universitaires de Louvain, 2012; trans. Stephen W. Sawyer as *Wrong-Doing, Truth-Telling: The Function of Avowal in Justice*, Chicago: University of Chicago Press, 2014.

Archival material

BANC   Manuscripts and tapes, Bancroft library, University of California, Berkeley.[2]

BNF   Archives et Manuscrits, Bibliothèque Nationale de France, Paris

IMEC   Fonds Michel Foucault, l'Institut Mémoires de l'édition contemporaine, l'abbaye d'Ardenne, Caen (formerly in Paris), http://www.imec-archives.com/

Catalogue numbers follow the archive abbreviation.

Other Texts

Classical texts are referred to by the usual conventions. I have generally used the bi-lingual editions in the Loeb library.

For the early Church Fathers, I have used J. P. Migne (ed.), *Patrologia Graeca*, Imprimerie Catholique, 161 vols., 1857–66; J. P. Migne (ed.), *Patrologica Latina*, Paris: Imprimerie Catholique, 217 vols., 1841–55 and *A Select Library of Nicene and Post-Nicene Fathers of the Christian Church*, eds. Philip Schaff and Henry Wace (series II), T&T Clark: Edinburgh, 14 vols., 1886–1900.

Note

Foucault and his editors are inconsistent in transliteration of Greek terms. I have tried to be consistent, and amended translations accordingly. The key changes are *tekhnē* instead of *techne*, *khrēsis* not *chrēsis*, *kharis* not *charis*, *parrēsia* not *parrhēsia*.

Introduction

On 26 August 1974, Michel Foucault completed work on *Discipline and Punish*, and on that very same day began writing the first volume of the *History of Sexuality*.[1] A little under ten years later, on 25 June 1984, shortly after the second and third volumes were published, he was dead.

This decade, the focus of this book, is one of the most fascinating in Foucault's career. It begins with the initiation of the sexuality project, and ends with its enforced and premature closure. Yet, in 1974, as he was writing the first lines of the first volume, he had something very different in mind from the way things were left in 1984. The introductory volume, uniquely among his studies, makes a number of assurances concerning what was to come. But Foucault wrote little of what was promised and published nothing. Instead he took his work in very different directions, studied and wrote about texts he had never even mentioned before, in periods that had not been his preferred focus in the past.

This book offers a detailed intellectual history of this final project on the history of sexuality. It is the story of an abandoned project – the original, thematic version of the sexuality work, presented in the first volume of the series in 1976 – and the story of an unfinished one – the more properly historical version which was left incomplete at the moment of his death in 1984. It is a history of that series, or those series. It therefore draws on all of Foucault's published work, including his lecture courses at the Collège de France, and unpublished material archived in France and California. It works in a textual and contextual way, offering close readings of Foucault's works and situating them in relation to his political activism and collaborative projects at the Collège de France and elsewhere. The arguments of those works are carefully reconstructed, filling in details and making links between published works, lecture material and unpublished projects.

Such a project is made possible, but also vastly more complicated, by the range of material we now have. Foucault published seven books in this decade: five authored and two edited. The edited books were *Politiques de l'habitat (1800–1850)* and the *Herculine Barbin* memoir; as well as the books already mentioned there was a co-authored study *Le désordre des familles* with Arlette Farge. For a while it seemed as if this would be all. In the letter written eighteen months before his death, which in the absence of a formal document has been legally interpreted as his will, Foucault made his views on this subject clear: 'No posthumous publications' (C 64/84).[2] Most importantly the fourth volume of the *History of Sexuality* series, *Les Aveux de la chair* [*Confessions of the Flesh*], which Foucault was revising at the time of his death, remains unpublished. Yet texts under the name of Michel Foucault have continued to appear. Ten years after his death a four-volume collection, *Dits et écrits*, was published, edited by his partner Daniel Defert and long-term colleague François Ewald.[3] This was produced with a strict interpretation of Foucault's wishes: only texts which appeared during his lifetime, or which were authorized by him and due to publishing delays appeared after his death, were included. Not a posthumous publication, but a posthumous collection.[4] While there were some important omissions from these volumes even within their own criteria,[5] one of the key contributions was to translate works originally published in a range of languages into, or back into, French. As well as some late texts delivered in English – a range of lectures and numerous interviews – there were texts that had been published in Portuguese, Spanish, German, Dutch, Japanese and English, for which no French edition previously existed. Equally, while there had long been collections of Foucault's shorter work in English and some other languages, this was the first collection of its kind in French. Its chronological ordering was revealing: it complicated and challenged dominant interpretations of Foucault's work along simple thematic lines, and fundamentally disrupted readings that focused on the discontinuities between major works. If the books he published in his lifetime were the peaks, these short works revealed the patient labour in the valleys.[6]

In addition, beginning in 1997, the lecture courses he delivered annually at the Collège de France have been published. It is a peculiar institution, and these are peculiar lecture courses. Rather than have students, professors there are said to have listeners; and rather than teach, they are expected to present their ongoing research. As such, they give an invaluable sense of how Foucault's work was developing, and again help to fill in much detail of planned, abandoned, or uncompleted projects. Initially, in order to circumvent the legal restrictions, Foucault's executors did not use the still extant lecture notes, but rather the audio recordings made at the time, which for some years have been accessible in various archives. Other than allowing these volumes' very existence, the advantage of such an approach meant that the texts were those Foucault actually delivered, along with extemporizations, developments and elucidations. This fidelity to the spoken word means that the notes are those of the editors, as is the punctuation and the division into paragraphs. Because the oral form can read rather awkwardly at times the editors exercised some discretion in sentence formulation. More seriously, due to recording deficiencies, there are passages that substitute ellipses for inaudible delivery. But, despite these problems, we now have the courses in a much more accessible form than the Paris tapes.

However, as the series progressed, the editors were allowed to interpret the restriction on posthumous publications in a much more liberal way. Foucault's manuscripts for the courses, and in some instances other preparatory material, were cited in editorial notes or scholarly apparatus. With some of the early courses tapes were not available, and so volumes were produced based on the manuscript alone, or a transcript made at the time, edited by Foucault himself. The second of these courses, *Théories et institutions pénales* [Penal Theories and Institutions], from 1971–2, for which only Foucault's preparatory lecture notes survive, was the last to be published.[7] The difference between the written and spoken style is important. Foucault's lecturing style is summed up, in a passage reproduced at the beginning of each lecture course, by a 1975 description by the journalist Gérard Petitjean, in a piece which also looks at the teaching of Lacan, Barthes, Derrida, Lyotard and others.[8] But Petitjean is somewhat misled: 'No oratorical effects. It is limpid and extremely effective. Not the least concession to improvisation.'[9] Looking at the notes used for the two courses where there are no extant tape recordings – the 1970–1 and 1971–2 courses – and comparing these to those which are transcripts shows that Foucault's lectures were often much less worked out in advance than his fluid delivery may have implied. Indeed, as Foucault himself said some years later in 1982:

> I understand that there are some people recording the lectures. Very well, you are obviously within your rights. The lectures here are public. It's just that maybe you have the impression that all my lectures are

written. But they are less so than they seem to be, and I do not have
any transcripts or even recordings. Now it happens that I need them.
So, if by chance there is anyone who has (or knows someone who has)
either recordings... or obviously transcripts, would you be kind enough
to tell me, it could help me. It is especially for the last four or five
years. (HSu 378/395–6)

The lecture courses provide a valuable insight into the development
of Foucault's research project from 1970 until his death, in much the
same way that Martin Heidegger's lecture courses in his *Gesamtaus-
gabe* have done.[10] However, Foucault's editor at Gallimard, Pierre
Nora, reports a conversation where Foucault himself was rather
disparaging about the material in his lectures: 'There is a lot of
rubbish, but also lots of work and ways to take it that might be useful
to the kids.'[11] Indeed, Foucault did throw a lot of this material away,
never working up many of the analyses and cases for publication.
Nonetheless, there is much that indicates the directions his major
publications would take, and would likely have taken, had he lived
to complete outlined and planned projects. Around June each year,
except when prevented by illness in 1983 and 1984, Foucault wrote
summaries of the courses, which were published in the *Annuaire de
Collège de France*. In these summaries he often emphasized aspects
of the course that he retrospectively saw as important even if he
underplayed them at the time, or neglected ones that had seemed
previously seemed crucial: the summary of '*Society Must Be
Defended*', for example, barely mentions race. Until the publication
of the full courses, these summaries, pirate versions, tape recordings
and eyewitness testimonies were all we knew of Foucault's lectures.
Now we have a huge amount of newly available material. Other
shorter materials have appeared in a variety of forms with a promise
of more to come, much authorized and some not. The 'no posthumous publications' injunction was once followed faithfully; then
interpreted generously; and is now almost completely disregarded.
Some more material is available in archives in Paris, Caen and Berkeley; other material is not yet publicly accessible.

The newly available material allows us to make connections and
discern continuities, when before there seemed to be breaks and divisions. It therefore provides a fundamental challenge to the periodizations of Foucault's work that have dominated much Anglophone
literature. It allows us to see how Foucault followed paths for much
longer than it may have appeared, only to track back to the departure
point and set off in another direction. His long-standing interest in
confession, both in relation to mechanisms of power and its role in
the production of truth and subjectivity, appears as a major thread

of continuity. We gain some insight into his working practices and modes of analysis, even if much remains unclear and key texts remain in the archive. Importantly we can also see something of his collaborative mode of inquiry, where his Collège de France seminar began to conduct work of many hands, something he intended to develop at Berkeley. And we have, preserved in audio and video recordings, now largely transcribed, an extensive though incomplete record of his practices as a teacher and lecturer.

While there have been fascinating developments, embellishments, appropriations and applications of many of the ideas discussed in this book since Foucault's death, including biopolitics, governmentality, sexuality and the care of the self, those are topics for different projects. Instead, here, the aim is to reconstruct as best as possible what Foucault himself was trying to do. This is a book about Foucault, not about Foucauldians; a contribution to, and not a book about, Foucault studies.[12] Accordingly, the focus is continually on what Foucault wrote, said, and did. It is not a biography, and the purely personal aspects of his life are not discussed. I have consulted some of his acquaintances, but with regard to his writing and teaching alone. The wider life is discussed only in relation to how it impacts on his work. The book seeks to outline how the originally conceived thematic plan for the *History of Sexuality* was abandoned; how it led Foucault through work on governmentality and technologies of the self; how he came to write the more chronological historical study he was working on at his death; and to open up some of the possibilities he himself left unexplored or under-developed. It discusses the key concerns of his work throughout this period and what he argues in well-known and unjustly neglected works. In providing this outline of his work in this decade, it seeks to show how, to a greater or lesser extent, all of concerns were connected in some way to this wider project. What may have appeared as separate links in important ways, seeming detours were often preparatory work. In its broadest sense, this is a book about a book, a history of the *History of Sexuality*. The inquiry is thus an exercise in the history of thought.[13]

This book is partnered by a separate study that traces the emergence of *Surveiller et punir*, which we know in English as *Discipline and Punish*, out of Foucault's initial lecture courses at the Collège de France: *Foucault: The Birth of Power*.[14] There, I examine *Lectures on the Will to Know* from 1970–1; *Théories et institutions pénales* from 1971–2, and *La société punitive* from 1972–3.[15] These courses develop key themes – Measure, Inquiry, Examination – in quite different historical periods: Ancient Greece, the Middle Ages to the seventeenth century, and the eighteenth and nineteenth centuries. This period, famously, sees an emergent focus on the question of power, working alongside Foucault's previous concentration on knowledge; and a supplement to, rather than a replacement of, his archaeological analyses with a genealogical approach. All of those courses, especially the third, with their conceptual innovations and historical detail, pave the way for the writing of *Discipline and Punish* between 1970 and 1974. Other material, particularly his 1973 lectures in Rio on 'Truth and Juridical Forms', which make use of Collège de France material, contribute to this account.

Foucault did not solely work on this project. In his 1973–4 course, *Psychiatric Power*, he makes use of the conceptual innovations around power to recast the analyses of his 1961 book *History of Madness*. Foucault returns to earlier themes and re-examines them, recasts their focus and elaborates on some of their blind spots. In other work, especially some important lectures given in Rio in 1974, he returns to themes examined in his 1963 book *The Birth of the Clinic* and looks at issues around hospital design, public health and disease management. *The Birth of Power* also examines his political activism, especially in the Groupe d'information sur les prisons, and parallel projects on health and asylums. Those political projects closely mirror his more academic interests. These projects – one on discipline, one on madness and one on illness – are all read through the dual lenses of power and knowledge, interpreted through the three concepts. As Foucault says in 1973, 'in their historical formulation, *measure*, *inquiry*, and *examination* were all means of exercising power and, at the same time, rules for establishing knowledge [*savoir*]' (DE#115, II, 390; EW I, 18).

In this productive relation between academic inquiry and political engagement, Foucault describes himself as an artificer, *un artificier* – a demolitions expert, a pyrotechnician, a sapper, a combat engineer (E 92). He claims that he wants his books to function as tools, 'like a kind of scalpel, Molotov cocktails, or undermining tunnels [*galeries de mine*] and to be burned up after use like fireworks [*feux d'artifice*]' (DE#152 II, 725). Books are to serve a purpose: 'a siege, a war, destruction'. His aim is not destroying things, but to get round a problem, past a blockage, over or through a wall. An artificer is, he says, 'primarily a geologist', someone who examines 'the layers of terrain, the folds, the faults'; they conduct a reconnaissance, keep watch, send back reports. What is needed, what can be done, what can be achieved? 'The method, ultimately, is nothing other than this strategy' (E 92). Such a description applies to his work, not just on madness, medicine and discipline, but also on sexuality.

The chapters in this book therefore follow from that study of the earlier period, though they are written to work as independent studies. The opening two chapters of this book outline the themes in his lectures of the mid 1970s, showing both their substantive focus and how these relate to the different subjects of sex as a knowledge and discipline. The third chapter looks how these are crystallized in the programme of work proposed in the first volume of the *History of Sexuality*. The arguments of that text are discussed in detail, but I also draw on the extant materials beyond the book itself to indicate where Foucault anticipated going with these ideas. The closing part of this chapter discusses how Foucault's project got into difficulties around the notion of confession, and led him to rethink its orientation. It therefore shows how the question of rule and regulation generally, and politics and ethics particularly, became concerns over the last few years of his life. Chapter 4 discusses the work on governmentality and a number of collaborative projects with which Foucault was engaged. Chapter 5 returns to the theme of confession, again a major focus of Foucault's writing and speaking in the late 1970s and early 1980s. Chapter 6 traces how Foucault deepens his historical inquiry with an analysis of pagan antiquity; Chapter 7 how this work led to the published second and third volume. The final chapter discusses his last lecture courses and the collaborative book with Arlette Farge. The book does not have a conclusion, not just because Foucault's work ends so abruptly with unfinished and unpublished projects, but because the archival traces remain incomplete and further posthumous publications are envisioned. Instead, it provides a brief summary of the research he conducted during this final decade, showing the continuity and transformation of his interests.

1

Pervert, Hysteric, Child

When he took up his chair at the Collège de France, Foucault did not just give lecture courses. He devoted much of his formal teaching time to constituting a research seminar. Foucault wanted to restrict the seminar to a small group of committed contributors, but the Collège authorities did not allow it and insisted on an open format. While this restricted the research he was able to conduct, it was nonetheless a productive working environment. The first year they found a case in the *Annales d'hygiène publique et de médecine légale*, the story of Pierre Rivière.[1] Further research uncovered a remarkable first-person memoir and witness accounts alongside medical and legal reports. Foucault and his colleagues published the documents and a number of commentaries in a small book in 1973.[2] Jean-Pierre Peter, who had links to the *Annales* school, was a crucial figure who did much of the archival work, including finding the original of Rivière's memoir in Caen.

Rivière was not the only case that Foucault and his colleagues discussed. In *The Abnormals* course in early 1975 Foucault refers to Peter's work in presenting him with material to analyse (A 94/102). In 1971 and 1972 Peter had published two articles in *Nouvelle revue de psychoanalyse* that were developed from work originally conducted in Foucault's seminar.[3] In the first of his two articles, 'Le Corps du délit', Peter briefly mentions the anonymous woman of Sélestat who killed and ate her daughter at the time of a famine in Alsace in 1817,[4] the shepherd Léger who killed and ate a young girl,[5] and Henriette Cornier.[6] These are all cases Foucault discusses in *The Abnormals*.[7] 'Le Corps du délit' is the French equivalent of *corpus deliciti*, the evidence concerning the fact and circumstances of a crime, but also the object upon which the crime was committed (i.e. a dead body). The piece appeared in an issue of the journal devoted to *Lieux du corps*, and Peter is interested in the corporeal nature of crimes, but the body of the criminal and the way medicine acts upon it, as much as the body of the victim. There are some phrases that anticipate claims Foucault would make later in the 1970s, especially in the 1974 Rio lectures on medicine and *The Abnormals*, but there are also passages that are explicitly supported by reference to Foucault's *Birth of the Clinic*, such as the discussion of medicine and space.[8]

The second piece comprises two archival documents presented by Peter. The issue is on the theme *Destins du cannibalisme*. There is a brief note from Peter introducing the two texts and then a reproduction of texts of 'Affaire de Sélestat' [The Sélestat Affair] and 'Procès de Léger' [The Trial of Léger].[9] The first case is a text that C. C. H. Marc had translated in the 1830s.[10] Foucault later describes the Sélestat case as 'the first recorded monster' (A 94/102). The second comes from Étienne-Jean Georget's *Examen médical des procès criminels...*[11] For no good reason, Peter's reproduction of the text breaks off two paragraphs before the end of Georget's text. It provides the legal charge, some interview material and some discussion of the case. As Foucault describes it, Léger 'killed a young girl, raped her, cut out her sexual organs and ate them, and tore out her heart and sucked it' (A 94/102).

The Sélestat, Léger and Cornier cases give some sense of how Foucault worked. The kind of meticulous, patient, documentary work on which his lecture courses, and later his books, depended was enabled by the collaborative work he undertook in his seminars. There are a number of such examples in the *Psychiatric Power* and *The Abnormals* courses. Foucault's examples can be grouped into several categories, including the monstrous and the perverse; women as hysteric and prostitutes; and the continual worry about children. In the first volume of the *History of Sexuality* Foucault would name these as three of the privileged subjects of sexuality, but the presentation of these examples in the lecture courses does not yet have that clear a focus. Foucault describes his work on these as 'dossiers' (i.e. in PP 239/239) – a cataloguing of a series of cases, with supporting evidence and archival work. In much of his analysis of men, women and children Foucault makes use of a similar tactic to the Rivière volume: he presents the documentary evidence of a case, drawing on medical, psychiatric and legal reports, and then draws out wider issues and principles. Indeed he makes explicit reference to the analyses of the Rivière documentary work as a complementary analysis (A 19–20/20–1).

The Monstrous and the Perverse

The preliminary discussion in *The Abnormals* course is centred on the role of such psychiatric expertise in the criminal trials (A 3–11/1–11), especially the relation of 'the grotesque' to the psychologico-ethical (or psychologico-moral) doublet of 'offence' [*délit*]. By 'grotesque' Foucault does not mean 'simply a category of insults...nor an insulting epithet...but a precise category of historical-political analysis' (A 12/11). This notion of the grotesque is linked to what Foucault called the 'ubuesque', a category deriving from Alfred Jarry's book *Ubu roi*.[12] Ubuesque is intended to designate someone who by their grotesque, absurd or cruel character resembles the character of this book. Foucault mobilizes the notion of the grotesque to look at sovereignty, drawing from examples in the history of the Roman Empire such as Nero. He also briefly touches on the links between the grotesque and administrative or bureaucratic power, not simply that found in the works of Balzac, Dostoevsky, Courteline or Kafka, but also modern bureaucratic grotesques in Nazism and Fascism (A 12–13/12–13). At this point Foucault breaks off and says that he has neither the force, the courage nor the time to give his course over to these topics (A 14/14). Nonetheless, these categories allow the analysis of the political monster, and Foucault draws parallels between acts of monstrosity such as vampirism, cannibalism and necrophilia and the literature on these figures. At times he will return to these themes, particularly in the analysis of Marie-Antoinette and Louis XVI (A 87–93/94–100). But more generally, the notion of the grotesque will serve as a guide in the texts that are read in the course (A 14–15/14–15).

Foucault turns in detail to the relationship between madness and crime, in relation to Article 64 of the 1810 Penal Code, which declared that there was no crime or offence if the accused had been in state of dementia at the time of the action, or under a force they could not resist. Once again psychiatric and medical expertise become central to the administration of the law. The double function of psychiatric expertise is to link offence and criminality on the one hand, and to link the author of the offence to the personage of the delinquent on the other. A third role is in the creation of the doctor-judge because of the legal powers the psychiatrist or the doctor came to have. On the other hand, the judge became a doctor of sorts, because the judgment was not simply over a legal subject of an offence defined

as such by the law, but over the individual with the character traits
so defined. The judge is able to prescribe a series of measures of
reform and rehabilitation for the individual. The nasty profession of
punishing thus becomes the fine profession of curing (A 22/23).

This creation of the personage of the delinquent leads to an examination of the concept of the 'dangerous individual', another subject
on which Foucault had intended to write a book (see Chapter 5). Just
as in *Discipline and Punish* and the 1974 Rio lectures on medicine,
Foucault then compares the treatment of lepers and plague victims.
The exclusion of the lepers is replaced with the confinement, observation, and the formation of a knowledge in the case of the plague. It
is a shift from a negative reaction to a positive reaction. It is, for
Foucault, the invention of the positive technologies of power, the
notion of discipline: it is the birth of administrative and political
strategies.[13] Foucault notes how these strategies might be thought of
as an art of governing, of children, the mad, the poor, and so on.
Though brief, this is one of the first times he had identified his object
of study in these terms.[14] By 'government' Foucault wants three things
to be understood: a juridico-political theory of power; the state apparatus and its subsidiary elements in diverse institutions; and disciplinary organizations (A 45/48–9). While it is clear that all three are
important, it is the last of these that Foucault concentrates on here:
what he calls the frame or apparatus [*dispositif*] of 'normalization',
which he outlines in terms taken from Georges Canguilhem's *The
Normal and the Pathological* (A 29–48/31–52). (*Dispositif* will
become an important technical term in Foucault's work, and is fully
discussed in Chapter 3.) This slow formation of a knowledge and
power of normalization is a crucial part of the way in which society
is defended, which links this period of Foucault's work with earlier
and later researches (see A 311/328–9). In the course manuscript,
Foucault closes the first lecture with the suggestion that he would like
to undertake 'the archaeology of the emergence of the power of normalization'. The spoken text simply says he would like to study it (A
24/26).

The realm on which the *dispositif* of 'normalization' is brought to
bear is that of anomaly or abnormality [*anomalie*]. In the second
lecture he notes that normalization was 'attempted in the domain of
sexuality' and that this will be the focus of his analysis (A 48/52; see
155–6/167–8). However some of the early discussion clearly relates
to the analysis of *Discipline and Punish*, with the comparison of the
scaffold and the prison, and the brief discussion of the *lettres de
cachet* (letters bearing the King's seal) relates to his long-term project
on these documents; a project he would later complete with the 1982

book *Le Désordre de familles* (see Chapter 8). In this course the notion of anomaly has three elements: the 'human monster', the 'individual to be corrected', and the masturbating child. The category of 'human monster' is formed in relation to the law – 'monster' is a juridical notion – but by its very existence it is a violation of the laws of nature as well as those of society. It appears in the domain Foucault calls the 'juridico-biological'. The monster is both an extreme phenomenon and an extremely rare one; it is the limit case, the exception that is only found in extreme cases. For Foucault the monster combines the impossible and the forbidden (A 51/56). It is essentially thought of as a mixture. 'The monstrous individual and the sexual deviant link up' (A 56/60). Foucault suggests that each age tended to have its form of 'privileged monster', a particular type that was emphasized. For the middle ages it was the bestial man – men with heads of cows, men with feet of birds. The monster is a mixture, a *mélange* of two species. These monsters transgress the table of classifications, they distort the laws of nature, they exceed the bounds of the possible (A 58–61/62–65). For the Renaissance the privileged monster was Siamese twins – one which is two, two which are one (A 61/66). But in the Classical age a third type of monster was emphasized: hermaphrodites (A 62/66–7).

The treatment of the issue of hermaphrodites is particularly detailed and interesting. Foucault notes that hermaphrodites were 'considered to be monsters and executed, burnt at the stake and their ashes thrown to the winds' (A 62/67). Initially, Foucault discusses the case of Antide Collas from 1599, who was accused of being a hermaphrodite. Doctors confirmed that two sexes were present in her, and that the second sex was a result of relations with Satan. Collas was burnt alive at Dôle. Foucault claims Collas was one the last cases of being burnt alive simply for *being* a hermaphrodite. This was followed by a period when hermaphrodites were allowed to choose their sex, 'to conduct themselves in the manner of the sex that had been so determined, and to take in particular its clothes [*les vêtements*]'. Foucault then recites the limitation of the acts allowed – to make use of the secondary sex would lead to their being condemned for sodomy. There were a number of such cases, including one where a hermaphrodite who had chosen the masculine sex had sexual relations with a man, and another of two hermaphrodites who lived together and were assumed to have had sexual relations (A 62–3/67–8). The course moves on to describe two later case studies in some detail: the affair of Marie/Marin Lemarcis (the 'hermaphrodite of Rouen') from the early seventeenth century, and that of Anne Grandjean from 1765. The first was born a girl, became a man, and then married a widow who had three children. But a medical examination found no sign of masculinity [*virilité*], so Lemarcis was sentenced to be hung, burnt and scattered, with the widow to witness this and be flogged. However, on appeal, one doctor recognized some masculine sign, so Lemarcis was acquitted, told to dress as a woman, and not live with anyone – of either sex – on pain of death (A 63/68). Foucault's interest, in part, is because the hermaphrodite was seen as a monster. One of the doctors – Riolan – thinks that 'the hermaphrodite is a monster because they are against the order and rule of nature, that which separates human gender [*genre*] into two: males and females. Because if someone has both sexes together, they must be seen as and labelled a monster.' The examination is therefore important for determining their conduct and ability to marry, and to whom (A 66/71). There is clearly a tension here which was not present in the case of Collas; nor in the case of Anne Grandjean.

Baptized as a girl, at the age of fourteen she realized 'attraction that she felt for girls of the same sex as herself'. Dressing as a boy, she moved town and married someone called Françoise Lambert. Denounced to the authorities, she was examined by a surgeon who decided she was a woman and therefore condemned: 'she had therefore used the sex that was not dominant in herself'. She was put in an iron collar, whipped and branded, but freed on appeal. Her obligation was to take the clothes of a woman and avoid both Françoise and other women. The difference between two similar cases, as Foucault notes, is that Lemarcis was prohibited from living with anyone; Grandjean just from women. This means Grandjean was allowed a sexuality and sexual relationship that was forbidden to Lemarcis (A 66/71–72). Foucault uses the two cases to suggest that during this time there was a fundamental shift in the treatment of hermaphrodites. Hermaphroditism is no longer seen as a 'mixture of sexes', but rather as the simultaneous presence of two sexes in a single organism and individual. The contemporaneous *Dictionnaire de médecine* declares all stories of hermaphrodites to be fables: there are those with predominant sexual characteristics but the generative organs are badly formed, and therefore they are not able to engender (either in or out of themselves). What was called hermaphrodism was physical malformation accompanied by impotence. In the case of Grandjean then, it was not that she was a hermaphrodite, but a woman 'with perverse tastes, she loved women, and it was that monstrosity, not of nature but of behaviour, which provoked the condemnation' (A 67/73).

Foucault points out that this history shows the disassociation of the juridico-natural complex of the monstrosity hermaphrodite, because the somatic anomaly is only an imperfection, with the monstrosity no longer conceived as juridico-natural, but as juridico-moral: 'it is a monstrosity of *behaviour*, and not a monstrosity of *nature*' (A 68/73). By the nineteenth century, difficulty in terminology emerges, as homosexuals – either men or women – were seen as psychic hermaphrodites (see HS I 134/101). Foucault's off-quoted suggestion of the birth of the homosexual in the nineteenth century is important in this regard (see HS I 59/43; and Chapter 3 below). In this course, Foucault notes the emergence of a species based on behaviour and not nature, from 'inherently criminal monstrosity' to 'monstrous criminality' (A 69–70/74–5). Foucault returned to the question of hermaphrodites in 1978, when he compiled the texts relating to the cases of Herculine Barbin, and in related material from 1979 and 1980. These texts will also be discussed in Chapter 3.

The individual in need of correction is similarly a species that arises in the Classical age, the period between the seventeenth and eighteenth centuries. While the monster is by definition the exception, the individual to be corrected is an everyday or common phenomenon. It is through such commonplaceness that it is a paradox – it is regular in its irregularity. The material here is rather sketchy, but we would expect that many of the techniques used to correct such individuals would bear comparison with those outlined in *Discipline and Punish* – the idea of dressage for one. Foucault suggests that these individuals are 'incorrigible' and that there is an ongoing tension between the techniques of correction, or rectification, and this status. The incorrigible is, like the monster, one of the ancestors of the nineteenth century notion of the 'abnormal' (A 53–4/57–8). Crucially there can be a blurring between categories, with the emergence of the 'sexual monster', who had been 'basically unknown to earlier periods' but now is where 'the monstrous individual and the sexual deviant link up' (A 56/60). While this naturally anticipates the work on sexuality, the link with *La société punitive* and *Discipline and Punish* is particularly evident in these particular lectures: 'the question of the illegal and the question of the abnormal, or that of the criminal or the pathological, are now linked – and not by a new ideology or state apparatus, but as a function of a technology characterizing the new rules of the economy of the power to punish' (A 85/92). Foucault also gives a couple of examples that could have easily sat in the place of Damiens at the beginning of *Discipline and Punish* – the execution of the assassin of William of Orange in the sixteenth century; and an execution in the papal state of Avignon (A 77–78/84–5). Just as the hermaphrodite becomes seen as a monstrosity of behaviour rather than of nature, no longer juridico-natural, but juridico-moral, so too does the notion of the monster with the emergence of the moral monster (A 75/81). The point of the preceding analyses is to trace the history of this moral monster, its conditions of possibility (A 85/92).

Foucault dates the birth of this modern monster to 1792–3, with the trial of Louis XVI. Indeed he claims that the King is the first juridical monster of the modern kind, and suggests that 'all human monsters are the descendants of Louis XVI' (A 87/95). There follows a discussion of the way the Jacobins, and particularly Saint-Just, constituted Louis XVI not as someone who had broken the laws from the inside, and that therefore could have the laws applied to them, but as an absolute enemy of the entire social body. He therefore had to be destroyed, as one would destroy an enemy or a monster. The action of the social body was at the same time the action of each individual, and therefore it did not matter who actually killed the King. As Saint-Just said, 'the right of men against tyranny is a personal right'. The discussion continues to bring in the figure of Marie-Antoinette, who was represented along with Louis XVI as the monstrous couple, blood-thirsty, at the same time jackal and hyena.

Many pamphlets at the time mobilized the notions of cannibalism, debauchery, homosexuality and incest – particularly the latter – to describe her. It was, suggests Foucault, with Marie-Antoinette that the thematic of the human monster became crystallized. But at the same time in the anti-Jacobin literature the idea of the monster was used in a different way, to characterize not the abuse of power, but the monster who broke the social contract by revolt. The blood being spilt was crucial again, with the revolution of the people, their regicide, being tied to cannibalism. Cannibalism and incest – an alimentary prohibition and a sexual one – are the central themes of the monster, shown in literary form in de Sade's work, above all *Juliette* (A 88–94/95–101). Cannibalism is also discussed in relation to the soldier Bertrand, the vampire of Düsseldorf, and Jack the Ripper (A 94–5/102). Foucault returns to the Bertrand case later in the course and apologizes for getting the date wrong, but more importantly for making an historical or epistemological error. As well as grave-robbing, desecration of corpses, and possible cannibalism, the authorities were alerted by the much larger number of female than male corpses involved. The corpses were especially those of young girls. Signs of sexual attention were found, including those corpses that were in an advanced state of decomposition. This leads Foucault to a discussion of different types of monomania – destructive and sexual – and to the difference between vampirism and Bertrand, who he calls an inverse vampire. For Bertrand, unlike vampires, was alive, preyed on *dead* bodies, and – to an extent – sucked their blood (A 267–71/283–6).

It is worth noting that some of Foucault's examples of criminal cases involving monstrosity or perversity are of women. One example is the anonymous woman of Sélestat who killed her daughter, chopped her up, and cooked and ate her thigh with some white cabbage at the time of a famine in Alsace (A 94/102, 102–3/110–12, 127–8/137–8). This was one of the texts that had been reproduced and discussed in Jean-Pierre Peter's archival work.[15] The key example, though, to which Foucault gives considerable attention, is the case of Henriette Cornier, who murdered her neighbour's daughter, seemingly without reason (A 103–5/112–13, 108–9/117–18, 114–24/122–34, etc.). Cornier became an application of Article 64. This case, which was also treated in Foucault's 1975 seminar (A 311/329), is important in understanding the relation of the criminal to psychiatry, particularly in the notion of the 'instinct'.[16] This leads into a discussion of how psychiatric models came to be applied to political regimes (A 140–5/151–7).

> These figures of monstrosity, of sexual and cannibalistic monstrosity, were the points of organization, the starting points, of all legal medicine. These themes, in this double figure of the sexual transgressor and the cannibal, are found throughout the nineteenth century. They are constantly found on the borders of psychiatry and the penal system and give stature to the great figures of criminality at the end of the nineteenth century: Vacher in France, the Düsseldorf Vampire in Germany, Jack the Ripper in England. (A 94–5/102)

The Family

Accompanying this analysis of individuals in both *Psychiatric Power* and *The Abnormals* are some detailed studies of the notion of the family. Foucault's examples seem to be of an almost entirely dysfunctional family, where the women are prostitutes or hysterical and the children are idiots or always masturbating. Yet despite the extreme examples, Foucault's analysis is of fundamental importance to his analytic of collectivity.[17] His claim is that the disciplinary society is not the model for the family, rather that the family bears more comparison to sovereignty. This is not to say it is a hangover from the past, but somewhat paradoxically that the family is an essential piece of the disciplinary system (PP 81–2/80). The family is for Foucault the hinge, the *charnière*, 'the absolutely indispensable interlocking point to the functioning of all disciplinary systems' (PP 82/81). There is an integral relation of the family to school, to the army, to work, and it plays a crucial role in fixing individuals into disciplinary systems: a similar role to the dual body of the King in sovereign systems (PP 83/82). In a sense, rather than being dysfunctional itself, the family is where dysfunction can be observed and controlled, functioning as a mechanism within disciplinary society: 'Disciplinary power is parasitic on domestic sovereignty, requiring the family to take the role of the agency that decides between the normal and the abnormal, the regular and the irregular, asking the family to hand over its abnormals, its irregulars, etc.' (PP 116/115).

The family is certainly one of the *dispositifs* of sovereignty, and has a particular role in those ways of thinking, particularly around the power of the father, though Foucault contends that it also plays a role in disciplinary societies, tied to economic questions of productivity. This role is different, obviously, but so too is the family itself. Increasingly it is 'concentrated, limited, intensified', it is reduced more and more down to the crucial relations of man-woman and parents-children (PP 84/83), the nuclear family (see A 229–39/243–54). These changes are in part related to class, with the formation of the urban proletariat, to work and housing conditions, and to child labour (PP 84–5/83–4). In sum then, between the disciplinary panopticism of society as a whole – an issue that is extensively discussed in *Foucault: The Birth of Power* – and the sovereign family there is a continual back and forth relation (PP 85/84). These analyses are primarily interesting because of the general claim that 'as a disciplinary system, the asylum is also a place of formation of certain type of discourse of truth' (PP 95/93). In this we see the relation between power and knowledge relations, or the political relation in the production of truth. This is not to say that other disciplinary places do not have this relation, nor that they do not have a relation to the family, but Foucault argues that this is particularly found and concentrated here (PP 96/94).

Foucault is often criticized for the lack of attention to women in his work; even though his work has proved extremely influential to some feminists. These courses provide some exceptions. He discusses the hysteric in *Psychiatric Power*, and sees hysteria as 'the great dividing point' in the history of psychiatry (PP 100/98), which for him is a history of the relation of psychiatric power to the disciplinary society. However, Foucault's language can be somewhat demeaning, referring to 'the famous, dear hysterics' (PP 253/253) and quoting one case study 'for amusement', before referring to it as a 'kind of bacchanal, this sexual pantomime' (PP 323–4/322). He is principally interested in the entry, not the appearance, of hysteria within the *dispositif* of psychiatric power. Indeed, Foucault says that 'the question of the historical existence of hysteria is a futile question'. Instead, he wants to examine how 'the emergence of hysteria within the medical field, the possibility of making it an illness, and its medical manipulation are only possible when this new clinical *dispositif*, which is neurological and not psychiatric in origin, was established; or when this new trap was set' (PP 306 /304). His key analysis is Jean-Martin Charcot and the work at the Salpêtrière hospital (where, coincidentally, he would himself later die). Foucault is interested in tracing how hysterics were understood, but more especially in terms of how different medical and psychiatric practices were directed towards them. As he says, 'I will not try to analyse this in terms of the history of hysterics any more than in terms of psychiatric knowledge [*connaissances*] of hysterics, but rather in terms of battle, confrontation, reciprocal encirclement, of the laying of mirror traps, of investment and counter-investment, of struggles for control between doctors and hysterics' (PP 310/308). Foucault is also interested in the relation between psychiatric power and hysterical resistance, describing hysterics 'as the true militants of anti-psychiatry' (PP 253/254). This is because, for Foucault, they are 'the front of resistance' to the 'double game of psychiatric power and asylum discipline' (PP 253/253). They adopt physical symptoms of the organically ill, as the body and site of genuine illnesses and symptoms (PP 253/253–4).

He also discusses the relation between hysteria and epilepsy (PP 311/310), an analysis that would be developed in *The Abnormals* lecture course when he shows how religious possession is in part an early form of what would come to be called mental convulsion (A 187–212/201–27).[18] Foucault briefly discusses the question of hystero-epilepsy, which he suggests was both demolished by Charcot and had previously been tangled up with Christian confession, monstrous crime and nervous convulsion (A 208/224). In addition, Foucault contends that what happened at Salpêtrière was a kind of founding moment for anti-psychiatry (PP 137/138). As he later notes in the course summary this was not a neutral medical experience: 'Charcot actually produced the hysterical fit he described' (PP 347/341).[19] Nonetheless, Charcot's failure left its trace in the three elements of 'questioning – language – hypnosis, and drugs...with which psychiatric power, within asylum spaces or in extra-asylum spaces, still operates today' (PP 290/288). Equally we can see the importance of psychiatric medicine, particularly in relation to the body of women, to the birth of the *dispositif* of sexuality. His analysis of the neurological body (PP 299–304/297–302) is crucial for understanding how discipline always directed its resources towards the corporeal, and for showing the emergence of issues of sexuality. As he claims, the neurological body, and the conflict between the body of the mad and the psychiatrist is entirely sexual. Struggles of power and domination are evident in the space of the asylum. 'This body, no longer the neurological body, is the sexual body' (PP 325/323).

> In breaking down the door of the asylum, in ceasing to be mad in order to become patients, in finally getting through to a true physician, that is to say the neurologist, in providing him with genuine functional symptoms, the hysterics, to their greater pleasure, but doubtless to our larger misfortune, gave rise to a medicine of sexuality. (PP 325/323)

Arnold Davidson has described this as 'a phrase that might have seemed enigmatic when pronounced by Foucault on 6 February 1974, but whose force is quite clear' viewed from *The History of Sexuality*.[20]

The other key women that Foucault discusses are prostitutes, who make a brief appearance in *Psychiatric Power* as an example of economic-political disciplinary mechanisms (PP 112–13/110–12). He relates this claim back to the analysis of the previous year's course, *La société punitive*, as an examples of how bourgeois society simultaneously found delinquency as a 'source of profit on the one hand, and of the reinforcement of power on the other' (PP 112/110). While the relation of 'prostitutes, clients and procurers' existed before the nineteenth century, from that date there was a shift to a tighter organization of property around hotels and brothels, and that this is coupled with the constitution and criminalization of delinquency (PP 112/110–11). The argument is that there is a contradictory, and yet, at the same time, reinforcing relation between profit and criminalization. Because it is prohibited it becomes more costly, and functions 'to bring back to capital itself, to the normal circuits of capitalist profit, all the profits that can be extracted from sexual pleasure' (PP 112/111). This prohibition/tolerance duality will reinforce surveillance and the constitution of discipline, as well as making profit for capitalism. In sum, 'sexual pleasure is made profitable...the profits from sexual pleasure flow back into the general circuits of capitalism...' and this fixes 'even more firmly the extreme effects, the synaptic relays of State power, which end up reaching into men's everyday pleasure' (PP 113/111–12). For Foucault, of course, this is only one example of the relation of discipline and production (PP 113/112), though the second element is underplayed in his published works such as *Discipline and Punish*, being much more explicit in the lecture courses.[21]

Foucault's analysis of children is more detailed, though there are promises that are not fulfilled. For example, in *Psychiatric Power* he says there will be a more thorough treatment of 'pedagogy and the dossier on childhood' (PP 239/239) in the following year's course, but this is only treated in part.[22] In fact, *The Abnormals* focuses almost exclusively on the theme of masturbation, and in the final lecture of that course Foucault notes that the 'recalcitrant child' is the missing figure from his genealogy, but that he has not had time to do more than outline it (A 275/291; see 258–9/274). In *Psychiatric Power* the analysis, while covering masturbation in part, is much broader. This is because Foucault claims that children play an important role in the birth of psychiatric power, effectively arguing that it develops from the psychiatrization of childhood (PP 199/201). In the literature of the time Foucault finds the argument that therapeutic inventions against madness cannot begin too young, and that it is important therefore not to wait until they are adults (PP 124–5/124–5). Equally, as is well known, incidents from childhood life are particularly significant in analysis (PP 125/125). Mechanisms of surveillance used against children – largely around masturbation and their sexuality more generally – provide models for surveillance more generally concerning the policing of normal and abnormal behaviour (PP 124/124).

One of the key figures in *Psychiatric Power* is that of the treatment of the imbecile, the idiot, the mad child (PP 201–21/201–23). Foucault goes so far as to suggest that 'the education of idiots and the abnormal is psychiatric power in its pure state' (PP 212/215). Why are idiotic children so important? Foucault's answer is that they are dangerous because they masturbate in public, commit sexual offences [*délits*], they are *incendiaires*, arsonists (PP 218/220). Foucault stresses that right from the beginning of the nineteenth century there is a clear argument that these children – though they are labelled as imbeciles, idiots, or later, as retarded – are not mad (PP 201/203). More generally the claim is that in the nineteenth century the question of anomaly in psychiatry is one that affects children rather than adults – leaving aside the question of physiology and anatomo-pathology. At this time, 'it is the adult who is mad; on the other hand, the child is the one who is abnormal' (PP 219/221). All sorts of problems can be traced back to the child.

The child therefore is seen as 'the bearer of anomalies [*anomalies*]' and Foucault discusses how around the figure of the idiot a whole range of practical problems are orientated: 'from the liar to the poisoner, from the pederast to the homicide, from the onanist to the arsonist', all this generalized field around the figure of anomaly, at the heart of which is 'the retarded child [*l'enfant arriéré*], the feeble child [*débile*], the idiot child' (PP 219/221). It is through these practical problems that psychiatry becomes something that does not seek to control and correct madness, but a much more generalized and dangerous power over the abnormal, 'the power to define who is abnormal, to control, and correct' (PP 219/221). Foucault's claims here are important in terms of the kind of analysis he is undertaking. His assertion is that 'anomaly is the individual condition of possibility of madness' (PP 274/272).

The disjuncture between the mad and the abnormal child is for Foucault therefore 'one of the fundamental traits of the exercise of psychiatric power in the nineteenth century' (PP 219/222). There are three consequences that he thinks can be traced from this. First, a series of disciplinary regimes emerge from the ideas behind this, which lead to a generalized science and power over the abnormal. This can be found in the discipline of schools, the military, and the family. Wider social controls arise and develop from the treatment of the child (PP 219–21/222–3). Second, the links between the abnormal child and the mad adult lead, in the second half of the nineteenth century to two key concepts: the notion of instinct and that of degeneration. The instinct, which is analysed in much more detail the following year (PP 213/215, 220/222; A 122–5/131–4; 128–9/138–9; 260–71/275–87) is important in terms of the moral tone adopted in response; whereas degeneration, particularly in the work of Morel, shows the intrusion of evolutionary biology into psychiatry, although it pre-dates Darwin, and is closer to the idea of inherited characteristics found in Lamarck, who was extremely important in his native France. In '*Society Must Be Defended*' degeneracy is linked to the general analysis of biological-racist discourses (SMBD 53/61, 225/252). The political question here is that of the spreading of anomaly into future generations: the disposition to anomaly makes possible the madness of adults (PP 220–1/222–3). The relation between anomaly and madness might be seen in this way: 'anomaly leads to madness and madness produces anomaly' (PP 221/223), though Foucault notes that this is because of the family. Third, the field of psychoanalysis emerges here, albeit in rather crude form. We can find it at work in the system of exchanges between children and parents, between ancestors and descendants, and in these questions of instinct and degeneration. For Foucault it is precisely in the generalization of the child and anomaly and not in that of the adult and illness that the object of psychoanalysis is formed (PP 221/223).

The masturbating child is a figure who begins to appear in texts at the end of the eighteenth century. Foucault says that it is looked at as a very frequent occurrence, where masturbation is the universal secret, the secret divided and yet shared across the world, as no one speaks to anyone else about it. In his archaeology and genealogy of anomaly, Foucault suggests that the abnormal of the nineteenth century is the descendant of the three individuals he has discussed: the monster, the incorrigible and the masturbator. Foucault discusses how the three types he is discussing here relate to the notion of sexual deviancy. Monstrosity and sexuality are closely linked, similarly masturbation and the notion of the incorrigible. But Foucault claims, and he stresses this is a crucial point, that the three types are kept quite separate in the seventeenth and eighteenth centuries. It is only in the nineteenth century, with the emergence of the technology of abnormal individuals that a broad field of knowledge and power can unite them. 'Masturbation is a kind of polyvalent causality to which one can attach, and to which doctors in the eighteenth century will immediately attach, the entire panoply, the entire arsenal of physical, nervous, and psychiatric illnesses' (A 54–6/59–60).

Foucault suggests that the discourse concerning masturbation is distinct both from Christian discourse on the flesh, and from what will come to be called *psychopathia sexualis*, sexual psychopathology (A 219/233). The discussion of masturbation led to careful control of the space of schools and the home, ensuring visibility and control (A 218/232–3, 231/245–6); manuals on how to prevent masturbation, detailing the disastrous physical consequences; brochures of medicines, apparatuses and bindings for its prevention (A 220–1/235); suggested preventative techniques such as tying children's hands to themselves, to an adult sleeping nearby, or to warning bells; and detailed information on how to spot the signs, traces and odours of arousal or ejaculation, the key times to check and so on. Foucault's examples are of both girls and boys (see, e.g., A 228/242–3). There are discussions of chemical solutions, permanent catheters, cauterization of the urethra, clitoridectomies and castrations (A 237–8/252–3). He talks of the medical manuals illustrating the dire consequences for masturbators, and a waxwork museum that turned these into even more vivid representations which parents and their children could attend (A 220–1/235). But as well as controlling the bodies of children, this new discourse places the fundamental blame on the parents, and puts the onus on them to prevent. Part of the emphasis is against the seduction of children by adults – particularly those in close contact with the children such as domestics, governesses, private tutors, uncles, aunts, cousins, etc. (A 228–9/243–4). This emphasis leads to what we might call the nuclear family as opposed to the larger 'household' of the past; new types of familial obligations; and new health principles regulated by external medical knowledge (A 232–9/246–54). 'The family becomes not only the basis for the determination and distinction of sexuality but also for the rectification of the abnormal' (A 239/254). Foucault suggests that what he calls this 'epistemophilic incest of touch, gaze and surveillance' is part of the foundation of the modern family (A 234/249; see 252/266). The crusade against masturbation – a new children's crusade – constitutes a new apparatus or *dispositif* of knowledge-power: it is linked to state strategies concerning education and population control (A 239–43/254–8).

Such strategies of population control are common themes in the final two lectures of *The Abnormals*, which discuss the normalization of the urban proletariat, the optimal division of the working-class family, the prohibitions on incest, and the link between instinct and sexuality in the context of the epistemologico-political task of psychiatry. Foucault recognizes that the prohibition on masturbation was aimed at the bourgeois family; the restrictions on proletariat families were rather against the danger of incest, to try to secure the institution of marriage, to prevent cohabitation. Whereas the anti-masturbation crusade encouraged parents to keep their bodies close to those of their children, here the aim was the separation of bodies, into spaces for parents and spaces for each sex of child (A 254–6/268–71). There follows a long discussion of Heinrich Kaan's *Psychopathia sexualis*, published in 1844, from which Foucault dates the emergence of sexuality and sexual aberrations in the field of psychiatry (A 262–7/278–83).[23]

Foucault discusses how the three types of abnormality – monstrosity, the individual to correct and the masturbator – can be seen to come together in the case of Charles Jouy (A 275–89/291–304), a figure he will go on to discuss in the *History of Sexuality* (HS I, 43–5/31–2). In this we can see one of the most explicit links between the course and that later book. In 1867 Jouy was charged with having had sexual relations with young girls, certainly paying for masturbation, but possibly including rape. Because Jouy was deemed to be educationally backward, 'more or less the village idiot' (A 276/292), Foucault is interested in the way that the case became an intervention for psychiatric expertise, and in seeing shifts in understandings around sexuality. It is doubtless one of a number of markers of a shift from an earlier tolerance of such behaviour to its entry into criminal and psychiatric assessment. But it has to be said the case is presented with unpleasant dismissal of how the victims may have felt, even hinting that they may have been responsible, or certainly complicit, and some weak attempts at humour.[24]

Foucault here outlines how this 'technology of anomaly' relates to 'other processes of normalization that were not concerned with crime, criminality, or great monstrosity, but with something quite different: everyday sexuality'. It is this he proposes to study as 'the history of sexuality, of the control of sexuality', in the period from the end of the eighteenth to the late nineteenth century (A 151/163). Foucault links these themes psychiatry and heredity (A 289–99/306–16); and then links these discourses to the modern notion of racism. Modern racism, returning this course to themes seemingly abandoned earlier, is an internal defence of society against the abnormals, and is born out of psychiatry (A 299–301/316–18). These themes provide a direct link to the 1975–6 course, *'Society Must Be Defended'*, discussed in Chapter 2.

The Constitution of the Normal

It is well known that Foucault's work has affinities with that of Canguilhem.[25] Canguilhem was the supervisor of Foucault's doctoral work, and they shared a common interest in Nietzsche (DE#330, IV, 436). In the book Foucault cites here, for which he wrote an introduction to the English translation, Canguilhem argued that 'the abnormal, [while] logically second, is existentially first'.[26] Like the argument made in *History of Madness*, where the notion of madness is able to constitute what we think of as reason – strikingly shown in Descartes' *Meditations* – we know that the 'normal' is often defined by what it is not. This understanding is clearly indebted to the examination Nietzsche made of slave morality in *On the Genealogy of Morality*. *The Abnormals* could therefore easily have been called *The Constitution of the Normal*. Constitution – legal, political, medical and biological – is a useful word in understanding Foucault's intent. A great deal of the material here is clearly connected not just to the *Sexuality* series which Foucault was working on at the time, but also to the researches of which *Discipline and Punish* was but one part, and to the work of the late 1970s on governmentality. *The*

Abnormals is therefore the bringing together of a number of problematics which coincide in the body of the abnormal.

What Foucault calls the *dispositif* of 'normalization' is an example
of his understanding of the relation between power and knowledge.
The negative formulation of the 'normal' through the knowledge of
what it is not – rather than what it is – is paralleled by the power
exercised in order to protect that normalcy.[27] This is how society is
defended: both an exclusion established through knowledge, and an
inclusion policed through power. The mechanisms of policing and
governmentality illustrated by the plague town are imposed over the
selected individual of whom the leper was but the striking historical
example. The notion of a norm is not a natural law, but is defined
by the role it plays in the domains it is applied to. The norm is not
simply a principle of intelligibility, one that allows us to compare and
contrast, but is an element in the exercise of power. It is a polemical
concept for Canguilhem, a political one for Foucault. And most
importantly for Foucault it is at the same time a principle of qualifi-
cation and a principle of correction. Rather than functioning to
exclude or reject, the norm is 'always linked to a positive technology
of intervention and transformation, to a sort of normative project'
(A 46/50).

However, the exclusion of the other or the abnormal in order to
constitute the same or the normal is not without risk. As the illustra-
tions of the nature of political leadership, bureaucracy and administrative power show, the mechanisms utilized to police normalcy
are often tainted by grotesque or abnormal elements. The original
preface to *History of Madness* made a very similar point, quoting
Pascal's aphorism that 'men are so necessarily mad that it would be
another kind of madness to not be mad' and Dostoevsky's admoni-
tion that 'it is not by imprisoning our neighbour that we become
convinced of our own sanity' (DE#4 I, 159). These lead Foucault to
write an investigation of what he calls 'the other form of madness'.
These lectures show elements of the other form of abnormality – the
categorization, delimitation, treatment of and cruelty towards the
'abnormals'.

As can be surmised from the preceding discussion the subject
matter of *The Abnormals* is almost entirely gruesome. The category
of the grotesque with which Foucault introduces the course does
indeed serve as a motto throughout. As Foucault notes, the themes
he is discussing bear relation to the gothic novel and to de Sade (A
69/75). Disease, death and torture shadow most lectures; cannibalism, incest, monsters and masturbation haunt its pages. Fascinating

though its themes are, it often reads as the accumulation of material, stories, and documents that Foucault is unable to fully come to grips with. That said, there is an important distinction between these two courses. At the time of its delivery, *The Abnormals* was clearly a project designed to try out material for the original plan of the *History of Sexuality*, but the vast bulk of the content of *Psychiatric Power* seems never to have been intended for publication.

2

The War of Races and Population

Towards the end of *The Abnormals* Foucault notes how modern racism, returning the course to themes seemingly abandoned earlier, is an internal defence of society against the abnormals, and is born out of psychiatry (A 299–301/316–18). In the final lecture he claims that all his courses to this point have shared a linked inquiry: 'the slow formation of a knowledge and power of normalization based on traditional juridical procedures of punishment'. He suggests that the next course, *'Society Must Be Defended'*, will 'bring this cycle to an end with the study of the mechanisms with which since the end of nineteenth century, we sought to "defend society"' (A 311/328–9).

Even before its publication this course was fairly well known, because the first two lectures had appeared first in Italian in the 1970s, and then were translated into English in 1980 (P/K 78–108). These discuss power relations in some detail and oppose models of understanding power on the basis of possessive right and the productive relation (liberal and Marxist), to those that seek to understand it on the basis of repression (Hegel, Freud and Reich are cited), and models based on war. Carl von Clausewitz's famous dictum is quoted, and then reversed – 'politics is *war* pursued by other means'. Foucault's focus for the courses is, therefore, war. He wants to examine how the clash of forces, or the question of struggle, is the 'foundation of civil society, at the same time the principle and the motor of the exercise of political power... where power has the role of defending society'. But the focus is not obvious theorists of war in society, such as Machiavelli and Hobbes. For Foucault, these are misleading.

Rather, he wants to examine 'the theory of war as an historical principle of the function of power, around the problem of race, since it is racial binarism that led – for the first time in the West – to the possibility of analysing political power as war'. The historical struggle between races, and the struggle between classes that follows it, are 'the two grand schemes by which we can map the phenomena of war and the relations of force in the interior of political society' (SMBD 18–19/18–19).

It is important that while Foucault emphases the question of struggle, either for classes or races, he is critical of the lack of attention paid by Marxists – though he exempts Marx and Trotsky somewhat – to what constitutes struggle when they talk of class struggle (DE#206, III, 310–11; P/K 208).[1] Foucault notes in 1977 that power, ultimately, is the 'class struggle...the entirety of relations of force', and that many of Marx's historical studies can be read in that way.[2] Indeed, in an interview with geographers in the *Hérodote* journal Foucault notes that Marx's work on 'the army and its role in the development of political power' had been unjustly neglected (DE#169 III, 39; SKP 182), and later stresses that he is interested in the second part of *Capital*, both because of its analysis of the genealogy of capital, but also because of the material on circulation (CMPP 106–7/100–1).[3] As Defert stresses, Foucault found Marx most useful as an historian, not for his economic analysis.[4] He suggests that the metaphors geographers claim are geographical are actually political, juridical, administrative and military. His interlocutors respond that some of these terms are both geographical and strategic, which is not surprising, given that geography 'grew up in the shadow of the military' (DE#169 III, 32–4; SKP 176–7). This interest can be seen as continuing in the discussions of the Peace of Westphalia and the invention of standing armies in the late seventeenth century in *Security, Territory, Population*, where Foucault discusses the permanent military apparatus, the advent of professional soldiers, the infrastructure of fortresses and transport, and the sustained tactical reflection that dates from this time (STP 308–13/300–6). We should not be surprised by the emphasis on war given the role the army and the figures of warfare play as constitutive elements in the genealogy of modern punitive society in *Discipline and Punish*. The rejection of Hobbes and Machiavelli is also important: more than just dismissing misleading precursors to this idea, Foucault is challenging a prevalent interpretation of their work (SMBD 51/59, 77–80/89–90).

Strategy and war are thus at the heart of Foucault's concerns in early 1976. Unusually, he followed up his interview with geographers by posing some questions back to them.[5] Strategy was, he contended, essential to understanding the relation of power and knowledge, but its relation to domination and war was more complicated. How, he asks, do we need to rethink strategy? (DE#178 III, 94; SKP 19). A similar set of questions are asked in the course summary to '*Society Must Be Defended*', written at the conclusion of the course and thus around the same time as the questions to *Hérodote*. He asks if war is the basis for social relations, and if 'all phenomena of social domination, differentiation, and hierarchization be regarded as its derivatives?' In particular, 'Do processes of antagonism, confrontations, and struggles among individuals, groups, or classes derive in the last instance from general processes of war?' And, 'can a set of notions derived from strategy and tactics constitute a valid and adequate instrument for the analysis of power relations?' (SMBD 239–40/266). But it is important to recognize that this is not necessarily a programme for future work, because there is an indication that his answers would largely have been in the negative. Indeed the lectures appear to be Foucault running ideas to ground, working them through to their logical conclusions and exhausting their possibilities before turning to other avenues. This course, as the last before his sabbatical, brings his initial research programme to something of a close. As Chapter 4 will discuss, picking up on his first post-sabbatical course, Foucault becomes more concerned with strategies for waging peace, examining how mechanisms employed in what he calls governmentality are only indirectly from mechanisms of war.

Indeed, a shift can be seen even as early as the course summary, which stresses the importance of war but makes only a passing reference to the role of race. Issues of security, violence, revolution, class struggle are much more to the fore. Foucault is interested in expanding his analyses beyond specific institutions to look at society as a whole, noting that disciplinary techniques and the law are increasingly interrelated. This is what he calls 'a "society of normalization"' (SMBD 34–5/38–9). That analysis is applied not just to liberal, democratic regimes, but also to totalitarian ones, with discussion of State racism in both its Nazi and Stalinist forms. This is, he suggests, 'a racism that society will direct against itself, against its own elements and its own products. This is an internal racism, a permanent purification, one of the fundamental dimensions of social normalization' (SMBD 53/62, see 71/81–2). What we find here is the replacing of the historical war with the biological struggle for life: 'differentiation of species, selection of the strongest, survival of the fittest races' (SMBD 70/80).

The project to be employed in the course looks, particularly, at how the writing of history is a political tool.[6] This is both in terms of history written in the interests of the state, or a particular class or race, and history written in opposition to it. That is both the focus of much of the analysis and explains his own genealogical approach, which is concerned with the 'insurrection of knowledges...an insurrection against the centralizing power-effects that are bound up with the institutionalization and workings of any scientific discourse organized in a society such as ours' (SMBD 10/9). Yet this emphasis on genealogy is not a replacement of his earlier approach. It is a supplement to it, an addition: 'Archaeology is the method specific to the analysis of local discursivities, and genealogy is the tactic which, once it has described these local discursivities, brings into play the desubjectified knowledges that have been released from them' (SMBD 11–12/10–11). In this he is explicit that he wants to avoid a totalizing answer to the question 'what is power?', but instead 'to determine what are, in their mechanisms, effects, their relations, the various power-apparatuses that operate at various levels of society, in such very different domains and with so many different extensions? (SMBD 13–14/13).

Reversing Clausewitz; Clausewitz's Reversal

Foucault begins the third lecture by suggesting that the juridical model of sovereignty is not suited to a concrete analysis of the multiplicity of power relations, and so dismisses that approach (SMBD 37/43). This was shown earlier in the course when Foucault contrasted his concern with that of Hobbes: 'Rather than pose the problem of the central soul [of the *Leviathan*], I believe that we must attempt...to study the peripheral and multiple bodies, those bodies constituted as subjects by the effects of power,' (SMBD 26/29). The question is thus not so much one of reversing Clausewitz's principle, but knowing what principle Clausewitz reversed, one 'which circulated since the seventeenth and eighteenth centuries, and which was both diffuse and specific' (SMBD 41/48; see 146–7/165). He traces this – as he says, 'schematically and rather crudely' – to the development of states throughout the Middle Ages until the threshold of the modern age. The practices and institutions of war became more and more concentrated in the hands of a central power; over time only state powers could engage in wars and use the instruments of war: the establishment of state-control over war [*étatisation...de la guerre*]. At the same time, because of this, the private wars of the social body are effaced (SMBD 41/48). War begins to only exist at the frontiers, at the external limits of these grand unified states. The social body is cleansed of the bellicose relations of the medieval period (SMBD 42/48).

Yet Foucault notes a paradox, one that arises at the same time, or maybe a little later, than this transformation. A new discourse appears, one which he describes as 'the first historico-political discourse on society', which is different from the 'philosophico-juridical discourse' which had held until then. This historico-political discourse is a 'discourse on war extended as a permanent social relation, as an ineradicable foundation of all relations and institutions of power'. This discourse dates from the end of the civil and religious wars of the sixteenth century, and is clearly formulated in the political struggles of seventeenth-century England, at the time of the bourgeois revolution. It appears in France a little later, at the end of the reign of Louis XIV (SMBD 42/49). Later Foucault calls this the first non-Roman history that the West had known, because it challenged the Roman notion of Sovereignty (SMBD 60/69). In both contexts the discourse is itself one of the means by which the aristocracy in France, or the bourgeois, petty-bourgeois and eventually the whole population in England, challenge the absolute monarchy; but more fundamentally challenge the idea that society is at peace. Beneath the façade of order is a raging battle. Foucault suggests a long list of writers that have contributed to this discourse – among them Edward Coke, John Lilburne, Henry de Boulainviller,[7] the Abbé Sieyès and Augustin Thierry. He analyses many of them at length in later lectures. He notes that the biological racists and eugenists of the late nineteenth century return to these themes.

He therefore rejects the 'philosophico-juridical theory' which claims political power begins where war ends: 'The organization, the juridical structure of power, of states, of monarchies, of societies does not emerge when the clash of arms ceases. War has not been averted. War presided over the birth of states: law [*le droit*], peace and laws [*les lois*] are born in the blood and mud of battle' (SMBD 43/50). It follows from this that the establishment of law is not a pacification, because beneath the law war continues (SMBD 43/50). 'It is a question of finding the blood which has dried in the legal codes' (SMBD 48/56). These codes, these constitutions, are not written in the ink of consent and contract, but with the blood of those defeated in war. But this is not a war of all against all, but of one group against another; one is either in one group or the other; there is no neutral. This is a binary structure: two groups, two categories of individuals, two armies present (SMBD 44/51). What becomes important is the division, and the reasons for it. Foucault suggests that therefore the principle of history becomes a series of brutal facts, ones we can call physico-biological: 'physical strength, force, energy, proliferation of one race, weakness of the other, etc.' (SMBD 47/54). It is precisely differences in these physico-biological aspects, along with ethnic differences or different languages that allow the separation of two races, that are at the root of social conflict. 'The social body is basically articulated around two races' (SMBD 51/60).

His point is not undertaking a history of 'racist discourse', but rather of 'the war or the struggle of races'. Modern racism is in a sense a reprise of this older discourse. He is undertaking a genealogical study of the struggle of races, in order to make more general points about modern racism, as a history of the present. As the editors of the course note, the contemporary context is set by the events of 1968 in Czechoslovakia and France, the Vietnam War, 1970s Black September in Jordan, student revolts against Salazar in Portugal in 1971, the IRA in Ireland, the Yom Kippur war, the Colonels regime in Greece, fascism in Italy, Francoism in Spain, the Khmer Rouge in Cambodia, and civil war in the Lebanon, Peru, Argentina, Brazil and several African states.[8] The first September 11th, when Salvador Allende was overthrown by a CIA-backed Augusto Pinochet, had taken place in 1973 in Chile. The French Left was struggling with the ideas of Eurocommunism and the unrepentant Stalinism of Georges Marchais, and it took five more years before a semi-united left facilitated the election of François Mitterrand. In the academy, numerous changes were taking place, particularly in the wake of the 1968 protests and those against the Vietnam War.

However, this older discourse, in socio-biological terms, served the ends of social conservatism and, in some cases at least, colonial domination (SMBD 57/64). Modern racism replaces the theme of the historical war with the biological theme, post-evolutionist, of the struggle for life. 'It is no longer a battle in a warrior's sense, but a struggle in a biological sense: differentiation of species, selection of the strongest, survival of the best adapted races. Similarly, the theme of the binary society... becomes replaced by that of a society which is, on the contrary, biologically monist.' This leads to a transition in the role of the state. It is no longer in the interests of one race against another, but 'the protector of integrity, of the superiority and purity of the race' (SMBD 70–1/80–1). The dominant race does not say 'we must defend ourselves against society' but 'we must defend society against all the biological perils of this other race, this sub-race, this contra-race which we are in the process of, in spite of ourselves, constituting'. It is not therefore simply a struggle of one social group against another, but a State racism, a racism society exercises throughout itself; an internal racism, a permanent purification, one of the fundamental dimensions of social normalization (SMBD 53/62, 71/80).

In the case of a society formed through contract, Foucault notes that for Hobbes 'sovereignty thus constituted assumes the personality of all'.[9] But, Foucault then asks, what about the other form of the constitution of republics, the mechanism of acquisition? (SMBD 81–2/94–5). Foucault notes that Hobbes's work, as is often observed, should be understood in the context of the civil struggles that divided England at the time of writing (SMBD 85/99), but also further back, as far as the Norman invasion by William the Conqueror, and suggests that the rituals of power established by this event continued until Henry VII (SMBD 86/99–100). This is particularly true with the figures of the Normans and Saxons, racial divisions which become transposed into more general high and low conditions or classes. 'Conflicts – political, economic, juridical – were…very simply articulated, coded and transformed into a discourse…which was that of the opposition of races' (SMBD 87/100–1). He suggests that the new forms of political struggle that emerged in the sixteenth and seventeenth centuries – between the bourgeoisie, aristocracy and monarchy – were still expressed in the vocabulary of the racial struggle (SMBD 87–8/101–2).

In Foucault's reading of the various interpretations of the Norman–Saxon conflict in England there is the suggestion that much of the literature represents William as the legitimate heir, but one whose sovereignty was limited by the laws of England. As Hobbes recognizes, a state formed by conquest can function as one formed by contract if the people recognize the ruler. As Winston Churchill – the seventeenth-century historian and ancestor of the twentieth-century politician – suggested, 'William did not conquer England; the English conquered William.'[10] The perfectly legitimate transfer of Saxon power to a Norman king was one thing; the later dispossessions, exactions and abuses of power another. This Normanization, the Norman yoke – this political regime favouring the aristocracy and the monarchy – was the target of the revolts of the Middle Ages, the Magna Carta, etc. *not* William himself. And this struggle was re-coded in the seventeenth century through the struggle between King and Parliament. Parliament was seen as the 'true inheritor of Saxon tradition' (SMBD 91/105). The Levellers, for example, viewed the Norman Conquest as the root of the contemporary social and political system; there was a direct relation between William and the lords of the manor and Charles and his colonels.[11] Foucault's point is that this is the first time that the binary schema of rich and poor was not simply a complaint or a demand, but one that was articulated as a fact of nationality: 'language, country of origin, ancestral customs, density of a common past, existence of an archaic right, rediscovery of ancient laws' (SMBD 95/110). This war is exactly what Hobbes is opposing: his philosophico-juridical discourse is a way of blocking what Foucault calls the 'political historicism' which was the dominant discourse or knowledge [*savoir*] in the political struggles of the seventeenth century (SMBD 96/111).

The Trojan myth of the French is that the French were descended from the Francs, who were themselves the Trojans who had left Troy under the King Francus, son of Priam, as the city was burned (SMBD 101/115). For Foucault, what is important is again the war of races: did the Francs conquer the Romans, or the Gauls? This stresses the same motif of invasion as was important in England (SMBD 104/118), and like the Normans and Saxons, the Francs and Gauls are essentially irreconcilable (see SMBD 141/159). The difference is that in this case, it is the victors, the aristocracy, who, portraying themselves as Germanic, write the history. Not only do they assert their separation from the bourgeoisie and proletariat (of Gallo-Roman pedigree), but they also limit the power of the king. These issues will be returned to later in the course, in a new context.

Boulainviller and the Generalization of War

'Until the seventeenth century war was essentially the war of one mass against another mass.' Foucault suggests that 'this generalization of war' is what characterizes Boulainviller's thought. Boulainviller saw how the relations of war worked in all social relations; how social relations were divided in a thousand ways; that war was a sort of permanent state between *groups* in society: not therefore a war of all against all in an individualistic Hobbesian sense, but a war of groups against groups (SMBD 144/162). It is interesting that Foucault takes a seemingly marginal figure to illustrate so many of his key themes, but as Renée Simon notes, 'we should ask ourselves how such a "famous" man in the eighteenth century (the word is Diderot's) could slip into such a complete lapse of memory'.[12]

Boulainviller is not just opposed to finding the constituent point in law, but also in nature. His thought is both anti-juridical and anti-naturalism. The key adversary of this kind of analysis is the 'the natural human, the savage'. This is understood in two senses. First, 'the savage, good or bad, the natural human that the jurists or the theorists of right dreamed up, before society, to form society, as an element from which the social body could constitute itself'. Second, the other aspect of the savage, the ideal element invented by the economists, the human without history or past, who is only moved by their own interest and who exchanges the product of their work for another product. So the notion of the savage that is opposed is simultaneously the one who leaves the forest in order to contract and found society, and also the *Homo oeconomicus* of exchange (SMBD 173/194). This double savage is the human of exchange: exchanger of rights or exchanger of goods. 'As the exchanger of rights, they found society and sovereignty. As exchanger of goods, they constitute the social body which is, at the same time, an economic body' (SMBD 173–4/194).

Foucault suggests that the figure which Boulainviller opposes to the savage is the barbarian. Unlike the savage the barbarian can only be understood, comprehended and described in terms of its relation to civilization. There is no notion of barbarism or cruelty [*barbarie*] without a civilization for it to be outside of. The barbarian is always trampling at the frontiers of states, crashing against the walls of the city. Unlike the savages, who rest at the foundation of nature, the barbarians only arise from the ground of civilization, but against which they will always be in conflict. Therefore the barbarian has a history – unlike the savage – because of the link to civilization. The barbarian is not an exchanger, but a dominator. Barbarians take, they appropriate: rather than cultivate the land, they plunder and pillage. Their freedom is only based on the freedom others have lost; whereas the savages give up some of their liberty to guarantee their life, security and property; the barbarians never give up their liberty. They create a king or elect a chief not to diminish their own power or rights, but to strengthen them, to be stronger in their relation with others. It is to multiply their own individual force that the barbarians put power into place. Their form of government is necessarily military, and does not rest at all on contracts of civil transfer (SMBD 174–5/195–6).

Boulainviller puts this notion of the barbarian to work in his histories, suggests Foucault, and it forms one of the four elements of his study: constitution, revolution, barbarism and domination. The question is one of finding what is useful in barbarism: 'how must one filter barbarian domination to achieve the constituent revolution?' It is the problem of finding within the field of historical discourse, the historico-political field, the tactical positions of the various groups, the various interests, the various centres of the battle of the nobility or monarchical power, of the bourgeoisie (SMBD 176/197). The question then is not a simple opposition of revolution *or* barbarism; but revolution *and* barbarism, 'the economy of barbarism in the revolution'. The contemporary opposition of revolution or barbarism (and here Foucault slips and references the journal *Socialisme ou barbarie*) is therefore a false problem, the true problem is revolution and barbarism (SMBD 176–7/198).[13] Through this move, Foucault suggests, Boulainviller has introduced the figure of the blond beast or barbarian, the juridical and historical fact of invasion and violent conquest, the conquest of land and the servitude of men, and finally an extremely limited royal power. Though Foucault thinks that there are many results of this move, he focuses on just three; which are politically and epistemologically most important, and which corre-spond to three clearly differentiated political positions (SMBD 177/199).

The first is the most vigorous, the absolute filter, where all the traces of barbarism are covered over. The example of France after the Germanic invasion is given: a complete denial of the roots of the nobility, from the other side of the Rhine. The invasion of the Francs is dismissed as a myth, an illusion, a creation of the works of Boulain-viller. The Francs, rather, were a small group of allies who were called upon to resist the Roman invasion. Not, therefore, invasion or conquest, but immigration and alliance. Their later dominant posi-tion – in particular that of the king – is due to invasion, conquest and dominance from within, rather than from without. The power of the nobility is analysed not as a result of a military invasion and the irruption of barbarism, but as a result of internal usurpation. The nobility are political swindlers rather than barbarians (SMBD 177–80/199–202). Examples of this interpretation are the Abbé Dubos and Jacob-Nicolas Moreau.

The second is closest to Boulainviller, and aims to disociate a Ger-manic liberty from the exclusive privileges of the aristocracy. In other words, it opposes the Roman absolutism of the monarchy to the primal liberties which the Franks and the barbarians brought with them. The barbarians did not create a small aristocracy, rather the body of the people. This idea supports a democracy rather than aris-tocracy; an egalitarian understanding of soldier-citizens. 'No author-ity to follow, no reasoned or constituted authority.' In this under-standing, the aristocracy are complicit in absolutism; they support the king, who supports feudalism. 'Of course, the aristocracy and the absolute monarchy will fall out one day, but one must not forget that they are, at root, twin sisters' (SMBD 180–1/202–3). The Abbé Gabriel Bonnet de Mably and Jean-Paul Marat are among Foucault's examples.

The third is, Foucault suggests, the most subtle, which, while it has had the greatest historical success, had less impact at the time when it was formulated. The central point is the distinction drawn between two types of barbarisms; the bad barbarism of the Germans, and the good barbarism of the Gauls, who alone truly possessed liberty. This allows two key moves: on the one hand to disociate liberty and the German; on the other to dissociate the Roman and absolutism. It discovers in Roman Gaul elements of liberty which Boulainviller and the other interpretations had suggested were imported by the Francs. Roman government had certainly included an absolute centralized power, but there was also a residue of the original liberties of the Gauls and Celts. Liberty is therefore compatible with Roman absolutism; a Gallic phenomenon, but above all an urban phenomenon. While the towns were destroyed by the invasion of the Francs, they were rebuilt and became a site for resistance to feudal power. Foucault suggests that clearly here is the root of the theory of the Third Estate, because for the first time the history of the town, the history of urban institutions is at the heart of historical analysis. The Third Estate is not simply formed by concessions from the king, but has a history, a strongly articulated urban right, in part imprinted with Roman right, but founded on an ancient liberty, that is to say on ancient Gallic barbarism (SMBD 181–3/204–6). A number of writers contributes to this interpretation, notably Augustin Thierry.

Foucault's general point is that Boulainviller has constituted 'an historical and political discourse whose domain of objects, pertinent elements, concepts and methods of analysis are all closely interrelated'. In the eighteenth century this historical discourse is held in common by a whole series of historians who oppose each other strongly in 'their theses, hypotheses and their political dreams', but who operate within 'a shared epistemic framework'. This does not mean, of course, that this epistemic frame requires them to think in the same way; rather it is the condition which allows them to think differently, and it is this difference which is politically pertinent. 'The tactical reversibility of the discourse is a direct function of the homogeneity of the rules of formation of this discourse. The regularity of the epistemic field, and the homogeneity of the mode of formation of the discourse, are useable in the struggles which are extra-discursive' (SMBD 185/207–8). These variations within these discourses, and the Rousseauesque juridicism of the noble savage to which they are opposed, are then utilized in a reading of the French Revolution (SMBD 186–9/208–12). What is important, suggests Foucault, is that there are several interpretations of the Revolution, and the political and social struggles within it, in terms of the history of races (SMBD 188/211).

It is therefore the discourse of history, rather than the discourse of right, or that of political theory, which has made war the principal analytic tool of political relations. Political theory, with its contracts, savages, inhabitants of prairies or forests, states of nature, war of all against all, and so on, is not sufficient. In the Revolution, this element of war is not entirely eliminated, but rather reduced, limited, civilized and pacified. The nineteenth-century historical discourse has a model of a final calm, or a perpetual peace not in the sense of an equilibrium (such as was found in the eighteenth century), but in the sense of a reconciliation (SMBD 193/215–16). The problem arises of how the notion of war shifts from being a condition of the existence of society to a condition of the survival of society; how war becomes reinscribed with a negative role, an exterior role; no longer constitutive of society but protector and conserver of society. This is because what appears at this point is the idea of a society that uses war internally as a defence of society against the dangers which are born in its own body and of its own body. It is, suggests Foucault, 'the great reversal from history to biology, from the constituent to the medical in the idea of the social war' (SMBD 194/216).

One of the crucial developments is the shift in the notion of the nation. In the eighteenth century, the idea of the nation, where it was deemed to exist at all, was associated with the body of the king. There was not a nation because there were a group of people who lived in a territory, who had the same language, customs and laws. Rather, individuals, who did not form a union, all had, individually, 'a certain relation, juridical and physical, with the real, living, corporal body [*la personne*] of the king. It was the body [*le corps*] of the king, in its physico-juridical relation with each of his subjects, which made the body of the nation.' This notion of the nation was used by the nobility when wars between nations were fought. In order to investigate this shift, Foucault cites the Abbé Sieyès's famous three questions: 'What is the Third Estate? Everything. What has it been in the political order until now? Nothing. What does it want to be? To become something' (SMBD 194/217).[14] Sieyès has another definition of the nation.[15] This is a two-part definition: on the one hand it is a juridical state or condition [*un état juridique*], with a common law and with a legislature (simply an ability to makes laws: it does not necessarily need a king, nor even a government); on the other it is a group of people held together by a certain interest, who would have certain things in common, like customs, habits, and eventually a language (SMBD 195–6/218). For Sieyès there is no distinction between the people and the nation – this means that the nation is constituted of ordinary people as much as the king or nobility. Indeed, at one point Sieyès falls back on the notion of race in relation to class: 'Those who are not of my species are not my fellow men; a noble is not of my species; he is a wolf and I shoot.'[16]

This political re-elaboration of a notion associated with the aristocracy in the eighteenth century, this reinscription of the nation, the idea of the nation, makes possible a new kind of historical discourse. This understanding of the nation becomes central to state power. It is the active nucleus, the constitutive nucleus, of the State. 'The nation is the State, at least in outline. It is the State insofar as it is in the process of being born, being shaped and finding its historical conditions of existence in a group of individuals' (SMBD 200/223). There is a straight line in the passage from national totality to state universality; and this opens up a way where relations of force are not relations of war, but an entirely civil relation. Foucault reiterates that in Boulainviller's work the confrontation of nations within one social body was made possible through intermediate institutions (economy, education, language, knowledges, etc.), but suggests that in that case there was no pretence that this was not war. In the nineteenth-century case the problem is entirely other; the problem is an internal tension against the universality of the State (SMBD 201/224–5). The question arises, however, as to how these internal struggles can be understood without recourse to military terminology. Can economic and political struggle be understood through properly economic-political terms? Or, on the contrary, must we return to the foundation of war that the historians of the eighteenth century tried to map? (SMBD 202/226).

A Matter of Life and Death

Foucault has therefore used war as a grid of intelligibility for historical processes, but this is a war understood as a war of races. That notion of war is finally eliminated in historical analysis with the principle of national universality, at the time of the French Revolution. The theme of race does not disappear, however, but rather, as has been intimated, becomes reborn as a State racism. It is reborn, because power takes control of life, in both general and specific terms, of the human as a living being and as part of a population, a sort of extension of state power [*étatisation*] over biology (SMBD 213/239–40). The sovereign could only directly take life to defend an attack on his body, or when the threat of external enemies was great he could expose people to the risk of death to defend him. The symbol of this was the sword [*le glaive*] (SMBD 214/240). The nineteenth- and twentieth-century development is that life can be protected, by death if necessary, through the defence of the social body as a whole. While the right of sovereignty was to make die or let live, the modern state can make live or let die (SMBD 214/240–1).

Foucault suggests that the modern formidable power of death is the counterpart of a power which administers life through precise controls and comprehensive regulations (SMBD 215/241–2). What happens is that politics becomes increasingly scientific: medical and mathematical. There is a discipline of the individual body – an *anatomo-politics* – and a regulation of the social body – a *bio-politics* of the population or human species (SMBD 216/243).[17] Not only does politics infiltrate biology, but biology also infiltrates politics. Politics becomes increasingly mathematical as it becomes medical. Bio-power had been a concern since at least 1974, but it is in *'Society Must Be Defended'* that it is first really developed. Bio-power involves the building up of profiles, statistical measures and so on, increasing knowledge through monitoring and surveillance, 'extremely meticulous orderings of space', and control through discipline. Birth and death rates and measures of longevity become important; fertility, illness, diet and habitation become measured; statistics and demographics come together with economics and politics.[18] This use of figures is pronounced in medical campaigns at the time (SMBD 215–7/241–3). Calculation is both a particular case of and the foundation of the more general science of ordering, with the reformulation of old ideas of *mathesis* into a general calculative, ordered, mode of thinking, a *savoir* which functions as a general domain or field, organizing the particular sciences. In *The Order of Things*, a decade previously, Foucault had aimed to show how general grammar, natural history, and the analysis of wealth became linguistics, biology and political economy: in *'Society Must Be Defended'* there is a politicizing of this argument (i.e. SMBD 170/190).

Foucault suggests that the end of the eighteenth century saw a shift from a concern with epidemics to endemics – 'the form, nature, extension, duration, and intensity of the illnesses prevalent in a population' (SMBD 217/243). The key is, of course, public health or hygiene, rather than just hospitals and clinical practice. The same sorts of mechanisms Foucault traces in *Discipline and Punish* can be found in public health: selection, normalization, hierarchisation and centralization (SMBD 161/181). As Foucault notes, 'the body is a bio-political reality; medicine is a bio-political strategy' (DE#196, III, 210; EW III, 137). The use of medical language is important. Because certain groups in society are conceived of in medical terms society is no longer in need of being defended from the outsider but from the insider: the abnormal in behaviour, species or race. What is novel is not the mentality of power, but the technology of power (SMBD 230/258). The recoding of old problems is made possible through new techniques. Issues such as geographical area, climate, and hydrography become important: there was a particular stress on the link between epidemics and proximity to swamps or marshes. One of the key concerns of this period was about water flow – the dangers of swamps and marshes for epidemics, and the need for circulation. The organization of the town becomes a central problem (SMBD 218/245). We find some discussion in *'Society Must Be Defended'* of these issues, which recall *Discipline and Punish*'s analysis of the military camp, in particular of the layout of rational towns, of working-class housing estates with their grid patterns and organizational design (SMBD 223–4/250–1). The organization of the town becomes a central problem (SMBD 218/245). Governments therefore are not just concerned with their territory and the individuals within it, but with an economic, political, scientific, biological problem, a problem of power, a collective problem: that of *population* (SMBD 218–19/245).

Population is a political, economic, political, scientific, biological problem. Population can be usefully conceived as bodies in plural, and while discipline works on the individual body, a multiplicity dissolved, the new technology of power works on the bodies accumulated, as a multiplicity, a species (see SMBD 216/242–3). This might be said to be the transition that takes place between *Discipline and Punish* on the one hand and *'Society Must Be Defended'* and *The Will to Knowledge* on the other, continuing into the work on governmentality. Foucault suggests this can be understood as two series:

> The series body – organism – discipline – institutions; and the series population – biological processes – regulatory mechanisms – State. An organic institutional ensemble: an organic-discipline of the institution, if you will, and on the other side, a biological and statist ensemble: bio-regulation by the State. (SMBD 223/250)

Foucault is keen to stress that there is not a clear separation of institution and state here: the disciplines tend to overflow their institutional context; the state is involved in the disciplines (SMBD 223/250). Equally, there is not a separation of these two understandings of power – as discipline and normalizing bio-power – in Foucault's work. They are not independent of each other, or one successive to the other, but rather are two conjoined modes of the functioning of knowledge/power.[19]

The reason that the problem of sexuality is so interesting is that it is situated at the crossroads of the body and the population; of discipline and regulation (SMBD 224/251–2). The creation of norms, by which the individual body can be measured and disciplined, and the social body can be measured and regulated, is central (SMBD 222/250). Foucault recognizes that any interpretation predicates a norm by which it measures: even if the normal is defined in terms of what it is not, as a consequence (see A 46/50). Understanding the demographics of a population could lead to campaigns to control birth-rates and prolong life: this was the power to 'make live' (SMBD 219–220/246). The extreme form of this is the power to make life, to make the monster, to make uncontrollable and universally destructive viruses (SMBD 226/254). The reverse side is the power to allow death. State racism is a re-coding of the old mechanisms of blood through the new procedures of regulation. For example, the old anti-Semitism based on religion is reused under the new rubric of state racism. The integrity and purity of the race is threatened, and the state apparatuses are introduced against the race that has infiltrated and introduced noxious elements into the body. The Jews are characterized as the race present in the middle of all races (SMBD 76/89). The use of medical language is important. Because certain groups in society are conceived of in medical terms society is no longer in need of being defended from the outsider but from the insider: the abnormal in behaviour, species or race. What is novel is not the mentality of power, but the technology of power (SMBD 230/258). The recoding of old problems is made possible through new techniques.

A break or cut [*coupure*] is fundamental to racism: a division or incision between those who must live and those who must die. The 'biological *continuum* of the human species' (SMBD 227/254–5) is fragmented by the apparition of races, which are distinguished, hierarchized, qualified as good or inferior, etc. The species is sub-divided into sub-groups which are thought of as races: the human continuum is divided, that is, made calculable and orderable. Foucault's claim is that modern discourses of class have their roots in the war of races, as does modern racism. He thus challenges ideas that racism is based on nationalism, or that class is the basis for racial claims. As emphasizing the biological, modern racism puts this in another way: to survive, to live, you must be prepared to massacre your enemies; a relation of war. As a relation of war this is no different from the earlier war of races that Foucault has spent so much of the course explaining. But when coupled with the mechanisms of mathematics and medicine in bio-power, this can be conceived of in entirely different ways. Bio-power is able to establish, between my life and the death of the other, a relation which is not warlike or confrontational, but a biological relation: 'the more inferior species tend to disappear, the more abnormal individuals can be eliminated, the less the species will be degenerated, the more I – not as an individual but as a species – will live, will be strong, will be vigorous, will be able to proliferate'. The death of the other does not just make me safer personally, but the death of the other, of the bad, inferior race or the degenerate or abnormal, makes life in general healthier and purer (SMBD 227–8/255).

Foucault argues that 'if the power of normalization wishes to exercise the ancient sovereign right of killing, it must become racist. And if, conversely, a sovereign power, that is to say a power with the right of life and death, wishes to function with the instruments, mechanisms and technology of normalization, it must also become racist' (SMBD 228/256). This holds for indirect death – the exposure to death – as much as for direct killing. While not Darwinism, this biological sense of power is based on evolutionism, and enables a thinking of colonial relations, the necessity of wars, criminality, phenomena of madness and mental illness, class divisions, etc. The link to colonialism is central: this form of modern state racism develops first with colonial genocide. The theme of the political enemy is extrapolated biologically. But what is important in the shift at the end of the nineteenth century is that war is no longer simply a way of securing one race by eliminating the other, but of regenerating that race (SMBD 228–30/256–8). In Nazism the two are combined. Eugenics and medical/mathematical techniques are coupled with the fantasy of blood and the ideal of the purity of the race. Foucault notes that there was immediate control of procreation and genetics in the regime, and that regulation, security and assurance were imposed over the disciplined ordered society; but at the same time the old sovereign power of killing traversed the entire society. This was not simply confined to the state, nor simply to the SA or the SS, but ultimately to everyone, as through denunciation everyone could have this power over their neighbour (SMBD 231/259).

Now while destruction of other races was central to Nazism, the other side of it was the exposure of the German race itself to death, an absolute and universal risk of death. The entire German population was exposed to death, and Foucault suggests this was one of the fundamental duties of Nazi obedience. Only this exposure of the entire population to the universal risk of death could constitute them as the superior race, regenerated in the face of those races either totally exterminated or completely subjugated. We have therefore, in Nazism, both the absolute generalization of bio-power and the generalization of the sovereign right of death. Two mechanisms: one 'classic, archaic', one new, coincide exactly. 'A racist state, a murderous state, and a suicidal state.' Accompanying the final solution was the order of April 1945 which called for the destruction of the conditions of life of the German people themselves. 'The final solution for other races, and the absolute suicide of the [German] race (SMBD 231–2/60).

Foucault wants to suggest that this is inscribed into modern states more generally, but as he is reaching the end of the course he does not really make good this claim. He looks briefly at how the theme of bio-power was not changed by socialism, but reprised by it – developed and modified certainly – but not fundamentally criticized. Foucault notes the anti-Semitism of French socialist parties during the Dreyfus affair; and earlier in the Paris Commune.[20] Equally the state took control over life, risk and reproduction in socialist states too. Its racism was not properly ethnic, but evolutionist, biological, and was found in its treatment of the mentally ill, criminals and political adversaries. More general than this Soviet model is the use of similar language in the class struggle. The idea of struggle against the enemy, eliminating the adversary within the capitalist society, thinking of physical confrontation with class enemies, all trade on the notion of racism. If it is simply economic elimination, of removing their privileges, it has no need of racism; but if it resorts to confrontation, to physical violence, to risking life and seeking to kill, then it rests on racism. Every time socialism resorts to the language of struggle, Foucault suggests, there is the model of racism (SMBD 232–4/260–3). Foucault therefore ends the course, inconclusively, questioning:

> How can one make bio-power function and at the same time exercise the rights of war, the rights of murder and the function of death, without becoming racist? It was the problem then, and I believe that it is still the problem. (SMBD 234/263)

3

The Will to Know and the Power of Confession

The Will to Know

That Foucault began writing the first volume of the *History of Sexuality* on the very day he finished writing *Discipline and Punish* is extraordinary for multiple reasons.[1] The first, and most obvious, is the driven nature of someone who can put one major work to rest and turn directly to the beginning of another. The second is that Foucault was drafting material for this book two years before he finished it in August 1976. He reveals in an interview that the book's form did not come easily: 'there were several successive drafts', including ones he rejected, and a reversal of approach 'that was only a game, because I wasn't sure' (DE#206 III, 312–13; P/K 210). The third is that Foucault began the second book with its last chapter,[2] which discusses race, the state, and the right of death and power over life. That chapter is very close to the final lecture of *'Society Must Be Defended'*, delivered on 17 March 1976. Eighteen months after beginning the chapter, Foucault elaborates its themes in a course where its argument is anticipated much more historically.[3]

There are hints of a project on sexuality much earlier in Foucault's career, including in *History of Madness*. Indeed, Eribon says Foucault told Gérard Lebruin in 1965 that this was his next project, having completed *The Order of Things*: 'It is almost impossible to do. One would never be able to find the archives.'[4] Foucault gave courses on sexuality at Clermont-Ferrand in 1964 (C 26/30), and at Vincennes in 1969 (C 34/41), and he was clearly thinking about possible ways to present this work (see DE#197 III, 229–30; P/K 184–5). Nonetheless it would be a decade before Foucault presented material in a form that is recognizable from the end product. Initially this was in a lecture in Berkeley on 8 May 1975 – Foucault's first visit to Berkeley, on the invitation of Leo Bersani and the French department[5] – and then almost the same paper to the 'Schizo-Culture' conference at Columbia University on 14 November the same year, shortly after he had delivered lectures on the theme in São Paulo.[6] Foucault begins the lecture by saying, 'I have taken on a piece of work that is a sort of sequel to my book on the history of madness.' He again notes that he could not find the documents for such a 'history of sexual repression', but now realizes that this was 'probably simply because such documents didn't exist', and that his focus needed to be elsewhere: it was not that there were no documents, but that the repression focus was misjudged (FL 154).

The book appeared in December 1976, and begins with two rather polemical chapters that highlight the problems of the approach through repression.[7] The first trades on Steven Marcus's work *The Other Victorians*, a book that examines sexuality and pornography in nineteenth-century England.[8] Foucault's chapter is entitled '*Nous autres, victoriens*' – 'We other Victorians' or 'We others, Victorians'. The point is that while, like the Victorians, we think we have a restrictive and restrained sexuality, it is actually quite different in practice. In particular, in this and the second chapter, entitled 'The Repressive Hypothesis', Foucault challenges the idea that sex is repressed in Western societies. This is an analysis proposed, in part, by Wilhelm Reich, but also Herbert Marcuse (see DE#297 IV, 198), that sees sexual repression as part of the tactics of capitalism.[9] An additional target is Jos van Ussel's history of sexual repression, a 1967 work which was translated into French in 1972 (see A 39/42; 221/235–6; FL 154).[10] Foucault characterizes this view as one where:

> Sexuality was carefully confined; it moved into the home. The conjugal family took custody of it. And absorbed it entirely into the serious function of reproduction. On the subject of sex, silence became the rule. The legitimate and procreative couple laid down the law. (HS I 9–10/3)

Foucault's critique of a Marxist mode of production argument is pronounced in these opening pages. His own view challenges 'a widely accepted thesis' and 'goes against the whole economy and the discursive "interests" which underlie it'. His historical analyses will provide 'a mapping [*repérage*] of some historically significant points and sketches of certain theoretical problems' (HS I 16/8). Foucault's point is that issues identified in other accounts need to be understood within a much wider complex of questions. The 'repressive hypothesis' sees 'defences, refusals, censorships, denials' as part of a 'grand mechanism'; Foucault wants to reconfigure them as 'only parts that have a local and tactical role to play within a putting into discourse, within a technology of power, within a will to know that are far from being reducible to them' (HS I 21/12). His aim is thus to write an historical account of their emergence, raising various doubts about the standard story that are 'historical...historico-theoretical... historico-political' (HS I 18/10; 21–22/13).

Foucault's key argument against the idea of a repressive age, tied to bourgeois societies, is that, far from their being censorship and muting of discussion, there was 'a veritable discursive explosion' (HS I 25/17). This does not mean that things were all said in the same way, but that there was what Foucault calls – in an explicit politicizing of the language of *The Archaeology of Knowledge* – a *'police des énoncés'*, a policing of statements; a 'restrictive economy' (HS I 26/18). This economy was part of 'the politics of language and speech [*la langue et de la parole*] – spontaneous on the one hand, concerted on the other – which accompanied the social redistributions of the classical period' (HS I 26/18). 'The policing of sex' in the modern era does not have 'the rigor of a prohibition but the necessity of regulating sex through useful and public discourses' (HS I 35/25). Historically there was a proliferation of specific discourses on sex 'within the field of the exercise of power itself' (HS I 26/18); of which his key example is the 'evolution of the Catholic pastoral and the sacrament of penance [*pénitence*] after the Council of Trent' (HS I 27/18).

This is a crucial point in Foucault's text, as he notes that even though there was an upheaval in the late Medieval Church, and 'the language may have been refined [*châtier*], the extension of confession, and the confession of the flesh [*l'aveu, et de l'aveu de la chair*], continued to grow' (HS I 27/19). The Counter-Reformation is the key example here. 'This scheme for "transforming sex into discourse" [*une «mise en discourse» du sexe*] had been devised long before in an ascetic and monastic setting. The seventeenth century made it into a rule for everyone' (HS I 29/18). He continues to suggest 'the reformed pastoral also laid down rules, albeit in a more discreet way, for putting sex into discourse. This notion will be developed in the next volume, *La Chair et le corps*' (HS I 30 n. 1/21 n. 4). It therefore makes sense that discussion of this topic in this book is quite limited, given the promise for the next volume. But that book never appeared, and so we are forced to analysis what Foucault thought of this on the basis of lecture material. These questions will be discussed later in this chapter and, with a different historical focus, in Chapter 5.

Foucault finds this urge to speak as much in memoirs and works of literature as in pastoral injunctions, looking at the Marquis de Sade and the book *My Secret Life* (HS I 31/21).[11] The later text is described by Marcus as 'the most important document of its kind about Victorian England, but one that at the time of his writing has been written about exclusively by those who have not read it'.[12] Foucault suggests 'this anonymous Englishman would be better than his sovereign [*sa souvereigne*] as the central figure for the history of modern sexuality which had already formed for the most part with the Christian pastoral' (HS I 32/22). Foucault's reference is of course to Queen Victoria, but it is another striking analysis of how an anonymous figure once more displaces a sovereign. The key point is that instead of a 'censorship of sex', there is rather 'an apparatus [*un appareillage*] to produce discourse on sex, ever more discourse, capable of functioning and taking effect in its own economy...a technique...a political, economical and technical incitement to talk about sex' (HS I 33/23). Yet it did not work in terms of the production and control of language alone. The 'policing of sex' takes place not only in the discursive, but also in the realm of power relations. This has implications far beyond a narrow focus on sex, even though that was at its core:

> One of the great innovations in the techniques of power in the eighteenth century was the emergence of 'population' as an economic and political problem: population-wealth, population-manpower or labour capacity, population as balanced between its own growth and the resources it used. Governments perceived that they were not dealing simply with subjects, or even with a 'people', but with a 'population', with its specific phenomena and its peculiar variables: birth and death rates, life expectancy, fertility, state of health, frequency of illnesses, patterns of diet and habitation...At the heart of this economic and political problem of population was sex: it was necessary to analyse the birth-rate, the age of marriage, the legitimate and illegitimate births, the precocity and frequency of sexual relations, the ways of making them fertile or sterile, the effects of unmarried life and of prohibitions, of contraceptive practices – of those notorious 'deadly secrets' that demographers, on the eve of the Revolution, knew were already familiar in the countryside. (HS I 35–6/25–6)

Foucault is here anticipating themes he would discuss in detail in subsequent lecture courses, but he also links the regulation of sex to that of race and racism from the course delivered earlier in 1976 (HS I 37/26). Yet in contrast to earlier courses, here Foucault tends to discuss institutions and practices rather than the lives of individuals.

Take the secondary schools of the eighteenth century, for example. On the whole, one can have the impression that sex was hardly spoken of in these institutions. But it is enough to glance at the architectural *dispositifs*, over the rules of discipline and the entire interior organization: it never stops being a question of sex. The builders thought of it explicitly. The organizers took it into account continually. (HS I 39–40/27–8)[13]

The key instance of a specific individual case being treated is the story of Charles Jouy, previously discussed in *The Abnormals* (and Chapter 1, above). There is less detail in this book than the course, and the possibility of rape is not mentioned. Foucault simply describes the event as 'At the border of a field, a few caresses from a little girl, just as he had done before and seen done by the village urchins round about him; for, at the edge of the wood, or in the ditch by the road leading to Saint-Nicholas, they would play the familiar game called "curdled milk"' (HS I 43/31). Foucault's point is that the significant thing is the shift in how such events were dealt with: 'the minor character of it all; the fact that this everyday occurrence in the life of village sexuality, these inconsequential bucolic pleasures [these minor rural delights – *ces infimes délections buissonnières*], could become, from a certain time, the object not only of a collective intolerance but of a judicial action, a medical intervention, a careful clinical examination, and an entire theoretical elaboration' (HS I 44/31). Yet once again he is a danger of marginalizing the others involved.

Part of Foucault's argument is that, while a lot of these discussions of sex can be traced back to the Middle Ages, there has been a shift. While there was a 'markedly unitary' discourse in the Middle Ages on 'the theme of the flesh and the practice of penance', this was now proliferating into 'a multiplicity of discourses produced by a whole series of mechanisms [*appareillages*] operating in different institutions...demography, biology, medicine, psychiatry, psychology, morals [*la morale*], pedagogy, and political criticism' (HS I 46/33). It is for this reason that there is a tension continuing: 'What is peculiar [*propre*] to modern societies, is not that they consigned sex to remain in the shadows, but that they dedicated themselves to always speaking of it, while valuing it as *the* secret' (HS I 49/35).

This focus was no longer on the heterosexual, monogamous couple, which 'tended to function as a norm, one that was stricter, perhaps, but quieter'. Instead, 'what came under scrutiny was the sexuality of children, the mad and criminals; the pleasure [*plaisir*] of those who did not like the opposite sex; reveries, obsessions, petty manias or great rages' (HS I 53/38–9). Earlier figures such as the libertine become marginalized, while new figures such as the pervert [*le pervers*]' (HS I 54/39) become more important. This category is both very specific – the individual cases Foucault has discussed in his lectures – and can be broadened to encompass a wide range of phenomena.

> An entire sub-race [*un petit peuple*] was born, different – despite certain kinship ties – from the libertines of the past. From the end of the eighteenth century to our own, they circulated through the interstices of society; they were hounded, but not always by laws; often locked up, but not always in prisons; were sick perhaps, but scandalous, dangerous victims, prey to a strange evil that also bore the names of vice and sometimes crime [*délit*]. They were children wise beyond their years [*enfants trop éveillés*], precocious little girls, ambiguous schoolboys, dubious servants and educators, cruel or maniacal husbands, solitary collectors, ramblers with bizarre impulses; they haunted disciplinary councils, the houses of correction, the penal colonies, the tribunals, and the asylums; they carried their infamy to the doctors and their sickness to the judges. This was the numberless family of perverts who were neighbours to delinquents and akin to madmen. In the course of the century they successively bore the stamp of 'moral folly', 'genital neurosis', 'aberration of the genetic instinct', 'degenerescence', or 'physical imbalance'. (HS I 55–6/40)

In order to address such questions, Foucault outlines a number of quite specific questions in summary form:

- how ancient prohibitions against consanguine marriage and adultery shifted into the modern medicalization of incest and the 'solitary habits' of children
- a 'new persecution of peripheral sexualities... an *incorporation of perversions* and a new *specification of individuals*'
- the continual observation and examination – a 'technology of health and pathology'
- the '*dispositifs of sexual* saturation so characteristic of the space and the social rituals of the nineteenth century'
- a proliferation of sex beyond the couple, such that through the examination and treatment it 'produced and determined the sexual mosaic', showing how modern society is perverse. (HS I 57–65/41–7)

In doing so, Foucault makes a number of indicative gestures about specific sexual characters. His comments on hermaphrodites in the first volume are rather restrictive: see, for example, the claim that 'Prohibitions bearing on sex were essentially of a juridical nature.

The "nature" on which they were based was still a kind of law. For a long time hermaphrodites were criminals, or crime's offspring [*rejetons*], since their anatomical disposition, their very being, confused the law that distinguished the sexes and prescribed their union' (HS I 52–3/38). Equally, his discussion of homosexuality is indicative rather than comprehensive:

> Sodomy – that of the ancient civil or canonical law – was a category of forbidden acts; its perpetrator [*auteur*] was only a juridical subject. The homosexual of the nineteenth century became a personage: a past, a history and a childhood, a character, a form of life; a morphology as well, with an indiscreet anatomy and possibly a mysterious physiology. Nothing that went into his total composition was unaffected by his sexuality...Homosexuality appeared as one of the figures of sexuality when it was transposed [*rabattue*] from the practice of sodomy onto a kind of interior androgeny, a hermaphrodism of the soul. The sodomite had been a throwback [*un relaps*]; the homosexual was now a species. (HS I 59/43)

This shift from an individual act to the description of a type is significant. But Foucault's major point in all this is to demonstrate the erroneousness of earlier work. He insists that the hypothesis of 'an age of increased sexual repression must be abandoned'. This is for two reasons: 'a visible explosion of heretical sexualities', but also because 'a *dispositif* quite different from the law, even if it is locally reliant on procedures of prohibition, ensures, through a network of interconnecting mechanisms, the proliferation of specific pleasures and the multiplication of disparate sexualities' (HS I 67/49).

His formulation of the problem revolves around two modes of knowledge [*savoir*]. One of these is a biology of reproduction, 'which developed continuously according to a general scientific normativity', while the other is a medicine of sex, dependent on 'quite different rules of formation' (HS I 73/54). Both of these have links to questions of the will to know of the book's title, and to the question of truth:

> For there can be no misunderstanding [*méconnaissance*] that is not based on a fundamental relation to truth [*vérité*]. Evading it, barring access to it, masking it: these were so many local tactics which, as if by superimposition and through a last-minute detour, gave a paradoxical form to a fundamental petition to know [*savoir*]. Choosing not to recognize [*reconnaître*] was yet another vagary of the will to truth [*la volonté de vérité*]. (HS I 74/55)

The play with words relating to *connaissance* – misunderstanding or failed knowledge, to recognize – and to *savoir* – knowledge, and to know – is important, but so too is the will to truth, familiar from at least as early as his first Paris course.

The latter of these two scientific knowledges is, in this volume, illustrated by the medical knowledge of Charcot at the Salpêtrière hospital.

> It was an enormous apparatus [*appareil*] of observation, with its examinations, interrogations, and experiments, but it was also a machinery [*machinerie*] for incitement, with its public presentations, its theatre of ritual crises, carefully staged with the help of ether or amyl nitrate, its interplay of dialogues, palpitations, laying on of hands, postures which the doctors elicited or obliterated with a gesture or a word, its hierarchy of personnel who kept watch, organized, provoked, monitored, and reported, and who accumulated an immense pyramid of observations and dossiers. (HS I 74–5/55–6; see DE#206 III, 319–20; P/K 218)

The linking of practices of power and procedures of knowledge, with its use in the examination and observation discussed in *Discipline and Punish*, makes several suggestive indications. But we now know how much of this, and the ensuing analysis, was dependent on the much more detailed discussion of hysteria in *Psychiatric Power*, and can imagine something of what was likely to come in the planned book on this topic. Some indications are given later in this chapter. Hysteria itself is only mentioned briefly in the published volume (HS I 75 n. 1/56 n. 1; 201–2/153).

Together biology and medicine constitute a *scientia sexualis*, a science of sex, which he contrasts to an *ars erotica*, an erotic art, such as can be found in 'China, Japan, India, Rome, the Arabo-Muslim societies' (HS I 76/57). This is a very bold – and, as he would later recognize, unjustified claim – that 'historically, there have been two great procedures for producing the truth of sex' (HS I 76/57).[14] What Foucault initially locates outside of the Western tradition would, in his last writings, be found in Ancient Greece:

> In the erotic art, truth is drawn from pleasure [*plaisir*] itself, understood as a practice and accumulated as an experience, pleasure is not considered in relation to an absolute law of the permitted and the forbidden, nor by reference to a criterion of utility, but first and foremost in relation to itself; it is known [*connaître*] as pleasure, evaluated in terms of intensity, its specific quality, its duration, its reverberations in the body and the soul. Moreover, this knowledge [*savoir*] must be deflected back into the sexual practice itself, in order to shape it as though from within and amplify its effects. (HS I 77/57)

Scientia sexualis is described as being a product of 'the only civilization to have developed over the centuries procedures for telling the truth of sex'. These are 'geared to a form of power-knowledge [*pouvoir-savoir*] strictly opposed to the art of initiations and the masterful secret: I have in mind the confession [*l'aveu*]' (HS I 78/58). This then is the general claim: the emergence of something called 'sexuality' is 'the correlative of that slowly developed discursive practice which is the *scientia sexualis*' (HS I 91/68).

This is then one of the key issues Foucault wants to address in this work. 'Let us put forward a general working hypothesis. The society that emerged in the eighteenth century – bourgeois, capitalist, or industrial society, call it what you will – did not confront sex with a fundamental refusal of recognition. On the contrary, it put into operation an entire machinery [*appareil*] for producing true discourses concerning it' (HS I 92/69). A whole set of procedures and practices exist within this. Towards the end of the chapter Foucault suggests that the *ars erotica* did not entirely disappear with the emergence of the *scientia sexualis*, nor was it entirely foreign to that science itself. His two examples are possession and ecstasy, both of which had been discussed in *The Abnormals* lecture course (HS I 94–5/70). But in sum he suggests that instead of the repressive analysis, we should interrogate 'the operation of a subtle network [*réseau*] of discourses, knowledges, pleasures and powers' (HS I 96/72).

The *Dispositif* of Sexuality

To interrogate this, he introduces the most important conceptual innovation of the first volume, the concept of the *dispositif*, an idea that has caused much confusion and debate. The existing English translation is extremely unhelpful on this point, rendering it most often as 'deployment', but also as 'apparatus', 'layout', 'device', 'construct', and 'organization'. *Dispositif* has some important uses in previous lecture courses and in *Discipline and Punish*, but by now it has taken on a much more significant role. It is more than just an apparatus or mechanism, but replaces the earlier notion of an *episteme* as a collection of rules for the formation of knowledge, now including relations of power, practices and actions. As Foucault's work on knowledge shifts to power-knowledge, so too does the *episteme* to the *dispositif*. The *dispositif* of sexuality therefore determines how we think about sex (HS I 205–6/155; see 207–8/156–7); it provides a context, framework or, even, a structure within which individual instances of behaviour, pieces of knowledge and acts of resistance find their place and their meaning. Foucault's best description comes in an interview shortly after the publication of the book:

> what I try to map with this term is, first, a thoroughly heterogeneous ensemble consisting of discourses, institutions, architectural forms, regulatory decisions, laws, administrative measures, scientific statements [*énoncés*], philosophical, moral and philanthropic propositions – in short the said as much as the unsaid. Such are the elements of the *dispositif*. The *dispositif* itself is the system of relations that can be established between these elements...what I call a *dispositif* is a much more general case of the *episteme*; or rather, the *episteme* is a specifically discursive *dispositif*, whereas the *dispositif* in its general form is both discursive and non-discursive, its elements being much more heterogeneous. (DE#206 III, 299, 300–1; P/K 194, 197)

The fourth section of the book, under the title of 'the *dispositif* of sexuality' is split into four chapters, and contains some crucial discussion. Foucault offers a compressed historical narrative; several crucial methodological precepts; crucial clarifications regarding his understanding of power, and an outline of how he intends to undertake his studies from this point on. Foucault suggests that he will 'put forward some general propositions concerning the objective [*l'enjeu*], the method, the domain to be covered, and the periodizations that can be provisionally accepted' (HS I 105/ 80). Short of quoting extensive passages at length it is difficult to do justice to the fecundity of the insights here.

Instead, this section will try to outline some of the most important claims. First, the objective. He wants to outline an analytic of power rather than a theory of power (HS I 109/82), putting it to work. But to do this he has to reject several elements of the standard, juridico-discursive, understanding of power, namely

1. the negative relation
2. the insistence [*l'instance*] of the rule
3. the cycle of prohibition [*l'interdit*]
4. the logic of censorship
5. the uniformity of its *dispositif* (HS I 110–2/83–5)

He suggests that that formation of power arose at a specific historical juncture, but that it is one we have gone beyond today. Foucault gives a compressed historical rationale for this transition, suggesting that the 'great institutions of power that developed in the Middle Ages – the monarchy and the state, with its apparatuses' were based upon but also in opposition to the multiplicity of existing powers that pre-dated them. Much of this is based on themes explored in *Théories et institutions pénales*. What seems striking here is that a lot of what he is talking about is the late Middle Ages or much of what we would call the Early Modern period.

> But such was the language of power, the representation it gave of itself, and the entire theory of public law that was constructed in the Middle Ages, or reconstructed from Roman law, bears witness to the fact. Law was not simply a weapon skilfully wielded by monarchs; it was the monarchic system's mode of manifestation and the form of its accept-ability. In Western societies since the Middle Ages, the exercise of power has always been formulated in terms of law. (HS I 115/87)

The use of Roman law immediately dates this to no earlier than the twelfth century, and probably the fourteenth. He references a tradi-tion dating back to the eighteenth and nineteenth century – i.e. the France of the Revolutionary period – that criticized absolutist power, and references Boulainviller for the only time in this book at this point. But the *ancien régime* was not a medieval monarchy. It was an absolutist modern monarchy, really established as such in the seventeenth century, and indeed Foucault describes it as 'absolute monarchic power' (HS I 115/87). It is this that leads to one of Foucault's most commonly quoted phrases:

> At base, despite the differences in epochs and objectives, the represen-tation of power has remained haunted by monarchy. In political thought and analysis, we still have not cut off the head of the king. (HS I 117/88–9; see DE#192 III, 150; EW III, 122)

In other words, we need to break with the model of law and sover-eignty to understand the workings of modern power (HS I 118–19/90). The tricky thing is how to examine sex, which seems to be accessed and shaped by power through repression. 'Through which mechanisms, or tactics, or devices?' (HS I 119/90). In distinction, Foucault proposes a 'technology' of sex, much more complicated and complex, and much more positive than merely prohibition: 'Think both of sex without the law, and power without the king' (HS I 120/91).

In the second chapter of this part Foucault makes use of the analy-sis developed in the lecture course earlier that year, though without the historical background he had there provided: 'Should we turn the expression around then and say that politics is war pursued by other means' (HS I 123/93). He then makes several significant propositions concerning power, which have become so ingrained in social science research since it is difficult to recognize the challenge they threw down forty years ago. Power is not possessed but exercised; power relations are immanent in other relations, not exterior to them; power comes from below; 'power relations are both intentional and non-subjective' (HS I 123–4/94); and that 'where there is power, there is resistance, and yet, or rather consequently, this resistance is never in a position of exteriority to power' (HS I 125–6/95). A whole industry has emerged to make sense and apply these insights, yet Foucault's own presentation remains the best introduction.

Foucault suggests that there are four rules to follow, understood as 'cautionary prescriptions' rather than 'Imperatives of method' (HS I 129/98).

1. Rule of immanence...'Between techniques of knowledge and strategies of power, there is no exteriority', power-knowledge (HS I 130/98)
2. Rules of continual variations – not who has power, and who is deprived of it; who has the right to know and who doesn't. 'Relations of power-knowledge are not static forms of distribution, they are "matrices of transformations"' (HS I 131/99)
3. Rule of double conditioning – relation between actions: 'one must conceive of the double conditioning of a strategy by the specificity of possible tactics, and of tactics by the strategic envelope that makes them work' (HS I 132/99–100)
4. Rules of the tactical polyvalence of discourses – not a simple relation, not uniform or stable, 'Discourse transmits and produces power; it reinforces it, but also undermines and exposes it, renders it fragile and makes it possible to thwart it' (HS I 133/100–1)

Later that year, in a lecture in Brazil, and building on insights he takes from Marx, Foucault declares that 'We must not speak of power, if we want to do an analysis of power, but we should speak of powers and try to localize them in their historical and geographical specificity...Society is an archipelago of different powers' (DE#297 IV, 187; SKP 156). In the third chapter, Foucault comes to more detail about how these propositions and sketches will be put to work in this and planned subsequent studies. He suggests that 'we can distinguish four great strategic unities [*ensembles*] which, beginning in the eighteenth century, formed specific *dispositifs* of knowledge and power centring on sex' (HS I 137/103).

1. a hysterization of the bodies of women
2. a pedagogization of the sex of children

3. a socialization of procreative behaviour
4. a psychiatrization of perverse pleasure (HS I 137–8/104–5)

These four *ensembles* are very significant, because after the projected volume on confession, they were to be the emphasis of the remaining planned volumes of the *History*. As Foucault elaborates:

> Four figures emerged from this preoccupation with sex, which mounted [*monte*] throughout the nineteenth century – four privileged objects of knowledge, which were also targets and anchorage points for the ventures of knowledge: the hysterical woman, the masturbating child, the Malthusian couple, and the perverse adult. Each of them corresponded to one of these strategies which, each in its own way, invested and made use of the sex of women, children and men (HS I 139/105).

The key point is that sexuality is not, for Foucault, something that exists and which is regulated, controlled or known, but something *produced*. Power does not seek to dominate it; nor knowledge to reveal or uncover it.

> Sexuality...is the name given to an historical *dispositif*: not a furtive reality that is difficult to grasp, but a great surface network in which the stimulation of bodies, the intensification of pleasures, the incitement to discourse, the formation of knowledges [*connaissances*], the strengthening of controls and resistances, are linked to one another, in accordance with a few major strategies of knowledge [*savoir*] and power. (HS I 139/105–6)

This *dispositif* is not the only one, because it was preceded by the *dispositif* of alliance, a different model of relating these questions. It is not, though, a simple replacement of the first with the second, but the second emerging around it, with 'the practice of penance, then that of the examination of conscience and spiritual direction' as 'the formative nucleus' (HS I 141–2/107). The problematic of the 'flesh': 'the body, sensation, the nature of pleasure, the more secret movements of concupiscence, the subtle forms of enjoyment [*délectation*] or acquiescence [*consentement*]' (HS I 142/108). The question of confession and its relation to the flesh and the body will be discussed below, but this is the key claim: ' "Sexuality" was being born, born of a technology of power that was originally focused on alliance' (HS I 142/108). All kinds of crucial figures, some of which Foucault had discussed in earlier lecture courses, and some of which he intended to discuss in subsequent volumes, emerge at this point:

Then these new personages made their appearance: the nervous woman, the frigid wife, the indifferent mother – or the mother beset by murderous obsessions – the impotent, sadistic, perverse husband, the hysterical or neurasthenic girl, the precocious and already exhausted child, and the young homosexual who rejects marriage or neglects his wife. These were the combined figures of an alliance gone bad and an abnormal sexuality; they were the means by which the disturbing factors of the latter were brought into the former; and yet they also provided an opportunity for the alliance system to assert its prerogatives in the order of sexuality. (HS I 146/110–11)

But before he can move to those different individuals, Foucault has a major project in mind: 'one of the most significant aspects of this entire history of the *dispositif* of sexuality'. This is something which has 'its beginnings in the technology of the "flesh" in classical Christianity, born itself on the alliance system and the rules that regulated the latter; but today it fills a reverse function in that it tends to prop up the old *dispositif* of alliance'. Thus the relation of these two *dispositifs* – alliance and sexuality – remains to be explored. The object of study is the Christian pastoral, in which they relative positions are reversed: 'in the Christian pastoral, the law of alliance codified the flesh which was just being discovered and fitted it into a framework that was still juridical in character; with psychoanalysis, sexuality gave body and life to the rules of alliance by saturating them with desire' (HS I 149–50/113).

The final chapter of this part of the book is on periodization, and suggests some of the key historical turning points or ruptures. Foucault outlines the possible economic story (HS I 150–1/114), but stresses other events he sees as more significant – notably the legacy of medieval Christianity, but also pedagogy, medicine and demography:

We must attempt to trace the chronology of these devices [*procédés*]: the inventions, the instrumental mutations, and the renovations [of previous techniques]...the calendar of their utilization, the chronology of their diffusion and of the effects (of subjectification [*assujettissement*] and resistance) they produced. These multiple datings doubtless will not coincide with the great repressive cycle that is ordinarily situated between the seventeenth and twentieth centuries...[it] must be sought in the penitential practices of medieval Christianity, or rather in the dual series constituted by the obligatory, exhaustive, and periodic confession [*l'aveu*] imposed on all the faithful by the Lateran Council and by methods of asceticism, spiritual exercise, and mysticism that evolved with special intensity from the sixteenth century on. First, the Reformation, then Tridentine Catholicism, mark an important mutation and a schism in what might be called the 'traditional technology of the flesh'. (HS I 152–3/115–6; see 158/119)

There is, in the two *dispositifs* he outlines, an uneven application, which provides a challenge, again, to the idea that repression was for the benefit of labour capacity. It was not directed predominantly towards the young adult man, nor towards the labouring classes (HS I 159/120). He notes that the working classes were able to escape the *dispositif* of sexuality for some time, though not the *dispositif* of alliance (HS I 160/121). The key point is not that the ruling classes imposed it on the working classes: 'Rather it appears to me that they first tried it on themselves' (HS I 162/122).

The Right of Death and Power over Life

The final chapter of the book is very close to the final lecture of *'Society Must Be Defended'*, with major themes repeated between the two. This was analysed in Chapter 2: the discussion here merely focuses on continuities and additions. However, seeing this final chapter in the light of the course is revealing of the much larger argument and supporting evidence concerning race. Foucault contends that the power of the sovereign over individual lives, whose symbol was the sword, was of course an ancient right, deriving from the Roman *patria potestas* (HS I 177/135); and by the time it was put on a contractual basis by the likes of Hobbes, it was already in a circumscribed and diminished form. In modern power, the state attempts to defend the social body through controls over life and death (HS I 178–9/135–6). Indeed, Foucault suggests that 'never have wars been so bloody as they have been since the nineteenth century, and all things being equal, never before did regimes visit such holocausts on their own populations' (HS I 179/136–7). This is, in part, because of the use of measures and regulations, a political and mathematical control that finds its application in the two registers of the anatomo-politics of the body and the bio-politics of the population (HS I 183/139; DE#297 IV, 193–4; SKP 161–2). The discussion of bio-politics in this book is heavily indebted to these earlier lectures; the opening up of the question of population is one that would occupy him for several years. As Foucault put it in a lecture on 1 November 1976, population is not merely 'a group of numerous humans, but living beings, traversed, commanded, ruled by processes and biological laws. A population has a birth rate, a rate of mortality, a population has an age curve, a generation pyramid, a life-expectancy, a state of health, a population can perish or, on the contrary grow' (DE#297 IV, 193; SKP 161).

In a contemporaneous review of Jacques Ruffié's *De la biologie à la culture*,[15] entitled 'Bio-histoire et bio-politique', Foucault suggests Ruffié is 'one of the most eminent representatives of the new physical anthropology' (DE#179 III, 96). One of the conclusions that Foucault draws from Ruffié is that 'although the species cannot be defined by a prototype but by a collection of variations, race, for the biologist, is statistical notion – a "population"' (DE#179 III, 96). Overall, as well as contributing to the bio-politics that Foucault has been advancing since 1974, Ruffié also helps with a project of bio-history, 'that would no longer be the unitary and mythological history of the human species through time' (DE#179 III, 97).

As the lecture course had noted, the reason that the problem of sexuality is so politically important for Foucault is that, like medicine, it is situated at the intersections of the body and the population; of discipline and regulation (DE#192, III, 153; P/K 125; HS I 191–2/145; SMBD 224/251–2). 'Sex was a means of access both to the life of the body and the life of the species' (HS I 192/146). The campaigns against masturbation and incest, which allow power to infiltrate the heart of the family are examples here (A 219–56/231–71). Trading explicitly on the course delivered earlier that year, Foucault suggests that 'The Constitutions written throughout the world since the French Revolution, the Codes drafted and revised, all this continual and noisy legislative activity should not deceive us: these are the forms which make acceptable this essentially normalizing power' (HS I 190/144). In this Foucault links his work on the disciplines explicitly to his work on warfare, and points towards the future work on governmentality, the regulation of populations.

> Wars are no longer waged in the name of a sovereign who must be defended; they are waged in the name of the existence of all; entire populations are mobilized for the purpose of wholesale slaughter in the name of life necessity. Massacres have become vital. It is as managers of life and survival, of bodies and the race, that so many regimes have been able to wage so many wars, causing so many men to be killed... The existence in question is no longer of sovereignty, juridical; but that of the population, biological. If genocide is truly the dream of modern powers, this is not because of a return today of the ancient right to kill; it is because power is situated and exercised at the level of life, the species, the race, and the large-scale phenomena of population. (HS I 180/137)

The shift Foucault thinks is interesting is what might be called a shift from sanguinity to sexuality: sanguinity in that it had an instrumental role (the shedding of blood), and a symbolic role (purity of blood, differences of blood); sexuality when mechanisms of power are directed to the body, to life. The theme of race is there in both, but in a different form (HS I 194/147). We have moved from *a symbolics of blood* to *an analytics of sexuality*. A contrast is established: 'Clearly, nothing was more on the side of the law, death, transgression, the symbolic, and sovereignty than blood; just as sexuality was on the side of the norm, knowledge [*savoir*], life, meaning, the disciplines and regulations' (HS I 195/148; see also DE#179 III 96). Racism, as biologizing, as tied to a state, takes shape where the procedures of intervention 'at the level of the body, conduct, health and everyday life, received their colour and their justification from the mythical concern with protecting the purity of the blood and ensuring the triumph of the race' (HS I 197/149). Foucault claimed in a 1977 interview that the final chapter of this book was frequently neglected in the literature, something that endured for some time and has only been partly redressed since the lecture courses have been published. Foucault suggested that though the book was short, he suspected people did not reach the last chapter. 'All the same', he added, 'it is the foundation of the book' (DE#206 III, 323; P/K 222). The lecture, though, is a much more logical conclusion to the course than the chapter is to the book, perhaps helping to explain the neglect.[16]

Right at the end of the chapter he links it back to the central conceptual innovation of this text:

> We must not refer a history of sexuality to the agency [*l'instance*] of sex; but rather show how 'sex' is historically subordinate [*dépendance*] to sexuality. We must not place sex on the side of reality, and sexuality on that of confused ideas and illusions; sexuality is a very real historical formation; it is what gave rise to the notion of sex, as a speculative element necessary to its operation. We must not think that by saying yes to sex, one says no to power; on the contrary, one tracks along the course laid out by the general *dispositif* of sexuality. It is the agency [*l'instance*] of sex that we must break away from, if we aim – through a tactical reversal of the various mechanisms of sexuality – to counter the grips of power with the claims of bodies, pleasures, and knowledges, in their multiplicity and their possibility of resistance. Against the *dispositif* of sexuality the rallying point for the counterattack ought not to be sex-desire, but bodies and pleasures. (HS I 207–8/157)[17]

In that, Foucault is opening the door to much of his future work. It is clear that the stakes are high, and that things are deceptive: 'The

irony of this *dispositif*: It makes us believe that it is our "liberation"'
(HS I 211/159).

Towards Future Volumes

While Foucault had gathered together multiple cases from the archives
in his lectures, the first volume rarely mentions specific individuals,
and departs quite radically from that documentary approach. This
material appears to be destined for future volumes. We are, instead,
presented with a critique of existing accounts, several methodological
and theoretical indications, and some rather sweeping historical generalizations. This is important to recognize, along with the way the
book is written with a rather different stylistic approach to some of
his other works. Foucault provides lots of orientations, indications
and outlines for future work, rather than asserts claims with the
confidence of his other major texts. He makes this claim in a 1979
interview: 'The first book is not one of theory. It is a series of hypotheses, methods, or, if you like, rules of the game for a future analysis.'[18]
With the exception of *The Archaeology of Knowledge*, there is more
explicit discussion of the approach he is taking to his work than his
other texts; less historical specificity; and a great number of promis-
sory notes.

The most important of such indications is, of course, that this is
the first volume of six. The book itself contains some gestures towards
future volumes, noted above, but a month before it was published,
on 5 November 1976, the front page of *Le monde* had carried an
advertisement for 'six volumes by Michel Foucault'.[19] In an article
inside Foucault provided a summary of the work to come:

> My project would be to trace the genealogy of this 'science of
> sex'...Starting from the Christian problem of the flesh, I would like
> to follow all the mechanisms which have given rise to a discourse of
> truth concerning sex, and have organized around it a mixed regime of
> pleasure and power. Recognizing the impossibility of following this
> genesis comprehensively, I will try, in separate studies, to locate some
> its most important strategies: concerning children, women, perver-
> sions, and birth control...I would hope that this fragmentary history
> of 'the science of sex' would equally be of value as an sketch of an
> analytic of power. (DE#181 III, 104–6)

Foucault clearly indicates here not just the fundamental theme of
the book – the relation of sex and truth to the question of power –
but also the specific topics of the following books. Early printings of

the book had carried a list of the projected volumes on the back cover:

1. *La Volonté de savoir* [*The Will to Knowledge*]
2. *La Chair et le corps* [*The Flesh and the Body*]
3. *La Croisade des enfants* [*The Children's Crusade*]
4. *La Femme, la mère et l'hystérique* [*The Woman, The Mother, and the Hysteric*]
5. *Les Pervers* [*The Perverse*]
6. *Populations et races* [*Populations and Races*]

That programme is clearly outlined in the argument of the first volume:

> Hence the domain we must analyse in the different studies that will follow the present volume is that *dispositif* of sexuality: its formation on the basis of the Christian notion of the flesh, and its development through the four great strategies that were *deployed* in the nineteenth century: the sexualization of children, the hysterization of women, the specification of the perverse, and the regulation of populations – all strategies that went by way of a family which must be viewed, not as a force of prohibition [*puissance d'interdiction*], but as a major [*capital*] factor of sexualization. (HS I 150/113–14)

As he outlines a few pages later, some of the modes of scientific knowledge of the new technology of sex being developed have specific targets: pedagogy, 'sexuality of children'; medicine 'the sexual physiology peculiar to women'; demography, 'the spontaneous or concerted regulation of births' (HS I 154/116); along with the medicine of perversions and the programmes of eugenics (HS I 156/118). Here, the future volumes are given a relation to models of scientific knowledge as well as the workings of power. The initially planned more thematic approach receives its rationale from the analysis in the first volume. As this chapter has shown, Foucault sees Christian practices of confession as central to understanding the birth of psychoanalysis and the discourse of sexuality, and had planned to analyse its understanding of the flesh as distinct from the body. Similarly sexuality's four constituent subjects were the masturbating child, the hysterical woman, the perverse adult and the Malthusian couple. These were to be the topics of the remaining volumes. There are reports that Foucault's original plan was to publish the six volumes of the series at the rate of one a year;[20] though Didier Eribon suggests they would have been even more rapid: one every three months – 'the sequels...were laid out, the files already prepared. On his desk there was a voluminous folder for each of the titles planned, awaiting the hour of its definitive elaboration, the moment when Foucault's prose – beautiful and precise, meticulously worked – would take hold of the material inside to transfigure it. A manuscript of Foucault is above all almost undecipherable handwriting, loaded with additions and scratched-out words.'[21]

As the analysis of those lectures in preceding chapters has shown, at this time he had much of the work of the subsequent volumes sketched out to various degrees of completeness. One of the ways we can read the lecture courses from the early to mid 1970s is as the most thorough treatment yet available of what would have been in the originally planned set of volumes. Some existed in manuscript status; others as 'dossiers' of notes, case files and written-out sections. The editors of *The Abnormals*, Marchetti and Salomoni, say that 'we call "dossiers" the collections of notes classified by Michel Foucault and preserved by Daniel Defert'.[22] Defert says that Foucault would take notes and file them thematically in these files, rather than chronologically.[23] Some of the lecture courses explicitly draw on this material. This is especially the case with regards to the lecture course *The Abnormals*. As the editors note, the course 'offers not only a very clear trace of these dossiers and manuscripts but it also allows us to reconstitute what is lost'.[24] The planned second volume on confession is the most important to the overall discussion, and will be discussed in detail in the next section of this chapter. Indeed, only his death stopped Foucault working on a book which bears strong relation to this projected volume.

Indications of the material for Volumes 3 to 6 are variable. *La Croisade des enfants* would surely have made much use of the analyses in *Psychiatric Power* and *The Abnormals*. The former takes a broader sweep of the question of childhood and psychiatry; the latter is primarily focused on the crusade against masturbation. We know little of this volume beyond these indications of possible material. Marchetti and Salomoni point to a dossier Foucault was building on onanism, which served to inform his work in *The Abnormals* and the first volume of the *History of Sexuality*, but they suggest that the analysis in both the course and the book 'seems quite limited'.[25] In particular, they argue that the presentation 'depends mostly – and sometimes without the necessary checking – on Léopold Deslandes's *Onanisme* of 1835'.[26] In addition, some of the material in the 1982 book on *lettres de cachet* discusses relations between parents and children (DF 157–73; see Chapter 8).

There is little in Foucault's lectures that fills in the details of what would have been in *La Femme, la mère et l'hystérique*. Foucault is often criticized for the lack of attention to women in his work, and treatment of women is almost completely lacking in the actually published volumes, with the exception of discussions of marriage in antiquity. While his courses in no way replace such a volume or entirely answer such criticisms they provide some indications of what Foucault thought about the subject. There is discussion of hysteria in *Psychiatric Power*, discussed in Chapter 1, but not much beyond this concerning the question of women, and little on motherhood apart from a few remarks here and there concerning the family. It is possible that Foucault would have elaborated on his brief remarks on prostitution in such a volume. According to Defert, Foucault did some research on the Charcot archives at the Salpêtrière hospital in January 1975, that is, almost a year after he gave the lectures on hysterics in *Psychiatric Power*, and almost two years before the first volume of the *History of Sexuality* was published (C 45/57). It would seem likely that he envisioned a much more detailed treatment in the projected fourth volume. The seminar of 1975, which began on 6 January, is on a more specific subject, 'the analysis of the transformations of psychiatric expertise in penal matters from the major cases of criminal monstrosity (the prime case being Henriette Cornier) to the diagnosis of 'abnormal' delinquents' (A 311/329). It seems unlikely that cases of criminal individuals such as Henriette Cornier would have found their way into this volume, rather than the next, but it is at least conceivable.

Foucault had much material that could have been used for *Les Pervers*. Marchetti and Salomoni discuss a dossier on 'the human monster' that Foucault was compiling, suggesting this was divided into three themes: on 'the juridical-natural and juridico-biological monster', 'the moral monster' and 'the founding monsters of criminal psychiatry'.[27] Much of *The Abnormals* would have found a natural home in a volume on the perverse, and it is clear Foucault had a huge amount of material to draw upon. Initially the material on hermaphrodites seems likely to have been in this volume, but later Foucault envisioned another volume on that topic. In the *Herculine Barbin* memoir, in 1978, Foucault talks of how 'the question of strange destinies like these and which posed such problems for medicine and law since the sixteenth century will be treated in the volume of the *History of Sexuality* that will be devoted [*consacré*] to hermaphrodites' (HB 131/119). Marchetti and Salomoni note that there exists a manuscript on hermaphroditism in Foucault's papers, which initially 'seems to be the extension of the dossier on monsters. However, it soon becomes autonomous.'[28] They suggest that the cases of Lemarcis and Grandjean (discussed in *The Abnormals* and in Chapter 1, above) 'derive from a wide collection of data, bibliographies, and transcriptions preserved in a box file that we have been able consult... and which clearly indicate the plan of publication of an anthology of texts'.[29] The *Herculine Barbin* memoir does not provide 'an exhaustive documentation', as did the Pierre Rivière dossier (HB 131/119). The reason for its absence is precisely because Foucault envisioned just such a volume: but the fact that it never appeared makes the lack more regrettable.

Foucault returned to this case the following year in a lecture which was later reworked as the introduction to English translation of the memoir, published in 1980.[30] This introduction claims that modern Western societies have decided that each individual needs a single *true* sex. This notion is in conflict, Foucault suggests, with 'an order of things where one might have imagined that all that counted was the reality of the body and the intensity of pleasures' (DE#287 IV, 116; HB vii). Indeed, says Foucault, research into medicine and law shows that this singularity was not always the case, and that such a demand has not always been made. In an Italian interview published around the same time, Foucault suggests that there now exists a 'rigorous correspondence between anatomical sex, juridical sex, and social sex'. These sexes must coincide and fall into one of two categories. Foucault suggests that before the nineteenth century, there was a 'fairly large margin of movement' between these understandings (DE#237 III, 624). Foucault is not suggesting that the situation in the past was perfect, and he mentions the executions that took place, but there appears to have been more of an element of choice in the role hermaphrodites would take in society. Initially the choice of sex would be made by the father or godfather, but this choice could be retaken by the person themselves at the time of marriage. This choice determined the person's civil status. The limit to this was the imperative that such a choice could not be unmade. To do so risked being labelled a sodomite. The shift from this to the modern position of one 'true' sex came, Foucault suggests, because of 'biological theories of sexuality, juridical conceptions of the individual [and] forms of administrative control in modern states' (DE#287 IV, 116; HB viii).

The role of an anthology on hermaphrodites changes from a section of or resource for *Les Pervers* to an additional volume, and again in 1979 it is referred to as the third volume, following one on confession.[31] From the material available, *Les Pervers*, whether in its original or revised form, could have been a great book. There is some fascinating documentary material and had Foucault continued to work in this area he would no doubt have both presented it in a more stylized manner and uncovered further stories. Miller claims 'at least one person has a partial manuscript of the volume on perversion ... but he has not shown it to me for the good reason that Foucault explicitly asked him to promise never to show it to anyone'.[32] Yet a different indication of its status comes from Arnold Davidson, who discussed the topic with Foucault in 1976, and who suggests that 'he soon reconceived the topics for his projected history of sexuality and never provided much historical detail to support his claims about perversion'.[33]

Work on these individuals, labelled as perverse or monstrous, links to several other projects Foucault discussed. One of these is the outline of an examination of the concept of the 'dangerous individual'. This topic was mentioned in the 1973 course (SP 182, see 190 n. 2), the seminar of 1975 (see C 45/57) and became the focus of 1976's seminar, which examined 'the category of the "dangerous individual" in criminal psychiatry', and linked this to the theme of 'social defence' and civil responsibility in the late nineteenth century (DE#187 III, 130; EW I, 64).[34] Foucault returned to this theme most fully in a Toronto lecture given in October 1977, 'About the Concept of the 'Dangerous Individual' in 19th Century Legal Psychiatry', in which he examined the notion of danger is some detail:

> The monstrous crime, a crime against nature and without reason, is the meeting point of the medical demonstration that insanity is ultimately always dangerous, and of the court's inability to determine the punishment of a crime without having determined the motives for the crime. The bizarre symptomatology of homicidal mania was delineated at the point of convergence of these two mechanisms ... In this way, the theme of the dangerous man is inscribed in the institutions of psychiatry as well as of justice. Increasingly in the nineteenth and twentieth centuries, penal practice and then penal theory will tend to make of the dangerous individual the principal target of punitive intervention. Increasingly, nineteenth-century psychiatry will also tend to seek out pathological stigmata that may mark dangerous individuals: moral insanity, instinctive insanity, and degeneration. (DE#220 III, 454; EW III, 189)

Perhaps if in 1977 Foucault still imagined he would complete the volume on the perverse he would have reframed some of its analysis around the concept of dangerousness. Some of the cases mentioned in previous lectures, including Cornier and Sélestat, reappear here.

> Thus, there appear in the field of legal psychiatry new categories – such as necrophilia around 1840, kleptomania around 1860, exhibitionism in 1876 – and also legal psychiatry's annexation of behaviour like

pederasty and sadism. There now exists, at least in principle, a psychiatric and criminological *continuum* that permits one to pose questions
in medical terms at any level of the penal scale. The psychiatric question is no longer confined to some great crimes; even if it must receive
a negative answer, it is to be posed across the whole range of infrac-
tions. (DE#220 III, 456; EW III, 191)

In a fascinating discussion with Jonathan Simon, dating from 1983,
Foucault returns to these questions, showing his undiminished interest in the material.[35] Yet there is another contender for the continuation of this theme, which is the idea of 'Lives of Infamous Men'. In
January 1977 Foucault had published an article with that title, which
was framed as the 'introduction to a work to appear, under the same
title, in the collection "Le Chemin"'.[36] Defert has suggested that the
introduction may date from 1975.[37] 'Le Chemin' is a series with Gallimard, and on the back cover of this journal issue Foucault's book
is listed as forthcoming. In the introduction, Foucault notes that all
the texts to be included in the book 'date approximately from the
same hundred years, 1660–1760, and all come from the same source:
archives of confinement, of the police, of petitions to the King, and
of *lettres de cachet*' (DE#198 III, 243; EW III, 164). That work eventually appeared, co-edited with Arlette Farge, as *Le désordre de
familles* in 1982, discussed in Chapter 8. Under the new name of
'Parallel Lives [*Les vies parallèles*]', a series did begin in 1978, but it
contained only two volumes. The second, of which Foucault has no
direct editor credit, is *Le Cercle amoureux d'Henri Legrand*;[38] the first,
of which Foucault is the named editor, is the case of *Herculine Barbin
dite Alexina B*.

For the last projected volume of the *History of Sexuality* as originally conceived, *Populations et races*, indications are similarly mixed.
While Foucault had running themes on the control of populations in
The Abnormals, this receives much more detailed treatment in the
following year's course. It would be easy to see parts of '*Society Must
Be Defended*' as a sketch of this volume, though it is likely that the
planned book would have a much broader focus than the lecture
course, with more on scientific work on fertility and the relation of
these concerns to the biologization of race. Such themes had been
explored in his Vincennes course of 1969, and Foucault's involvement
with abortion rights struggles in the early 1970s was likely also
important.[39] Foucault of course continued to work on the question
of population in his writings tracing the history of governmentality,
a theme that will be discussed in Chapter 5.

There is another book lurking behind all this. Foucault begins *The
Abnormals* by discussing the role of psychiatric expertise in criminal

matters, a theme he had concentrated on in the previous year's *Psychiatric Power*. Foucault is interested in the use of this expertise in trials, from both an historical and a contemporary perspective. In *The Abnormals* Foucault initially cites contemporary events (one from 1955 and one from 1974), before quickly moving to an examination of the history that informs them. In a sense then, his work on this topic, like *Discipline and Punish*, can be read as a history of the present. But in a 1975 interview, shortly after that book came out, published in June, Foucault indicates another text: 'I am currently preparing a work on psychiatric expertise in penal matters. I will publish some dossiers, of which some go back to the 19th century, and others are more contemporary, and which are quite astonishing' (DE#156, II, 746; P/K 45). This was a topic he was working on in his Paris seminar at the time, mentioned in the discussion of women above (A 311/329). How far he was advanced in this project is unclear, but it is not a project that would have easily found its way into the *History of Sexuality* plan, though there is of course overlap, especially to *Les Pervers* and perhaps to a volume on women, as well as being yet another way to approach the question of confession. From Foucault's comment it seems conceived to be more like the Barbin memoir; related to themes of the wider series but a discrete publication of archival material. Marchetti and Salomoni suggest 'this work appears at several points in the course of the lectures in the form of dossiers already prepared and almost ready for publication'.[40] Marchetti and Salomoni discuss this dossier in some detail, noting the three main parts, on 'contemporary expert opinion'; more historical accounts from the early nineteenth century; and material from later in the nineteenth century to the present. They suggest that this research informed the three lecture courses preceding *The Abnormals* as well as *Discipline and Punish* and the first volume of the *History of Sexuality*, but also draw links to previous and forthcoming work that they suggest are anticipated here.[41]

Yet another book is promised in the first volume of the *History of Sexuality*. Following a discussion of the relation between torture and confession as the 'dark twins' (see below), a note clarifies 'Greek law had already paired torture and confession [*l'aveu*], at least for slaves. Roman imperial law had developed this practice. These questions will developed in the *Pouvoir de la vérité* [*The Power of Truth*]' (HS I 79 n. 1/59 n. 2). The English translation omits the last sentence of the note entirely, even though in the main text Foucault makes reference to this 'political history of truth' shortly afterwards (HS I 80–1/60). Paul Veyne notes this planned book on truth and power relations, especially ordeals, and recalls that 'Foucault wrote a long draft for such a work, which, he said a year or two before his death, he would have liked to develop much further.'[42] The reference given is to the 1973 'Truth and Juridical Forms' lectures (DE#139 II, 538–53; EW III, 1–16), but research on this theme extends far beyond – in scope and duration – this work, as future chapters will show.

It is important to recognize, however, that the courses only give indications of where published volumes might have gone. With the important exception of its final chapter, little of the first volume of the *History of Sexuality* was dependent on lecture courses, and it is likely that Foucault anticipated including much new material in the subsequent volumes. None of these promised volumes appeared; what was drafted was apparently destroyed; and it was to be several years before any new books were published. Defert suggests that Foucault signed an exclusive five-year contract in 1975 with Gallimard to fund the *Moi, Pierre Rivière* film, and that he therefore decided his next book 'would be very short and that he wouldn't write another one for five years (something that many people have interpreted as a crisis in his thought)' (C 50/61).[43] A different story tells of an argument with the editor Pierre Nora, over the launch of *Le Débat* in 1980 and Foucault's perceived lack of support for François Mitterrand. 'The outcome was a violent quarrel with Nora. Foucault even threatened to leave Gallimard, and to publish the remaining volumes of his history of sexuality elsewhere.'[44] And yet, all Foucault's future major works, including the *Herculine Barbin* memoir, and after the five years, the second and third volumes of the *History of Sexuality*, were published by Gallimard.[45] *Le désordre des familles* was published by Juilliard, in the Archives series co-edited by Nora and Jacques Revel, and was subsequently reissued by Gallimard.

Defert has additionally suggested that, even as the first appeared, Foucault confided to him he did not intend to write the subsequent volumes. 'He envisages changing his mode of writing: that form of rather anonymous speech, shrouded in the Pierre Rivière documents, had captivated him. This is how he wants to deal with hermaphroditism, or the question of true sex, using the documents about the Alexina B. case that he found in the *Annales d'hygiène*' (C 49/62). This is revealing, but it still raises intriguing questions. Fundamental to these is that if the Rivière case had fascinated him so much in terms of writing style, why did he subsequently write two books – *Discipline and Punish* and the first volume of the *History of Sexuality* – that departed so much from that mode of presentation? And why did both, especially the latter, make so little use of the documents of individual cases that we know, from his lectures, he and his research colleagues had gathered so extensively? Aside from these questions, we know from Defert's other indications, and much other evidence, that Foucault continued to work on the topic of the planned second volume of that initial plan, on the question of the body, flesh and confession, for many more years.

The Power of Confession

Of course, between the first volume and the publication of *The Use of Pleasures* and *The Care of the Self* in 1984, Foucault changed his project radically. Future chapters will discuss how, realizing some of the first volume's claims were misleading, he moved to a far more historical study, tracing the subject backwards, through early Christianity initially and then back to antiquity. Fundamental to this work is the question of confession. When Foucault first outlined his project for the *History of Sexuality*, in 1975, he made clear the importance of this theme. He suggested that confession was older than the eighteenth century, and was already found in the Middle Ages.[46] Foucault frequently underlines that sexuality is something that *is* talked about, rather than subject to taboo and silence. 'In the West sexuality has not been something that you hide but something that you confess. And it is to the degree that sexuality has been caught within the techniques of confession that it must consequently become silent at a particular moment or in a particular situation' (FL 163; see A 157/169). This requires a history of confession since the Middle Ages, which would include study of judicial confession, particularly the Inquisition; the penitential confession; and confession of sins against the sixth and ninth commandments.[47] Foucault suggests that at least the first two are recent developments (FL 163–4). Foucault dates this from the Lateran Council of 1215, and discusses some of the crucial aspects he had outlined in earlier lecture courses.

The most extensive discussion of the body, confession and possession we have to date is contained in the lectures of 19 and 26 February 1975 of *The Abnormals*. The *Théories et institutions pénales* course had discussed related issues in more detail, albeit with a very different focus. Chapter 1 showed how Foucault argued that the three types of abnormality are related to the notion of sexual deviancy. This is most clearly the case with the masturbating child. To make sense of the injunction against this, Foucault makes a long detour through Christian procedures of confession and penitence, and the separation of the notions of the body from the flesh, in order to trace how this has informed psychiatry (A 158–80/171–94). As such this touches upon themes that would have likely been treated in the projected second and third volumes. Foucault's aim in the course – and there is a clear sense of this being a very preliminary sketch – is not to write a history of the silencing or censorship of sexuality, but rather of 'the history of the confession of sexuality', through the ritual of penance (A 158/170–1). Confession existed alongside 'other forms of enunciation [*énonciation*] of sexuality' (A 157/169). Foucault's critique of the role of capitalism here is less stark than it would be in the first volume of the *History of Sexuality*, and he adds that the medieval aspects of the question have not been adequately explored by historians (A 157/169–70).

The appearance of the sexual body of the child in the eighteenth century has a pre-history that dates back to the Council of Trent, interpretation of the sixth (seventh) commandment concerning adultery, Augustine's *Confessions* and various other places and times. Masturbation emerges as a sin in relation to fornication, adultery, debauchery, rape, molestation, sodomy, incest and bestiality (A 172/185). These discussions lead Foucault to sum up the development as there being alongside 'the political anatomy of the body, a moral physiology of the flesh' (A 180/193). Foucault traces how this leads to a pedagogical medicine of masturbation and the linking of the notion of desire with that of instinct. Together this returns problems of sexuality to the field of abnormality. In tracing this question, Foucault discusses the relation of the body to concupiscence, the problem of the charnel, witch-hunts, possession and the Inquisition (A 187–212/201–27). The theme of sexuality is continued throughout. The nature of the pact with the devil is discussed in terms of a transgressive sexual act – 'the visit to the incubus, kissing the goat's arse on the Sabbath'; the idea of possession on the other hand is described as an invasion, a penetration of the body (A 193/208). Foucault draws a strict line between witchcraft and possession; the former trading on his earlier work on this topic. For the latter, Loudun serves as Foucault's principal example here – the point is to highlight the differences in the conception of the body. The inner struggle made visible by convulsion is that between medicine and Catholicism, at the level of the individual body (A 198/213). Bringing in the theme of the hysteric briefly, Foucault notes the correspondence between Loudun, Lourdes and Salpêtrière. This triangle is one where possession, cure, hysteria and faith relate in various ways. All of these themes, demonstrating the battle between ecclesiastical and medical power, help us to understand the emergence of sexuality within the field of medicine (A 210/226). In the next lecture he notes that here he has sketched a genealogy of the 'Christian discourse of the flesh' (A 219/233).

At the beginning of the treatment of this question in *The Abnor-mals*, Foucault notes how 'two or three years' ago he had discussed the emergence of confession within the ritual of penance, and traced the development of it from the Middle Ages to the seventeenth century (A 158/171). Foucault summarizes two points he says he discussed in more detail there: 'confession [*l'aveu*] was not originally part of the ritual of penance', but emerged belatedly and only later became 'necessary and obligatory' (A 158/171); and 'the effectiveness of this confession and its role in the practice of penance underwent considerable changes between the Middle Ages and the seventeenth century' (A 158/171). While this links to the 'ordeal test' examined in *Lectures on the Will to Know*, especially in the second lecture and returned to in the third and ninth, it is mainly a reference to *Théories et institutions pénales*, which included a substantial discussion of these topics in the second half of the course. The focus there had not been on sexuality, but the broader question of the inquiry, proof and the test of truth in judicial procedure.[48] All his subsequent discussions of confession and avowal link back to this initial outline, and it appears elements within it may have been what Veyne was referring to in the suggestion of a book on 'truth and power'.[49] Foucault had briefly discussed confession [*l'aveu*] in psychiatry in *Psychiatric Power*, where it becomes important for the patients to acknowledge their symptoms: ' "Yes, I hear voices! Yes, I have hallucinations!"; "Yes, I think I'm Napoleon!"; "Yes, I rave!" ' (PP 276/274). He notes that this is based 'on the assumption and with the claim that if one avows the madness, one gets rid of it', and that this has links to religious confession (PP 276/274; see 175/177). Confession continues to be an issue in subsequent courses, and *Discipline and Punish*, before becoming a major focus in the *History of Sexuality*.

The claims in the first volume are clearly summaries of all this work and gestures towards a much more detailed discussion to come. He suggests that this dates from at least the Middle Ages, and that confession or avowal [*l'aveu*] is 'one of the main rituals we rely on for the production of truth'. Several topics need to be analysed:

> the codification of the sacrament of penance by the Lateran Council in 1215, with the resulting development of confessional techniques [*techniques de confession*], the declining importance of accusatory procedures in criminal justice, the abandonment of ordeals of guilt [*épreuves de cupabilité*] (sworn statements, duels, judgments of God) and the development of methods of interrogation and inquiry [*enquête*], the increased participation of the royal administration in the prosecu-tion of infractions, at the expense of procedures leading to private settlements, the setting up of tribunals of Inquisition: all this helped to

give the confession [*l'aveu*] a central role in the order of civil and religious powers. (HS I 78/58)

This notion is therefore a crucial focus of his work here, and continues to be so for the rest of this decade. 'The evolution of the word *avowal* [*l'aveu*] and of the legal function it designated is itself emblematic of this development: from *l'aveu* being a guarantee of the status, identity and value granted to one person by another, to *l'aveu* as someone's acknowledgement [*reconnaissance*] of their own actions and thoughts'. As individuals make a 'discourse of truth' about themselves, 'the truthful confession was inscribed at the heart of the procedures of individualization by power' (HS I 78–9/58–9).

> In any case, next to the ritual ordeals [*rituels de l'épreuve*], next to the guarantees [*cautions*] given by authority and tradition, next to testimonies, and the learned methods of observation and demonstration, the confession [*l'aveu*] became one of the West's most highly valued techniques for producing the true. We have since become a singularly confessing [*avouante*] society. The confession [*L'aveu*] has spread its effects far and wide. It plays a part in justice, medicine, education, family relationships, and love relations, in the most everyday affairs of everyday life, and in the most solemn rites; one confesses [*on avoue*] one's crimes, one's sins, one's thoughts and desires, one's childhood, one's illnesses and troubles; one goes about telling, with the greatest precision, whatever is most difficult to tell. One confesses in public and in private, to one's parents, one's educators, one's doctor, to those one loves; and to oneself, in pleasure and in pain, confessions [*des aveux*] impossible to [tell] another, the things people write books about. One confesses – or is forced to confess [*On avoue – ou on est forcé d'avouer*]. When it is not spontaneous or dictated by some internal imperative, the confession is extorted; it is driven from its hiding place in the soul, or extracted from the body. Since the Middle Ages, torture has accompanied it like a shadow, and supported it when concealed: the dark twins. The most defenceless tenderness and the bloodiest of powers have a similar need of confession. Western man has become a confessing animal [*une bête d'aveu*]. (HS I 79–80/59)[50]

The Fourth Lateran Council passed Canon 21, *Omnis utriusque sexus*. Indeed, Oscar Watkins's extensive study of penance in the Church ends with this, as the 'modern system of the Latin Church is henceforth in force'.[51] The Canon begins by stipulating that

> All the faithful of both sexes [*omnis utriusque sexus fidelis*], after they have reached the age of discretion, must confess all their sins [*solus peccata*] at least once a year, to their own priest, and perform to the

best of their abilities the penance imposed...otherwise they will be denied entry into the Church in life and a Christian burial in death...But if anyone should wish to confess their sins to another priest, with just cause, let them demand and obtain licence first from their own priest, as otherwise this other is not able to loose or bind them.[52]

The Church is therefore given extensive power over the individual, with a right to excommunicate, and grant access to other priests or not. Later developments would include the Council of Narbonne in 1227, which enforced confession for those over fourteen; and the Council of Toulouse, which called for three confessions and three communions a year, with those who failed suspect of heresy.[53] Peter Lombard later made confession a sacrament, a decision which was ratified by the Council of Trent.[54] The Council of Trent ended on 4 December 1563, and was the basis for the reorganization of Roman Catholic Church. The Catechism ordered by the Council defined confession as 'a sacramental accusation of one's sins, made to obtain pardon by virtue of the keys'.[55] The keys here are the keys to heaven, the power Jesus gave to his disciples: 'I will give you the keys of the kingdom of heaven; whatever you bind on earth will be bound in heaven, and whatever you loose on earth will be loosed in heaven.'[56] The basis of the Church was from this point on centred on the individual rather than the group, with a stress on individual prayer and the sacramental system, but with a great deal of power in the hands of the priest.[57]

Claude Mauriac recounts a conversation from 30 November 1976 where he tells Foucault that he does not agree with all he has written on confession. Foucault's response: 'But it is the heart of the book!'[58] It is clear from Foucault's outline that the importance of this notion is at least in part because of the uses to which it is put. He notes how in the eighteenth century mechanisms of confession are deployed in the crusade against childhood masturbation – children must confess to their family, to their family doctor, or to doctors specializing in sexuality. He suggests, but does not elaborate, that 'this same confessional technique appears in general medicine at the end of the eighteenth century'. Central to understanding its impact, of course, was the use to which it was put in psychiatry. 'In nineteenth-century psychiatry, the sexual confession became one of the cornerstones of the 'curative' operation. It is this same confessional practice that Freud brought back in the technique of psychoanalysis' (FL 164). Equally we might anticipate that Foucault's research in this period would have looked in detail at the role of the Inquisition, which, when it started to look at the offences of common people, including blasphemy, bigamy or superstition, discovered how little confession was actually practised.[59]

Therefore 'for the past six or seven centuries, sexuality has been less something that you do than something that you confess, by which and through which are established a whole set of obligatory procedures of elocution, enunciation and confession; the obligations of silence are doubtless the counterpart of these'. Confession is the first trait of this technology of sexuality: 'sexuality is something that must be talked about inside a ritual discourse organized around a power relationship' (FL 164; see A 157/169). We find this notion of confession played out in the first volume, where for example Foucault contrasts two texts: one religious, one secular.

> Tell everything...not only consummated acts, but sensual touchings, all impure gazes, all obscene remarks...all consenting thoughts.[60]

> Your narrations must be decorated with the most numerous and searching details; the precise way and extent to which we may judge how the passion you describe relates to human manners and character is determined by your willingness to disguise no circumstance; and what is more, the least circumstance is apt to have an immense influence upon what we expect from your stories.[61]

The first comes from St Alfonso Maria de Ligouri's eighteenth-century commentary on the sixth/seventh commandment; the second from de Sade's *120 Days of Sodom*.

> Confession [*L'aveu*] is a ritual of discourse where the subject who speaks is also the subject of the statement [*énoncé*]; it is also a ritual which unfolds within a relation of power, because one does not confess without at least the virtual presence of a partner who is not simply the interlocutor, but the authority [*l'instance*] who requires the confession, who prescribes, appreciates, and intervenes to judge, punish, pardon, console, reconcile; a ritual where truth is corroborated by the obstacles and resistances which needed to be overcome for it to be formulated; and finally, a ritual in which the enunciation alone, independent of external consequences, produces intrinsic modifications in the one who articulates it: it exonerates, redeems and purifies, discharges faults, liberates, and promises salvation. (HS I 82–3/61–2)

The confession has of course changed, and Foucault points to 'Protestantism, the Counter-Reformation, eighteenth-century pedagogy, and nineteenth-century medicine' as detaching it from its specific reference (HS I 84/63). 'A dissemination, then, of procedures of confession, a multiple localization of their constraint, a widening of their

domain: a great archive of the pleasures of sex was gradually constituted' (HS I 85/63).

The key is how 'sexual confession' became 'constituted in scientific
terms'. He points to five reasons.

1. the combination of confession with the examination [*l'examen*]
   and other practices of knowledge, putting the 'procedure of confession in a field of scientifically acceptable observations'
2. through understandings of causality, and claims that sex was a
   'cause of anything and everything'
3. 'the principle of a latency intrinsic to sexuality' – not just a question of the subject revealing what they wished to hide, but also
   what was hidden from themselves
4. the interpretation of confession, the crucial role of the person to
   whom the confession is made in giving it scientific validation, a
   hermeneutic role; no longer confession as 'a proof [*une preuve*],
   but rather a sign'
5. 'the medicalization of the effects of confession' – no longer 'error
   or sin, excess or transgression, but was placed under the regime
   of the normal and the pathological (which was only the transposi-
   tion of the former categories)' (HS I 87–90/65–7).

What we have in these discussions is a mix of earlier claims about
knowledge, statements, inquiries, examination, tests, rituals and the
production of truth and new claims of power.

According to the editors of *The Abnormals*, *La Chair et le corps*
existed in a manuscript form, and Foucault had used it when delivering the lecture course. This would indicate that Foucault had written
it by early 1975, though how much existed at this point is unclear.
The discussion of confession in *The Abnormals* course is not always
convincing, and it seems to make sense that it was the analysis of this
material for *La Chair et le corps* that led Foucault to abandon the
original plan and work more historically than thematically. In these
extant discussions Foucault ranges over a vast amount of material,
and several centuries, and some of the more sweeping claims may not
have been sustainable on more detailed examination. Foucault's argument seems to rely on relatively few sources, and primarily secondary
accounts, notably Henry Charles Lea's *History of Auricular Confession*, rather than primary documents.[62] If Foucault did indeed rely on
a much more extensive manuscript, the extent and detail of what was
drafted is likely to remain unknown. Foucault apparently worked on
the text again in August 1977, looking at the early Church Fathers,
and in January 1978, with Defert reporting that he intended 'to focus

on the Christian idea of the flesh. It will be a genealogy of concupiscence that addresses the practice of confession in Western Christianity
and the direction of conscience as it developed after the Council of
Trent' (C 53/64, 53/66).[63] Concupiscence is strong, especially sexual,
desire or lust – from the Latin *concupiscere*, to covet. Defert says that
this 1978 version was destroyed, and told the editors of that course
that Foucault had destroyed the manuscript used in 1975 (C 53/66).[64]
A short fragment from around 1978 has however survived (see
Chapter 7).[65] The material in the lectures in *The Abnormals*, along
with some poor-quality recordings of four lectures given between
October and November in São Paulo, remains our main indication
of material which existed in 1975.[66]

There are, in addition, already hints of where his future work
would take him even in 1975, with formulations such as 'the techniques of the government of souls' (A 217/231); 'Christian technique
of the government of individuals' (A 217/232). It is clear that Foucault did not abandon the theme, because the issue of confession is
repeatedly returned to in lectures, both in the analysis of the Christian
pastoral in the lectures on governmentality, and in *On the Government of the Living* and *Wrong Doing, Truth Telling*. Crucially, rather
than beginning his inquiry into confession with the late Middle Ages,
in the lectures he goes back to the early Church Fathers. In April
1978 Foucault suggests that the departure point is at least since
Augustine, since the first centuries of Christianity (DE#233 III, 555).
Subsequent chapters will discuss these themes in more detail, but it
is already clear that the working through of the themes of confession
tied Foucault up for many years, and the unpublished *Les Aveux de
la chair*, even though it treats a different historical period to *La Chair
et le corps*, may well be the key to the whole *History of Sexuality*
series.

Beyond the Series as Planned

Foucault delivered *'Society Must Be Defended'* in the first three
months of 1976. He had a sabbatical in academic year 1976–7, and
as his lectures ran most years from January to March, this allowed
him effectively twenty-one months' absence. When he returned to the
Collège de France in early 1978 he appeared to have shifted direction.
Yet the intervening period is revealing. After some lectures in Montreal, Berkeley and Stanford in Spring 1976, he spent the next few
months completing Volume I, which was submitted in August 1976
(C 49/61).[67] Given his seeming discontent with what he had done, as

evidenced by remarks in the course, it is perhaps surprising that he spent this time perfecting the plan of a project he had already decided was flawed. Defert suggests in his chronology that even at this point Foucault did not intend to write the promised volumes (C 49/62). Instead, it appears at least part of his efforts was towards a related yet distinct set of concerns. In a letter he wrote in August 1974, at the time of completing *Discipline and Punish*, he confessed he was bored with the subjects he had been working on and that 'political economy, strategy, politics' would be his new concerns (cited in C 45/56). Equally in April 1976 he notes that 'his next book will treat military institutions' (DE#174 III, 89).[68] We get an initial glimpse of this in '*Society Must Be Defended*', when he suggests that if the previous five years had been given over to the disciplines, in 'the next five years, it will be war, struggle, the army' (SMBD 21/23). Had this been followed through, Foucault would have been treating these subjects until 1981, but of course we know that this was not the case. Although that year he did again suggest war as future theme of research: 'the problem of war and the institution of war within what one might term the military dimension of society' (WDTT 246/246).

So, if Foucault had so much of the material of the subsequent volumes already worked out in 1976, why did he abandon the project? Various reasons have been given in the literature – a crisis in his thought; a wish to avoid giving the subsequent volumes to Gallimard; or more fanciful explanations based on personal biography and a dubious grasp of dates and causality. The next chapters will advance a more modest claim, better grounded in the documentary evidence, and, for all that, much more interesting and revealing. Foucault gives a number of indications, principally in interviews. In early 1977, shortly after he had published the first volume, he was involved in an interview with the Freudian journal *Ornicar?*[69]

A. Grosrichard: It is time to turn to this History of Sexuality of which we have the first volume, and which you have announced will comprise six.

M. Foucault: Yes, I would first like to say that I am very happy to be here with you. This is partly why I wrote this book in this form. Up until now, I wrapped things up – I spared no citation, no reference, and threw rather heavy cobblestones, which remained for the most part unanswered. From this came the idea of the book programme, a sort of gruyère cheese, with holes which could be filled in. I did not want to say 'this is what I think', because I am still very unsure of what I put forward. But I would like to see if it could be said, and how far it could be said, and, of course, that risks being very disappointing for you. And that there are uncertainties in what I have written is certainly uncertain. There is no trick, no rhetoric. And I'm not certain either what I will write in the following volumes. That is why I wanted to hear the effect of this hypothetical discourse, in overview. It seems to me that this is the first time I have met people who want to play the game that I propose in my book. (DE#206, II, 298)[70]

In an interview published in January 1977 he admitted that the project had a different focus to how it might appear: 'For me, the whole point of the project lies in a re-elaboration of the theory of power. I'm not sure that the mere pleasure of writing about sexuality would have provided me with sufficient motivation to start this sequence of (at least) six volumes, if I had not felt impelled by the necessity of re-working this problem of power a little' (DE#197 III, 231; P/K 187).

In March 1977, in an interview with Bernard-Henri Lévy, he is asked what justifies a project of such a scale: His response is intriguing: 'Of such a scale? No, rather of such restriction. I do not intend to write the chronicle of sexual behaviour over the ages and civilizations. I want to follow a narrower thread: the one that through so many centuries has linked sex and the search for truth in our societies' (DE#200 III, 256; PPC 110). This is, at least not yet, a turn away from the planned sequence of volumes, as he responds to one of Lévy's questions concerning the question of sexual poverty or misery [*misère*]: 'In subsequent volumes, concrete studies – on women, children, the perverted – I will try to analyse the forms and conditions of this misery' (DE#200 III, 258; PPC 112). Yet later in the interview he notes he is recognizing a shift in his preoccupations, when he frames the question as 'the economy of untruth. My problem is the politics of truth. I have spent a lot of time realizing it' (DE#200 III, 263; PPC 118; see DE#216 III, 404). While power remains important alongside truth, there is perhaps a small move away from the conceptualization at the beginning of the chapter on method in the first volume: 'analyse the formation of a certain type of knowledge concerning sex, not in terms of repression or law, but in terms of power' (HS I 121/92; see FL 167). There were certainly doubts quite early. In a preface written in September 1977 for the German translation of the first volume, he announced that 'for the moment, the volumes which will follow can only be announced provisionally' (DE#190 III, 136); and 'I know that it is imprudent to send out first, like an illuminating flare, a book which constantly makes allusion to publications to come' (DE#190 III, 137).[71] It is worth noting that the German series title *Sexualität und Wahrheit* would translate as *Sex and Truth*, not *History of Sexuality*, which Foucault says was the original title (DE#206 III, 312; P/K 209), but which was turned down by the publisher.[72]

These points and doubts are telling, especially as they come mid-way through the sabbatical year. A year later, in a lecture in Japan on 20 April 1978, shortly after the *Security, Territory, Population* course, he was clearer that the series was not going to work out in the way planned: 'I promised with the greatest imprudence that I would have six volumes. I certainly expect that I will not arrive at the very end, but I believe, all the same, that this problem of the history of sexuality will continue to concern me' (DE#233 III, 553). Another year on, in an interview on 29 May 1979, Frank Mort and Roy Peters ask Foucault: 'Is the overall project which you outline in *La volonté de savoir* still underway?' They receive an intriguing response: 'Well, you see, I don't want to write those five or six books. Just now I am writing the second one about the Catholic Christian confessional, and also the third one on hermaphroditism'.[73] Yet by this point Foucault had taken his work in seemingly different directions, notably in terms of two detailed courses on the history of what he called governmentality.

4

From Infrastructures
to Governmentality

Foucault's Collaborative Projects

Foucault was unhappy at the outset of 'Society Must Be Defended'. The lecture as performance, with the assumed role as expert, was not to his liking, and he felt that the preparation was getting in the way of the research itself. He speculates about the possibilities if 'thirty or forty of us could get together in a room. I could tell you roughly what I've been doing, and at the same time have some contact with you, talk to you, answer your questions and so on, and try to rediscover the possibility of the exchange and contact that are part of the normal practice of research or teaching' (SMBD 4/3; see BB 155 n. **/150 n. *). As Ewald and Fontana note, 'he dreamed of holding a seminar in which truly collective work could be done. He made various attempts to hold such a seminar'.[1] Foucault was rather self-critical, suggesting how little he felt he had achieved (SMBD 5–6/3–4), but in terms of his collaborative work at least, this seems overly negative. The two most famous results are the publication of the dossier on the case of Pierre Rivière, which occupied Foucault's seminar in Paris for a number of years; and The Foucault Effect, a collection which appeared after his death, but which collects a number of papers from colleagues in his seminars, especially from the late 1970s. But there are many other outputs from Foucault's collaborative projects, especially in the mid 1970s, when he operated as a research team-leader, a facilitator, a colleague. His courses frequently make use of material that finds its most explicit expression in his work with others. Almost none of this material is available in English; some is not even published in French. As well as reports, journal issues and books, this section therefore draws extensively on materials archived at IMEC.

The collective projects examined here provide valuable background and a more general contextualization to his courses, and especially their focus on technologies of government, normalization and the mechanisms of peace. They emerge out of work in the early 1970s, conducted by the Centre d'Études, de Recherche et de Formation Institutionnelle (CERFI), which was a group founded in 1967 by Félix Guattari, as a formalization of the 1965 Féderation des Groupes d'Études de Recherches Institutionnelles (FGERI). Research was conducted on a series of projects with Gilles Deleuze, Guattari and François Fourquet into urban infrastructure, public utilities and related themes. It first output was a collaborative work by Lion Murard and Fourquet entitled *Les équipements du pouvoir*, which contained discussions with Foucault, Deleuze and Guattari.[2] *Équipements* are infrastructure or public amenities, such as roads, transport systems, and institutions. That work is analysed more extensively in *Foucault: The Birth of Power*, but it was the beginning of a productive research process, culminating in three volumes of reports under the general title *Généalogie des équipements collectifs* published in 1975 and 1976. The first of these was written by Anne Querrien, and was a study of the primary school; the third was authored by François Fourquet and was entitled *Histoire des services collectifs dans la comptabilité nationale*. Both were subsequently republished as issues of *Recherches* or as books by the associated press.[3] The second was led by Foucault on hospitals, and later reappeared in substantially revised and expanded form as the collective work *Les machines à guérir (aux origines de l'hôpital moderne)* published in 1976 and reissued in 1979. It developed from CERFI work, Foucault's independent research and another research project under the leadership of Bruno Fortier. A related study Foucault edited was entitled *Politiques de l'habitat (1800–1850)* from 1977; and a final project was planned on the 'green spaces' of Paris.

These are the key collaborative projects of this period, which are in various ways related to his work at the Collège de France, but were not the only projects he was involved in. Others include one where although he was the titular head, Robert Castel actually led the research team. This was research in 'resistance to medicine and the reduction [*démultiplication*] of the concept of health'. Conducted in the late 1970s, Castel and his research team – which initially comprised Jean Carpentier, Jean-Marie Alliaumé and Jacques Donzelot – analysed the way in which medicine exceeded a narrow definition as concerned with sickness and began to engage with a much wider set of concerns, including mental health, well-being and public health.[4] The working hypothesis was that resistance to medicine was more than 'a simple refusal' but was targeted against precisely this 'proliferation of new means of intervention'.[5] Psychiatry and psychoanalysis accordingly were a major part of their concern, as they traced the way that health became more than the simple 'reverse [*envers*]' of illness.[6] While the final report did not follow what was originally intended, it comprises a series of papers on the outlined themes.[7]

Foucault was also involved in research projects in his role as visiting professor at other universities. The best-known output from these is the *Technologies of the Self* volume from the University of Vermont, but another volume from his time at the Catholic University of Louvain in 1981 will be briefly discussed in Chapter 5. Shortly before his death Foucault also planned a collaborative project with students at Berkeley from his *parrēsia* seminar in late 1983. This will be discussed in Chapter 8, but it is worth noting that one of its themes was how mechanisms of war were continued in peacetime. This closely relates to themes of the *'Society Must Be Defended'* course, when Foucault notes how war itself can change, from a concentration on the battle to 'a war that begins before the battle and continues after it is over' (SMBD 141/159), which he suggests derives from Boulainviller (see also SMBD 146–7/165). For while *'Society Must Be Defended'* is explicitly orientated around questions of war, it is implicitly about the tactics that must operate in peacetime. Such themes would continue in the 'governmentality' lectures courses of the later 1970s, discussed in the second half of this chapter, but they were also ones Foucault anticipated returning to in the 1980s.

Hospitals and Normalization

The second volume of *Généalogie des équipements collectifs* was the project led by Foucault. The CERFI plan for the project looked beyond the institutions of hospitals and schools to wider concerns with sanitary norms and 'the power of the state in the determination of sanitary mechanisms'.[8] The resultant report was entitled *Généalogie des équipements de normalisation: Les équipements sanitaires*, all of which was designated as 'sous la direction de Michel Foucault' – under his direction, or edited by him.[9] The volume is in three parts, only one of which is directly associated with Foucault: *L'institution hospitalière au XVIIIᵉ siècle*. The other parts are on psychiatry and mental health, authored by Gaëtane Lamarche-Vadel and Georges Préli, and Fourquet and Murard, respectively.[10] Foucault's own part is divided between an essay by him, entitled 'The Politics of Health in the Eighteenth Century' and a seventy-page unsigned text on hospitals, illness, public health and the organization of urban space. Foucault's essay was reprinted in a book, *Les machines à guérir*, which itself appeared in two very different editions, but the remaining material has never been republished.

As well as Foucault's essay, *Les machines à guérir* contains contributions from four colleagues from his research seminar in Paris, and an extensive dossier on the architecture, equipment, chronology and organization of the hospital. The 1979 re-edition has several changes, including to Foucault's own essay. Three of the other essays are revised to greater or lesser extents; Bruno Fortier contributes an entirely different piece.[11] As well as the CERFI project led by Foucault, the book is also informed by research conducted on the politics of space in Paris at the end of the Ancien Régime, led by Fortier, with the Comité de la Recherché et du Développement en Architecture (CORDA) and the Délégation Générale à la Recherche Scientifique et Technologique (DGRST). The research from the second contract, in which Foucault was not directly involved, was published as a separate volume in 1975.[12]

Foucault's essay is closely related to the three lectures on medicine given in Rio in October 1974. In the second lecture Foucault refers to the collective work at the Collège de France: 'some of us are studying the growth of hospitalization and its mechanisms from the eighteenth century to the beginning to the nineteenth, while others are concentrating of hospitals and are moving towards a study of habitat and what surrounds it: the roads system, transport routes, and the collective infrastructure [*équipements*] which assure the functioning of everyday life, particularly in urban environments' (DE#196, III 208; EW 135). *Les machines à guérir* is therefore the product of the research contract Foucault headed, the one on Parisian space by the team apart from him, and his own interests from lectures. This is a productive set of concerns. Blandine Barret-Kriegel demonstrates how the hospital functions as a tool of cure, through its architectural design and organization. Similar issues emerge in the public health concerns of the time, along with the emergence of the notion of population. Observation and quantification are the two privileged methods – the politics of calculation (MG 22). Mortality rates, birth and baptism figures, and the other mechanisms of modern demography. Water, air seasons, climate, dietary regimes and their influence on mortality, and other medical concerns (MG 24–5). The population emerges as a site of medical knowledge – distinct and yet dependent on the individual bodies that make it up (MG 23).

> To calculate is to establish a statistical quantity to the detriment of aesthetic composition, the estimation [*le chiffre*] of the physician, the chemist and even the demographer, to the place of architectural proportion. Power is to command and realize the operation. (MG 26)

Dispersion and circulation become the keys to the hospital – the placing of objects, bodies and equipment within the space of the hospital itself and its situation in the town and surrounding area (MG 26).

Anne Thalamy's work also contributes to this general approach, noting the military model behind the hospital, with the traditional discipline, unified command and absolute hierarchy, but also more concretely to issues of circulation, the keeping of detailed notes and records, and the cataloguing of resources (MG 32–3). Thalamy finds in medical writing of the time 'the sign of a functional space and of a perpetually updated knowledge, which analyses the illness in the continuity of observation [*le regard*], and positions it in the duration of medical practice...It is the essential support of an illness, which becomes an object of treatment, of a hospital conceived as a space of recovery' (MG 36). François Béguin offers some further analysis, particularly around the object of the bed, with objectives of separation, rest and recovery. Again the idea of the physical design of the hospital comes through, with a particular stress here on architecture (MG 39). Bruno Fortier's chapter again treats similar themes, arguing that the hospital is a 'political tool', a step in a wider political project of the control and organization of the population, particularly in the urban setting. Similar concerns are found in the prison and school, and 'spaces of work and exchange' (MG 45).

In the first version of 'The Politics of Health in the Eighteenth Century', from 1976, Foucault notes that 'police...is the ensemble of mechanisms through which order is ensured, the channelled growth of wealth and the conditions of preservation of health "in general"' (DE#168 III, 17; P/K 170). In the revised version of this, written as his researches into government developed for the revised 1979 edition, the role of the police is seen as the management of the social 'body'. He stresses that this should not merely be understood metaphorically, but as depending on the material bodies of individuals, and the material conditions of life. Population in this sense is more than merely the people in a particular area, but also individuals taken both as individuals and as a whole. The conditions of their existence, survival and well-being are controllable, but this is only possible with control and surveillance of the population as a whole (DE#257 III, 730–1). Something similar had been argued as far back as *The Birth of the*

Clinic, where he suggested that 'a medicine of epidemics could exist only if supplemented by a police'.[13] It is important to realize that this is not the police in the modern sense. As Farge and Foucault note in 1982, 'A science of police is in place in the eighteenth century, certainly, but not really a police' (DF 345).[14]

The Politics of Habitat

Politiques de l'habitat contains a brief, unsigned, introduction and chapters by a range of Foucault's colleagues: Thalamy, Barret-Kriegel, Alliaumé, Béguin and Danielle Rancière. It includes detailed analyses of cholera epidemics, public health initiatives, housing projects and the emergence of the notion of habitat. This was a sequel to the communal work on hospital architecture. What we find in this book, as well as pieces of Foucault's own work of the same time, is an attempt to broaden the institutional analysis of prisons, hospitals and asylums to society as a whole. In the 'Avant-Propos' there is a list of the topics that make the determining factors of the urban environment or habitat: 'medicine and hygiene, architecture, civil engineering, the social sciences and jurisdiction'.[15] Again this was the product of a research project, conducted between September 1975 and May 1977, funded by DGRST-CORDA, this time on 'the history of the appearance of the notion of habitat in the architectural thought and practice of the eighteenth and nineteenth century'.[16]

The initial themes of this research included the notion of habitat-salubrity and the establishment of health norms, procedures of normalization that followed from that, and administrative practices and social habitat.[17] Originally planned in the Summer of 1975, this project included many of the same colleagues as the previous projects, along with the architect Bernard Mazeret, who did not contribute to the published volume. The team was interdisciplinary in design, and the research proposal itself makes much of the inclusion of historians and architects, because of the importance of the analysis of architectural techniques and plans.[18] The documents indicate that in 1975 Foucault intended to publish the work of a seminar entitled *L'architecture du surveillance*. This is likely to be an early description of the work that led to *Les équipements sanitaires* and *Les machines à guérir*.[19] It clearly indicates the continuity of concerns, stressing the relation between these earlier architectural analyses of hospitals, work on prisons, and the work to come.

The work included in this volume on the notion of habitat includes studies of medical epidemics, statistical measures used to combat disease, the production of urban space and the mechanics of the transition to public spaces within towns and the organization and control of these spaces. Foucault's colleagues provide rich empirical work to supplement and enhance the work that Foucault himself had done, both in *Birth of the Clinic* and the 1974 Rio lectures. It is notable that the volume has a much less obviously negative tone to it than some of Foucault's own work on these subjects, recognizing the means through which environments are developed and controlled. There is an identification of the ways in which these tools of government are utilized to work on and with the urban population, to provide satisfactory environments or milieus for their habitation, to serve capitalism, and in order to constitute security. One of the key themes is the spatial distribution of individuals, and the theme of public goods or collective infrastructure is continued from the earlier projects.

The project proposal is equally revealing, showing an interest in the organization of space in the urban environment, and the key theme is the tracing of the evolution of public space to a more concentrated concern with habitation. The proposal sets the dates as between 1750 and 1830, while the published work limits the study to 1800–50. Concerns with surveillance and circulation reoccur here, especially as the spaces (of particularly Paris) are opened up, destroyed and renovated.[20] Themes from the Rio lectures and *Les machines à guérir* are also found in the interest in the relation between the police and hygiene, in particular in the police as a means of intervention of the public in the private, especially in terms of the control of the circulation of elements. The point of intersection of public and private spaces – for instance pavements, roads and crossroads – are crucial here.[21] Issues outlined in detail in *Discipline and Punish* and elsewhere are found here, in terms of the spatial distribution of individuals, particularly as a means of social control. There is also a recognition that the development of notions of salubrity was related to that of the pathological character of the city, analysed in detail in the published work through the cholera epidemics.[22]

This reorganization of urban space is found in these hygiene projects, but not simply for the physical life and health of its occupants, but also because of a concern with their moral existence.[23] In particular, developments relating to earlier changes in hospitals with the emergence of *pavillonaire* architecture and the removal of communal beds are found in the new partitioning of domestic space.[24] These were concerns in *The Abnormals* with the campaigns both against masturbation and incest. Increasingly private space contains a reserved element for state observation [*regard*].[25] To study such issues requires issues around medicine naturally – hygiene, pathology, biology – but also sociology, economics and architecture. Laws and regulations, as well as practices all need to be studied. Making use of previous techniques of analysis developed in the work on public utilities, they propose to carefully study architectural plans and commentary on those plans.[26] While Foucault and his team think they can date the emergence of the term 'habitat' relatively precisely, they are concerned with the notion itself, which is later named, rather than simply its discursive constitution.[27]

The same folder at IMEC contains an untitled article by Bruno Fortier.[28] Although not formally part of this research team, this article touches on a number of related themes, including concerns about cemeteries in an urban environment, the washing of the laundry of the sick in the Seine, and what he calls a 'logic of spatialization' about the circulation of water, air and light.[29] One of the most interesting parts is the suggestion that dating is possible for the medicalization of spatial categories:

- Prisons 1765–1770
- Hospitals 1770–1785
- Industry 1770–1810
- Houses 1830-[30]

Clearly related to the Parisian context, this is interesting in terms of Foucault's own researches on the first two categories, and the more general research outlined here for the other two. Fortier also raises issues about the class relations at the heart of urban development – crucial of course in a slightly later period of Haussmann's reforms – the legal reforms and legal codings of space.[31] His study includes the following summary paragraph, which brings together much of the work he and Foucault had been leading:

> The question at the end of the eighteenth century was thus not the presence of the working classes in the town, but the screen which it represents in the control, knowledge and production of space. It is a power which is concerned with confiscating, not a presence that is concerned with spatializing. The dream at the end of the eighteenth century, and the reality of the nineteenth, is therefore that of a generalized coding of space, as transparent to the State as it would be foreign to working-class knowledge.[32]

Green Spaces

The last of these projects seems only to have got to proposal stage, but intended to look at the 'green spaces', *les espaces verts*, of Paris.[33]

This was one of the five themes of the CERFI-led 'Equipments of Power' project, but in its expanded form was intended to provide a mapping and analysis of the material and cultural underpinnings of 'green spaces'. The attempt was to trace the relation between administrative strategies concerning public hygiene more generally with the development of green spaces.[34] The budget for the eighteen-month project was over a quarter of a million francs, and as well as the core team of Foucault, Barret-Kriegel, Alliaumé and Thalamy from earlier work, included the architect Henri Bonemazon and the geographer Alain Demangeon.[35] Demangeon would later collaborate with another colleague of Foucault's, Bruno Fortier, on the book *Les vaisseaux et les villes*, on the arsenal at Cherbourg, which appeared in the same series as the reissue of *Les machines à guérir*.[36]

One of the issues that seems remarkable to the team is the increasing scarcity of green spaces in Paris, but also in other major towns, and the way in which the discourse of salubrity 'seems to have systematically excluded green space from its preoccupations'.[37] Why this should have come to pass is a crucial issue, and needs to be situated in relation to the control of dangerous populations. The fairly detailed proposal notes the Ministry of Construction's realization in 1958 that Paris was seriously lacking in both parks and gardens, and that the key was to preserve what did exist from development and auto-routes.[38] While distancing themselves from the *paysagistes* or *Robinsonnades* with their wish for a return to nature, the research recognized their importance, and particularly their use by the old, women, and children.[39]

The key green spaces – the Bois de Vincennes and the Bois de Boulogne to the east and west – need to be related to the planning of Baron Haussmann in the Third Republic, and along with the establishment of the Parc de Buttes Chaumont and Parc Montsourris at this time. This is all related to the transition from Royal gardens to public parks and squares, but questions need to be asked about the 'amputation' of parks such as the Luxembourg gardens just south of the Latin Quarter, and the Parc Monceau, and why public places such as the Champs Elysses and Les Invalides did not become parks. These are perhaps the most crucial issues, but what is also notable is the lack of individual or communal private gardens on the English model.[40] While the research looked to this specific example, it is clear that it was an opportunity to approach familiar questions from a new angle. The stated aims of the research to be undertaken in this project cover the recurrent themes of public hygiene; urban surveillance; and industrialization and the urban.[41] In sum though, this projected research was concerned with the problem of 'verdure', of 'greenery', what they state to be 'a recent problem, more exactly environmental' of green belts, barriers.[42] Of marginal interest perhaps, but notable for the geographical and environmental angle on a continuing set of concerns, and for the interest in this shown by Foucault, not noted for his love of the non-built environment.

As Chapter 2 noted, one of the themes of *'Society Must Be Defended'* was on the use of history as a political tool, not simply reporting struggle, but as a weapon itself. This is not merely during the war, but in the ensuing peace. How do models of war move from being the means of the constitution of society to the conserver of society, when struggle gets turned inward as a defence from within rather than against what is without? This is a society that uses war in peacetime, internally rather than externally, as a defence of society against the dangers that are born in its own body. This too was a concern of some of Foucault's colleagues. Notable here is the work of Kriegel, who wrote a thesis under Foucault's supervision on the question of historiography in France, particularly legal and political history. It was published in four volumes in 1988.[43] Its title is not a history *of* the classical age, but history *in* the classical age. Kriegel's earlier *L'état et les esclaves: Réflexions pour l'histoire des états*, originally 1979 and revised in 1989, then translated into English in 1995 as *The State and the Rule of Law*, makes use of some similar ideas.[44]

This collaboration is not to diminish Foucault's work, but to suggest that seeing him as a *sui generis* figure can be misleading. He is both inspired by others of his generation – Deleuze and Guattari, Peter Brown, Veyne, Pierre Hadot, and others – and inspirational. Perhaps here we can see the model for the sort of work that Foucault hoped would follow him, work that was going on in his lifetime but remains largely unknown even in his native France. In this respect we should also look at some of the work done by colleagues since that date, including studies by Donzelot, François Ewald, and Kriegel, and, a little later, his colleagues and students in Berkeley.[45] All of these projects demonstrate the way in which Foucault was concerned with numerous techniques of normalization, categorization and control, with truth as a political force, and modalities of government. These are, of course, concerns of his books and lecture courses, but were also worked through in his seminars and other collaborative projects where mechanisms of security extend through the social fabric.

And the hoarse songs of the races that clashed in battles over the lies of laws and kings, and which were after all the earliest form of revolutionary discourse, become the administrative prose of a State that defends itself in the name of a social heritage that has to be kept poor. (SMBD 73/83)

Foucault's work, and that of his collaborators, demonstrates that the formation of a knowledge and power of normalization is a crucial part of the way in which society is defended and security attained.

The Governmentality Lectures

After his sabbatical year, Foucault returned to the Collège de France to give two important lecture courses – *Security, Territory, Population* and *The Birth of Biopolitics* – which seemed to suggest a break with the interest in sexuality. Yet they link in crucial ways, and certainly the project was still being worked upon, with Defert noting that Foucault wrote on the Church Fathers in August 1977 while at his family home at Vendeuvre-du-Poitou, and that he was redrafting the second volume in early 1978, just as he began the *Security, Territory, Population* course (C 51/64, 53/66). The focus of this course intersects at times with the wider project, though it predominantly develops questions in a range of other directions. It begins with three lectures on town-planning, famines and smallpox, in order to illustrate the themes of the spaces of security, the aleatory, normalization and the birth of the modern conception of population. The third lecture is especially interesting: to the medical examples of leprosy and the plague, familiar from previous courses and *Discipline and Punish*, Foucault adds procedures to deal with smallpox and inoculation. The contrast between leprosy and the plague marks for him the break between sovereign and disciplinary power. But in these lectures the mode of dealing with smallpox epidemics is a good indication of a new mode of government that emerges. It makes use of a different set of practices, knowing, calculating and planning – a 'general economy of power' that Foucault calls security (STP 12/10). These three lectures are followed, on 1 February 1978, by the famous 'Governmentality' lecture. It is clear now how this lecture, for so long seen out of context, is the opening up of a problematic that Foucault then treats in sustained detail for the rest of that year's course and the next. Foucault therefore suggests that the title of the course should have been 'history of governmentality' (STP 111/108). Indeed, five months after the end of the second course, in October 1979 at Stanford, Foucault talks of his work in broad overview as 'the rudiments of something I've been working at for the last two years. It's the historical analysis of what we would call, using an obsolete term, the "art of government"' (EW III 324; DE#291 IV, 160). Government, in its multiple forms, becomes a concern from this point on, and the sexuality series, with its emergent focus on the question of subjectivity, is reconfigured in its light.

In this course though, Foucault is concerned with rereading the history of the state from the perspective of practices of government in a more specific sense, and he suggests three key models for the West. These are the Christian pastoral, with its themes of the flock, confession and the government of souls; the diplomatic-military technology which emerges following the Peace of Westphalia; and the notion of the police (i.e. STP 320/312). These 'were the three major points of support upon which that fundamental phenomenon in the history of the West, the governmentalization of the state, could be produced' (STP 113/110; see 126 n. */122 n. *). Population, police and governance were all themes that had been in his work before, but are now given new pre-eminence and a much more explicitly political twist. As Foucault suggests: 'The constitution of a knowledge [*savoir*] of government is absolutely inseparable from the constitution of a knowledge [*savoir*] of all the processes revolving around population in the wider sense of what we now call "the economy"' (STP 109/106). The inquiry begun here was developed the following year in *The Birth of Biopolitics*, a course that has a misleading title. It is Foucault's most detailed study of the twentieth century, analysing various issues around liberal thought and modern political rationalities.

At the outset of the first of these two courses, Foucault suggests that his initial focus will be on biopower, picking up on themes outlined in the pre-sabbatical course '*Society Must Be Defended*'. He recognizes that his earlier use of the term was somewhat vague, but quite quickly the course shifts to the question of government (STP 3/1; see 77/76).[46] In this Foucault is therefore returning to some crucial themes from *The Abnormals*, left rather underdeveloped at that time. In that course Foucault had stressed the importance of understanding government in a broad sense. He stresses the point again here, noting the return to Stoicism in the sixteenth century as a way of governing the self; the Christian practices of 'the government of souls and of conduct', the government of children, and then government of the state (STP 92/88). It is the last that will be the key to this course: government in a narrower, more specific and traditional sense, rather than the broader one. As we know, in his later courses he will again return to the wider question of the government of the living, of the self and others. The most important of these previously discussed themes, apart from the question of government itself, is the

Christian pastoral, described in 1975 as a 'technique for the government of souls' (A 165/178). That theme, outlined in 1975 as part of the preparatory work for *La Chair et le corps*, in a version that was at least partly destroyed, is again central as he attempts to redraft the volume in 1978.[47] There is at least one key difference between 1975 and 1978: Foucault has shifted his analysis from the late medieval and early modern period to the early centuries of Christianity.[48]

These two lecture courses – *Security, Territory, Population* and *The Birth of Biopolitics* – have been extensively discussed in the twelve years since their publication. I have elsewhere analysed and criticized their claim of a shift of the object of government from territory to population.[49] Foucault's analysis of developments in government is crucial in seeing the emergence of a category of population, with its measured, calculated nature and the specific political technologies that develop to shape, manage and direct it. Foucault stresses the importance of calculative practices, for example, in the claim that 'police make statistics necessary, but police also make statistics possible' (STP 323/315). He suggests that statistics is key both to the diplomatic-military equilibrium and the police, because 'statistics is the state's knowledge of the state, understood as the state's knowledge both of itself and also of other states. As such, statistics is the hinge of the two technological *ensembles*' (STP 323/315). He also links the analysis made to some of his previous writings. Notably the three domains of knowledge of life, labour and production, and language, which he had discussed at length in *The Order of Things* more than a decade before, are now explicitly politicized (STP 78–81/76–9). How did we move from natural history to biology, analysis of wealth to political economy, and general grammar to philology? Now Foucault has a crucially amended answer: 'if we look for the operator that upset all these systems of knowledge, and directed knowledge to the sciences of life, of labour and production, and of language, then we should look to population' (STP 80/78). Thus the earlier theme of man and the 'human sciences' should be understood 'on the basis of the emergence of population as the correlate of power and the object of knowledge... man is to population what the subject of right was to the sovereign' (STP 81/79). With the stress on the notion of *governing*, rather than earlier forms of rule, Foucault suggests that 'one never governs a state, never governs a territory, never governs a political structure. Those whom one governs are people, individuals, or groups' (STP 126/122).

The question of population is a major contribution in Foucault's work, but rather than territory being eclipsed by this development, it makes more sense to suggest that they are co-produced, at around the same time, through markedly similar processes and actions. Just as population codifies and directs formerly vaguer notions of the people or the populace, so too does territory superimpose itself over inchoate senses of land and terrain. It is simply misleading to suggest, as Foucault does, unless concepts have no specificity, that 'from the Middle Ages to the sixteenth century, sovereignty in public law is not exercised on things, but first of all on a territory, and consequently on the subjects who inhabit it' (STP 99/96). That argument – which is both inspired by Foucault and critical of the details of his analysis of territory – will not be rehearsed further here.[50] Instead, the reading of these lecture courses takes three key themes as its focus: the role of the Christian pastorate; the emergence of the *Homo oeconomicus*; and the question of government and its relation to the state.

The Christian Pastoral

Foucault suggests that if we are looking for the basis of the idea of governing people then we will not find it in Greek or Roman thought. In those traditions, he suggests, there are ideas of governing as steering, but this is of the city-state, of the ship of state and not the sailors (STP 126–7/122–3). Rather, he locates it in the idea of a shepherd of men, a flock, 'a multiplicity on the move' (STP 130/125), in Eastern thought – Egypt, Assyria, Mesopotamia, and especially the Hebrews (STP 128/123). He clarifies in his October 1979 Tanner lectures at Stanford University that this does not describe Hebrew power before the fall of Jerusalem, but only the flock in exile (EW III, 303; DE#291 IV, 138). This is a power exercised over each individual as much as it is power over the flock taken as a whole. The title for those lectures is 'Omnes et Singulatim', all and each, which describes a technique that is both totalizing and individualizing. As he suggests there, 'If the state is the political form of a centralized and centralizing power, let us call pastorship the individualizing power' (EW III, 300; DE#291 IV, 136; see STP 132/128).[51] The key is how these two elements combined. The pastor has to take responsibility for each individual but also the whole community, 'the whole town and the *orbis terrarum*' (STP 172/168; see 157/154).[52] For Foucault this is a crucial development: 'The modern state is born...when governmentality becomes a calculated and reflected political practice. The Christian pastorate seems to me to be the background of this process' (STP 169/165).

Foucault suggests that there is a key distinction between the Greek god and the Hebrew god. The Greek is 'a territorial god, a god *intra muros*', within the walls of the *polis*, rooted or perhaps even born from the very soil of the place, and located in a temple. The Hebrew god, in contrast, is one who 'marches, displaces, wanders' (STP 129/125). As such, the Hebrew model of politics is entirely distinct from the Greek *polis*, and even from the Roman *imperium* (STP 133/129). This is a model Foucault will call the pastoral, which is found in some Greek texts, notably Plato's *Statesman* and some minor references in other dialogues, but predominantly developed in texts from other traditions (STP 133/129, 142–5/138–41; EW III, 304–5). Foucault's references to Greek and Roman texts suggests a familiarity with the material, even though he would return to them with renewed focus and greater depth over the next several years. As well as classical political theory and philosophy, Foucault reads literature such as the *Iliad*, the *Odyssey* and *Beowulf*, suggesting that similar models can be found there (STP 140–141/136–7; EW III 304). Nonetheless, the key point is that the figure of the pastor as ruler or the shepherd as magistrate develops from sources outside the Greek tradition. The route through which this pastoral tradition came into the West was Christianity, which developed ideas from the Judaic and Eastern traditions. A key moment was when the Western Roman Empire became Christian, and the Church established its home in Rome. Foucault notes the importance of Veyne's work in shaping his argument (STP 151/148, 245/239).[53] The paradox is that the Christian West, born out of this technique of tending a flock, is also the most creative, conquering, arrogant, bloody and violent civilization (STP 133–4/130). Nonetheless, 'pastoral power is a power of care [*soin*]. It looks after the flock, it looks after the individuals of the flock, it sees to it that the sheep do not suffer, of course it goes in search of those that have strayed, and it treats those that are injured' (STP 131/127).

In this discussion there are at least two parallel projects in play. The first, pre-eminent in this course, is the way that the Christian model is important in providing a source for the transitions in government in the Latin West in the fifteenth and sixteenth centuries. The second is the continued attempt to draft the second volume of the *History of Sexuality*, on confession and the Christian distinction between the body and the flesh. Both are concerned with modes of government: the former in the narrower, more specific sense of government of a polity; the latter with the wider sense of the government of souls, something Gregory Nazianzen called the *oikonomia psuchon*, the economy or household or management of souls, or 'the conduct of souls' (STP 196–7/192–3). The 'art of governing men by the pastorate', the *oikonomia psuchon*, is defined by Gregory Nazianzen as the 'art of arts [*tekhnē tekhnōn*] and the science of sciences [*epistemē epistemōn*]'[54] (STP 154/150–1), something Foucault calls an 'ensemble of techniques and procedures' (STP 196/192). For Gregory the Great, this becomes the *'ars atrium est regimen animarum'*,[55] the art of arts is the regimen or government of souls, which becomes a standard formula (STP 154/151).

Foucault argues that 'the government of souls was formed in the Christian Church as a central and learned activity indispensable for the salvation of all and of each' (STP 374/364). The pastorate thus forges the link between new ways to govern children, family, the domain, and the principality. It is 'a complicated technique that demands a certain level of culture, not only on the part of the pastor but also among his flock' (EW III, 312; DE#291 IV, 148). We know from Defert that at the time Foucault was delivering these lectures he was also redrafting the second volume and reading widely in Christian thought (C 53/66). The figures that would have played a major role in the book are also crucial for this course. For these lectures, John Chrysostom's *De sacerdotio*; Cyprian's *Epistles*; John Cassian's *Collationes* and the *Cenobite Institutes*; Ambrose's *De officiis* and Jerome's *Epistolae* are all important, but Foucault suggests that Gregory the Great's *Regula pastoralis*, sometimes known as the *Liber pastoralis*, will become the core text of the Christian pastoral until the seventeenth century, while Benedict's *Regula* would be the foundational text of monasticism (STP 155–7/152–4, 169–73/166–70, 179/176). These figures and texts, and others, also play a crucial role in the 1979–80 course *On the Government of the Living*, where, like the 1979 Tanner lectures (EW III, 308–11; DE#291 IV, 145–7), there is a discussion of Christian monasticism.

Only occasionally in *Security, Territory, Population* does Foucault make the explicit link of his inquiry here to the earlier work, such as when he suggests that 'the institutionalization of the Christian pastorate is very important for Christian morality, both in the history of ideas and for the practice itself, as also for all the problems of what is called the "flesh" in Christianity' (STP 181/178). Even here, it is interesting that he is hinting at a need to take his historical analyses further back, suggesting that the notion of *apatheia*, which comes to Christianity through Greek and Roman moralists, is transformed in Christian thought. Whereas for pagan philosophy this renunciation of 'the pleasures of the flesh and the body' was for self-mastery, for Christianity he suggests it was the denial of egoism, a singular will. *Apatheia* is an 'absence of *pathē*, of passions' (STP 181–2/178–9). Elsewhere he draws some quite sharp distinctions between pagan and Christian thought in the question of spiritual direction. He suggests, for example, that in antiquity individuals approached others to direct them, paying a fee for the service; that direction was for specific moments or periods of a life; and principally for comfort, for benefit of the one directed. In Christianity, these codes were not voluntary, not dependent on circumstance and therefore about a life of obedience, and not about self-mastery, but a position of subordination to the director (STP 180–1/177–8, 184–6/181–3).

> The Christian pastorate is not fundamentally or essentially characterized by the relationship to salvation, to the law, and to the truth. The Christian pastorate is, rather, a form of power that, taking the problem of salvation in its general set of themes, inserts into this global, general relationship an entire economy and technique of the circulation, transfer, and reversal of merits, and this is its fundamental point. (STP 186/183)

The Christian pastorate is 'the birth of an absolutely new form of power' (STP 187/183). And the link to a still broader project, the reformulation of the entire *History of Sexuality* to a history of the emergence of the modern subject, can also be traced here: 'the history of the pastorate involves...the entire history of procedures of human individualization in the West. Let's say also that it involves the history of the subject' (STP 187/184).

Foucault's sketches of this work are illuminating, and yet the detail he would surely have added to a finished book remains lacking. In that sense the outline here is similar to the treatment in *The Abnormals* lectures from 1975 (A 155–180/167–94). Here, the long time period he is trying to cover in just a few lectures is one of the major issues: from the second and third centuries through to the eighteenth. Foucault recognizes the challenges, and is explicit that there is not an invariant and fixed structure to the pastorate over this millennia and a half (STP 152/148). He even doubts that the eighteenth century is an adequate end date for this history, suggesting it continues to play a crucial role up to the present. He notes the provisional nature of the inquiry (STP 139/135–6), and his point here is not, he stresses, to try to write the history of the pastorate, although he claims that this is a history others have not really undertaken and therefore is generally told inadequately (STP 153/150; 169/166; 197/193–4). While there may have been histories of ecclesiastical institutions, of doctrines, beliefs, and religious representations, and of religious practices such as how people confess and take communion, but the history of the techniques used, reflections upon them, and their 'development, application and successive refinements', along with knowledge relations, has not been made (STP 153–4/150–1).

The shift from the 'pastoral of souls to political government of men' is thus a complicated story in political thought, related to the English Glorious Revolution, the Reformation and Counter-Reformation, and 'resistances, revolts and insurrections of conduct' more generally (STP 234–5/228–9). For Foucault this goes beyond theology, but characterizes politics more generally: the 'Western sovereign is Caesar, not Christ; the Western Pasteur is not Caesar, but Christ' (STP 159/156). Yet if we are to look for the link between religion and politics it is not between 'Church and state, but rather between the pastorate and government' (STP 195/191), that is on processes and relations, rather than institutions. Governmentality in its modern form builds on the pagan and Christian notions of the conduct of the self, of children, and of the family, through to the flock, and we can see clearly here how this anticipates later work on technologies of self.[56] 'With the sixteenth century we enter into the age of conducts, the age of direction, the age of governments' (STP 236/231). In summary, then, Foucault contends that we a have shift in political rationalities from *ratio pastoralis* to *ratio gubernatoria* or *raison status*: pastoral reason, governmental reason, reason of state (*raison d'État*) (STP 238/232, 243/237–8). Yet Foucault does not just find the relation between pastorate and conduct of men important for the emergence of modern governmentality, because he notes the parallel emergence of what he calls counter-conducts, which will also run alongside governmentality (STP 362–3/355).

> Whether one opposes civil society to the state, the population to the state, or the nation to the state, it was in any case these elements that were in fact put to work within this genesis of the state, and of the modern state. It is therefore these elements that will be at issue and serve as the stake for both the state and for what is opposed to it. To that extent, the history of *raison d'État*, the history of the governmental *ratio*, and the history of the counter-conducts opposed to it, are inseparable from each other. (STP 365/357)

He briefly hints at the resistance of populations to conversion to Christianity, and 'the long-standing resistance to the obligatory practice of confession imposed by the Lateran Council in 1215', but says his focus here is elsewhere (STP 197/194). The Lateran Council is important for the institutionalization of the practice as obligatory, but Foucault notes its general development between the eleventh and twelfth centuries as something done between confessor and priest, rather than earlier less discriminate models (STP 207/203, 213/209–10; PPC 102).[57] Foucault says little about mysticism in the course, but also sees it as a form of resistance or counter-conduct, because instead of confession to another, the soul 'sees itself in God and it sees God in itself' (STP 216/212).

Christianity, Sexuality and Power

Foucault finished the delivery of this course in April 1978,[58] and shortly afterwards flew to Japan for a three-week visit. He gave two important lectures there, along with some interviews.[59] These were published in Japanese translation, but were not available in France until they were translated back into French for *Dits et écrits*. The first of the lectures, 'Sexuality and Power', was delivered in Tokyo on 20 April 1978. Interestingly it still makes the *scientia sexualis* versus *ars erotica* claim, even in Japan (DE#233, III 556–7; RC 115–30; see also DE#230, III, 525–6). Foucault summarizes some of the claims of the discussion of pastoral power, but explicitly situates it in relation to the *History of Sexuality* project, which is clearly underway, although he admits he may not complete all the volumes of the original plan (DE#233, III 553; RC 116).[60] Nonetheless he opens with remarks about hysteria and psychoanalysis (DE#233, III 553–5; RC 116–18) and his final point about the pastorate is one he thinks 'will bring us back to our initial problem, i.e., the history of sexuality – the pastorate brought with it an entire series of techniques and procedures concerned with the truth and the production of truth' (DE#233, III 564; RC 124–5). This analysis is worth a little discussion.

Christianity, in the second and third centuries, was 'concerned with a Roman society which had already accepted, for the most part, its morality – the morality of monogamy, of sexuality, of reproduction', but its own practice was a 'model of an intensely religious life', the ascetic practices that had been developed from Eastern antecedents. Christianity occupies a position 'between a civil society which had accepted a certain number of moral imperatives and this ideal of complete asceticism' (DE#233, III 565; RC 125). The 'conception of the flesh' was at the heart of this balance between an ascetic refusal of the world and a secular society, a balance between a radical refusal of the body and a common morality in the service of a society that required reproduction and families (DE#233, III 565; RC 125–6).

> It is by the constitution of a subjectivity, of a consciousness of the self perpetually alert to its own weaknesses, to its own temptations, to its own flesh...this technique of interiorization, the technique of taking conscience, the technique of alerting oneself to oneself, with respect to one's weaknesses, with respect to one's body, with respect to one's sexuality, with respect to one's flesh – this is, it seems to me, the essential contribution of Christianity in the history of sexuality. Flesh, the

subjectivity itself of the body, Christian flesh, sexuality taken inside this subjectivity, inside this subjection of the individual to himself, is the premier effect of the introduction of pastoral power within Roman society... It did not prohibit and refuse, but put in place a mechanism of power and control that was, at the same time, a mechanism of knowledge [*savoir*], of knowledge of individuals, of knowledge over individuals, but also of knowledge by individuals over themselves and with respect to themselves. All of this constitutes the specific mark of Christianity, and it is in this measure, it seems to me, that one can do a history of sexuality in Western societies starting with mechanisms of power. (DE#233, III 566; RC 126)

He does stress that this is a framework and hypotheses (DE#233, III 566; RC 126), but it is a very revealing insight into where, as early as April 1978, he thought this work was going, and why the pastorate was so crucial to his ongoing work. The second lecture, on 27 April 1978, discusses philosophy, power and the state. He returns to antiquity and the themes of the 1970–1 course concerning Solon and the role of the philosopher in the *polis* (esp. DE#232, III 536–8), but also brings the analysis up to the modern period and makes some comparative remarks with China and Japan. It closes with a return to the theme of pastoral power, which is of principal interest for its relation to Feudalism within Europe and Confucianism in the East (DE#232, III 548–51). On this trip Foucault also spent time in a Zen temple, clearly fascinated by the rituals and rules, in which he saw both parallels and distinctions from Christian monasticism and mysticism (DE#236, III 618–24; RC 110–14; see DE#230, III, 527–8).

On his return to France in May 1978, he participated in a round-table discussion with historians about *Discipline and Punish* on 20 May, in which he first introduced the notion of a 'regime of veridiction' (DE#278 IV, 20–34; EW III, 223–38).[61] This discussion included Arlette Farge, who would go onto to collaborate with Foucault on the *lettres de cachet*. He also gave a major lecture on 27 May to the *Société française de philosophie* on the question of critique and enlightenment in Kant.[62] While the explicit discussion of Kant looks forward to his more worked through analysis of 1983–4 (see also EW III 298–9; OHS 127–9), culminating in the 'What is Enlightenment?' essay, the opening part of this lecture links to his current preoccupations with 'the direction of conscience; the art of governing men' (QC 36). In September and November 1978 Foucault undertook his two visits to Iran (see C 55/69–70). His reports, principally for the Italian newspapers *Corriere del Sera*, have provoked controversy both at the time and since.[63] Much of their detail is now of historical interest, and the way that events developed has outstripped what is, in truth, journalism and prediction rather than the more considered work of his lectures, books or other writings. Others have presented and debated his arguments in considerable detail.[64] The key resonance that these works have to the concerns of this chapter is in Foucault's interest in the 'political spirituality' he saw developing among the Iranian people, which has parallels to his interest in Christian practices of which the West has lost sight (DE#245, III, 694).[65] Indeed it may well have been his interest in the history of Christianity that attracted him to the developments in Iran. But while Christianity was, at this time in his work, important for the way its practices of the pastorate were crucial to the development of the state; with Islam his interest concerned how they could be seen as a viable alternative to the state regime of the Shah.

Neoliberalism and the Birth of *Homo Oeconomicus*

Defert notes that in January 1979 – that is a full year before he delivered *On the Government of the Living*, and in parallel with *The Birth of Biopolitics* – Foucault was again working on confession, and his research was taking him further back in time:

> The history of confession led him to study the early texts of the Church Fathers, Cassian, Augustine, and Tertullian. A progressive birth of new subject material for the second volume of the *History of Sexuality: Les Aveux de la chair*. The study of the early Christian texts turns his genealogical research towards the Greek and Latin texts of late antiquity. (C 56/70)

This indication is telling for at least two reasons. First, because it suggests that as early as 1979 Foucault was working on pagan antiquity, and second, because the book being drafted had a new title, *Les Aveux de la chair*, rather than the originally announced title of the second volume. This revised title would be the one announced as the forthcoming fourth volume in 1984. In 1979 its placing in the series remains the same, but the title has already changed. We therefore know that Foucault was working on this volume for at least five years in something approaching the form in which it was left at his death. The key change in that period is that it moves from being the projected second volume to the drafted fourth, as the books on Greece and Rome are introduced and therefore move it down the plan. It is something of a surprise, then, that Foucault's course of 1979 does not report on this work, or even relate to the material being read in its preparation. Instead, Foucault turns to a very different time period, both in the course and the seminar.

The focus of the 1979 seminar was on the 'crisis of juridical thought in the last years of the nineteenth century' (BB 329/324). In the course summary Foucault lists the papers that were given in the seminar, on civil law, public and administrative law, penal law, legislation concerning children, security and police and health policy; while at the end of one of the lectures he describes it as 'the transformations of juridical mechanisms and judicial institutions, and of legal thought, at the end of the nineteenth century' (BB 155 n. */150 n. *). Foucault notes that the first session, to take place on 26 February 1979, would be on 'some problems of method and possibly some discussion on the things I am talking about in the lectures' (BB 155 n. */150 n. *).[66]

This 1979 course, *The Birth of Biopolitics*, has received a lot of attention for its analysis of neoliberalism.[67] Foucault's prescience is indeed remarkable: Margaret Thatcher would be elected exactly one month after the course finished; Ronald Reagan at the end of the following year. But Foucault identifies elements of this practice in the contemporary chancellorship of Helmut Schmidt in West Germany (BB 25/22), and in the French government of Valéry Giscard d'Estaing and Raymond Barre (i.e. BB 199/194). The Autumn 1978 austerity plan of Barre was an especially important context.[68] Foucault traces earlier models of this economic model of thinking, looking back to classical liberalism on the English model of the eighteenth century through to Weimar-era German economics and contemporary Chicago debates. The analysis is detailed and illuminating, even if somewhat outdated in the light of subsequent events. Even more explicitly than the previous course, the interest is in the extent of the state and the limits of its power. For Defert, 'the critique of the state appealed to him, but more as anarchist than as liberal'.[69] Yet his focus, contrary to those who wish to appropriate him as either a supporter or critic of neoliberalism, is historical rather than political. Or, perhaps better, it is an attempt to grasp the historical conditions of possibility of political order, rather than an endorsement of or opposition to a specific political programme. In that light, rather than a detailed exposition of this course, the reading here will focus on one key aspect, the emergence of the category of *Homo oeconomicus*.

Foucault begins the course with a summary of the questions discussed in the previous course, and stresses that he was not so much interested in what government meant in practice, 'the way in which governors really governed' (BB 4/2). Rather, his focus was on 'the level of reflection in the practice of government and on the practice of government...government's conscience of itself' (BB 4/2), although he stresses he is not fully comfortable with that latter term. Foucault identifies an important historical shift between the *raison d'État* period he had studied in the previous course and the eighteenth century. It is no longer a question of government addressing all aspects, both in foreign and domestic policy, as it had been with the diplomatic-military technique and the constitution of the police, but it is the question of knowing the 'principle of limitation...an internal regulation of governmental rationality' (BB 12/10). Foucault outlines a range of ways that this limitation can be understood, but his key point is that the 'intellectual instrument, the type of calculation or form of rationality' which acts as the 'self-limitation of governmental reason' shifts from being the law to political economy. This is a shift between the mid seventeenth and the mid eighteenth century (BB 15/13). *The Birth of Biopolitics* then, is both a direct continuation of the analysis in *Security, Territory, Population* and concerned with a fundamental break in governmental practice.

What does political economy mean at this time? Foucault notes that it signifies both a very specific sense of 'the production and circulation of wealth', but also a broader meaning of 'any method of government that can procure the nation's prosperity' (BB 15/13). But the key question is not about how much government can be conducted to achieve that aim, but how little. It is a matter of knowing where not to govern, what to leave alone, the well-known notion of *laissez faire*. The new form of rationality, which consists in the idea of leaving things alone as much as possible, is, Foucault explains, the question of 'liberalism' (BB 22–3/20). Liberalism, his manuscript clarifies, should be understood broadly, as both a limitation of government and as the practice of working out where that limitation is found and how its effects might be calculated, and narrowly, as the specific way in which government is limited, through institutions such as the constitution, the parliament and commissions or inquiries (BB 23 n. */20–1 n. *). It is this that is the focus of the course as actually delivered, rather than as planned or titled: 'The emergence of this regime of truth as the principle of the self-limitation of government' (BB 21/19). Yet this focus is really intended as illustrative of a much larger theme, which has characterized Foucault's researches since at least the early 1960s:

> The point of all these investigations concerning madness, disease, delinquency, sexuality, and what I am talking about now, is to show how the coupling of a set of practices and a regime of truth forms a *dispositif* of knowledge-power that effectively marks out in reality that

which does not exist and legitimately submits it to the division [*partage*] between true and false. (BB 22/19)

While there is an element of retrospective reinterpretation here, as is common in his successive formulations of his overall project, it does provide a strong thread of continuity between his perhaps rather disparate inquiries. And while the work of the later 1960s in *The Order of Things* and *The Archaeology of Knowledge* might appear to be absent from the overview, this is perhaps explained by their focus on knowledge rather specifically, at the expense of the specific focus on power. The question of truth, though, is central to all these projects, and here Foucault suggests that his analysis is moving from 'a site of jurisdiction' to a 'site of veridiction': 'The market must tell the truth [*dire le vrai*]'; it must tell the truth in relation to govern-mental practice. Henceforth, and merely secondarily, it is its role of veridiction that will command, dictate and prescribe the jurisdictional mechanisms, or absence of such mechanisms, on which [the market] must be articulated' (BB 34/32).[70] This is why he suggests that there are three features of liberalism: 'veridiction of the market, limitation by the calculation of governmental utility, and now the position of Europe as a region of unlimited economic development in relation to a world market' (BB 62/61).

In the main body of the course, which will not be discussed in detail here, Foucault shows how German political practice was dependent on decisions made in the post-war period. It was, Foucault suggests, the Socialist Party's rejection of the idea of planning, even flexible planning, in 1963 that meant it had 'entered fully into the type of economic-political governmentality that was adopted by Germany in 1948'. This was so successful that an SPD candidate became Chancellor six years later (BB 92/91). In other parts of the discussion he notes how the decisions shaping this were born out of a reaction to the Nazi period and the perceived growth of state power (BB 115/111). All the defects of the market economy could be effec-tively blamed on the state, on excessive state intervention. What they therefore proposed was the opposite of what had come before: 'a state under the supervision [*surveillance*] of the market rather than a market supervised by the state' (BB 120/116).

Foucault suggests that in the classical conception the *Homo oeconomicus* is 'the man of exchange, the partner, one of the two partners in the process of exchange' (BB 231/225), a man of exchange or consumption. But in neoliberalism he is instead 'the man of enterprise and production' (BB 152/147). In University of Chicago

economist Gary Becker's theory of human capital, the *Homo oeconomicus* is 'an entrepreneur, an entrepreneur of himself' (BB
232/226).[71] From this theory of the individual comes a proposal for
society. He finds this, for example, in Adam Smith's famous 'invisible
hand' proposal. For Foucault this functions as a kind of 'correlate of
Homo oeconomicus', a 'kind of bizarre mechanism which makes
Homo oeconomicus function as an individual subject of interest
within a totality which eludes him and which nevertheless founds the
rationality of his egoistic choices' (BB 282/278). In other words, as
Bernard Mandeville suggested centuries before, from private vices
come public virtues, collective self-interest can create a model society.

> Economic science never claimed that it had to be the line of conduct,
> the complete programming of what could be called governmental
> rationality. Political economy is indeed a science, a type of *savoir*, a
> mode of *connaissance* which those who govern must take into account.
> But economic science cannot be the science of government and eco-
> nomics cannot be the internal principle, law, rule of conduct, or ration-
> ality of government. Economics is a science in a lateral relation to the
> art of governing. One must govern with economics, one must govern
> alongside economists, one must govern by listening to the economists,
> but economics must not be and there is no question that it can be the
> governmental rationality itself. (BB 290/286)

The object of government is therefore not the economy itself, but civil
society (BB 290/286; see 299/295). 'Civil society is, I believe, a
concept of governmental technology, or rather, it is a correlate of a
technology of government the rational measure of which must be
juridically pegged to an economy understood as a process of production and exchange' (BB 299–300/296). It thus follows that we need
to interrogate *Homo oeconomicus* and civil society together. The first
is 'the abstract, ideal, purely economic point that populates [*peuple*]
the dense, full and complex reality of civil society'. In reverse, 'civil
society is the concrete ensemble within which these ideal points,
economic men, must be placed so that they can be appropriately
managed'. So, *Homo oeconomicus* and civil society belong to the
same ensemble of the technology of liberal governmentality (BB
300/296). In all this the political stake is 'the problem of the survival
of capitalism' (BB 170/164).

The Question of Government and the Problem of the State

It is easy to forget, through Foucault's long discussions of specific
economic theorists and the actions of particular regimes, that his core

interest in these lectures remains the question of government. He stresses that he is not interested in German politics for its own stake – either to understand the basis of Christian democracy or denounce the Brandt and Schmidt governments for their lack of socialism. He suggests that the basis of the analysis remains a study of power relations, and the question of conduct and government (BB 191/185–6). There are therefore some important asides about how political philosophies or theorists offer programmes of government. For one, he suggests that 'utilitarianism is a technology of government, just as public law was the form of reflection, or, if you like, the juridical technology with which one tried to limit the unlimited tendency of *raison d'État*' (BB 42/41). He makes that claim of historical figures too: 'Locke does not produce a theory of the state; he produces a theory of government' (BB 92/91). In terms of the left he is more ambiguous:

> In short, whether or not there is a theory of the state in Marx is for Marxists to decide. As for myself, I would say that what socialism lacks is not so much a theory of the state as a governmental reason, the definition of what a governmental rationality would be in socialism, that is to say, a reasonable and calculable measure of the extent, modes and objectives of governmental action. (BB 91–2/93)

Socialism has, he claims, an historical rationality; an economic rationality; and even an administrative rationality, but it lacks a governmental rationality: 'there is no governmental rationality of socialism' (BB 93/92).

The course is therefore very much a continuation of his studies of governmentality. He even suggests that his earlier work on power needs to be subsumed within that inquiry, arguing that the term 'power' 'does no more than designate a [domain] of relations which are entirely still to be analysed, and what I have proposed to call governmentality, that is to say, the way in which one conducts the conduct of men, is no more than a proposed analytical grid for these relations of power' (BB 191–2/186). Governmentality, then, is a useful frame for understanding means of 'conducting of conduct of the mad, the sick, delinquents, children', and in these lectures he is seeing how far it is useful for studying questions of a 'different scale, such as a political economy, or the management of a whole social body' (BB 192/186). This brings him to an important methodological clarification: his emphasis on micro-powers is 'not a question of scale, it is not a question of region of analysis [*secteur*], it is a question of a point of view' (BB 192/186). It is for this reason that the emphasis on micro-powers, of power relations, of governmentality allows him to study the state. Different models of government – rationality of the sovereign state, rationality of economic agents, rationality of the governed – can be conceived as 'different arts of government... different types of ways of calculating, rationalizing, and regulating the arts of government' (BB 316/313). This leads to Foucault's final claim of the course, that politics is the 'interplay of these different arts of government with their different reference points and the debate to which these different arts of government give rise': this is where 'politics is born' (BB 317/313).

This conceptualization of politics as the interplay of different arts of government helps to ground Foucault's attitude to the state, which has long been the subject of criticism. His work on institutions such as the prison and the army in the mid 1970s had been intended to move analysis to other levels, to examine the way in which power relations operated within society generally, rather than operating simply from a single central source. In these courses he provides a nuanced set of reformulations of this overall project and his position in relation to state theory. In particular, in *The Birth of Biopolitics* he takes issue with critics who suggested the absence of a theory of the state in his work marginalized 'the presence and the effect of state mechanisms' (BB 78–79/77). Foucault claims the opposite: 'the problem of bringing under state control, of "statification" [*étatisation*] is at the heart of the questions I have tried to address' (BB 79/77). Yet he does not approach this problematic in the same way as others. He does not begin with as if it is a universal political form the state or talk of the essence of the state (BB 79/77). He claims he has avoided a theory of the state as 'one must forgo an indigestible meal' (BB 78/76–7). Instead, we should try to make sense of the state through its actions, its practices; asking not what the state *is*, but what it *does*. In *Security, Territory, Population* he had asked: 'what if the state were nothing more than a way of governing? What if the state were nothing more than a type of governmentality? (STP 253/248). Here he elaborates on the question in greater detail.

> The State is not a universal or in itself an autonomous source of power. The State is nothing else by the effect, the profile, the mobile shape of a perpetual statification [*étatisation*] or statifications, in the sense of incessant transactions which modify, or move, or drastically change, or insidiously shift sources of finance, modes of investment, decision-making centres, forms and types of control, relationships between local powers, the central authority, and so on... The state is nothing else but the mobile effect of a regime of multiple governmentalities. (BB 79/77)

The key to this, as with so much of his work, is to avoid thinking that concepts of our present can be used as analytical tools to make sense of previous eras. It is not simply that different times, and different geographies, operated with different understandings within existing concepts, but that they operated with entirely different concepts. This is why Foucault suggests that the relation and distinction between the state and civil society should not be seen as 'an historical universal enabling us to examine every concrete system'. Rather, it is 'a form of schematization peculiar to a particular technology of government' (BB 325/319). Looking back on the course in June 1979, when he wrote its summary for the *Annuaire de Collège de France*, Foucault stressed that he had spent the entire course on what was originally intended only to be an introduction, and that the discussion of the political rationality of liberalism was to make sense of the emergence of biopolitics and regulation of population. Regulation, while a key topic in earlier work, is now the core concern of Foucault's interest in government. Ultimately, this is how the course does deliver at least something of the promise of its title. Population is the key object of the modes of government and the limitations of liberalism, and this is 'the basis upon which something like biopolitics could be formed' (BB 23–4/21).

The Birth of Biopolitics would remain Foucault's most contemporary course, and his last course to treat the modern era at all. He suggests the potential of continuing this analysis, especially in terms of the governmentality of the party in totalitarian states, in the following year's course (BB 197/191), though this was not fulfilled, as he turned back to Christian thought and practice. That and subsequent courses would, of course, make his analysis more explicitly linked back to the long-running project on sexuality, but even in this course there are important indications that the project remains a current focus. As he says in the second lecture:

> studying the genealogy of the object 'sexuality' through a number of institutions meant trying to locate [*repérer*] in things like confessional practices, direction of conscience, the medical relationship, and so on, the moment when the exchange and cross-over took place between a jurisdiction of sexual relations, defining the permitted and the prohibited, and the veridiction of desire, in which the basic armature of the object 'sexuality' currently appears. (BB 36/35)

But it may be in other respects that Foucault felt there was a deeper link. As he says in a number of places, the history of sexuality was intended, in large part, as a history of the subject, tracing its emergence in order to circumvent it. In the emergence of *Homo oeconomicus* there is a crucial element in that story. There are many aspects of that outlined in this course, but it is telling that Foucault suggests that it is in English empiricism, with the emblematic figure of Locke, that there is the introduction of a different kind of subject to ones that have gone before. In this instance it is not a question of freedom, of the soul versus the body, or concupiscence marked by the Fall or sin, but 'a subject of individual choices which are both irreducible and non-transferable' (BB 275–6/271–2).

Although his lecture courses and principal publications from this point on would turn to the early Church and antiquity, Foucault would continue to work on these topics of politics and government. His 1980 seminar in Paris, running in parallel with *On the Government of the Living*, would be on liberal thought in the nineteenth century (GL 320/325), with presentations by, among others, Didier Deleule, François Ewald, Pasquale Pasquino, and Pierre Rosenvallon.[72] Michel Senellart notes a manuscript entitled 'Libéralisme comme art de gouverner' dating from 1981 which trades on the seminar and his earlier analysis (BB 336 n. 13/331 n. 13).[73] That would be the final seminar Foucault would lead at the Collège, deciding that he would increase the hours of his lectures instead, and sponsor or contribute to, rather than run, other seminars, such as one on the sociology of law in 1981, led by Ewald, and on the philosophy of law in 1982–83 (C 58–9/74). As well as this manuscript on liberalism, following his suggestion in the 1979 course that socialism lacked a governmental rationality, he had implied this was a project to be undertaken: 'I do not think that for the moment there is an autonomous governmentality of socialism...it is not hidden within socialism and its texts. It cannot be deduced from them. It must be invented' (BB 94–5/93–4).

This was a project that took on a special urgency with the election of François Mitterrand in 1981. Foucault had previously taken part in a discussion in 1977 around future Socialist minister of justice Robert Badinter's collection *Liberté, libertés*; a book which has a preface by Mitterrand.[74] Yet despite his engagement, Eribon notes the disappointment felt when he was not offered an active role on behalf of the new government.[75] In a November 1981 interview with Clare O'Farrell, Foucault equally expressed regret the new government had not asked for his views on prisons.[76] As his disillusion grew, there was an unfulfilled plan to produce a collaborative book on the failure of left-wing governments in France, one of which was precisely this lack of an 'art of government'.[77] Eribon says this was to be a collaborative book of interviews under the title *La tête des socialistes*; though Defert is sceptical about the extent of Eribon's involvement.

He suggests rather that this project developed from a working group known as the *Académie Tarnier*, after the hospital where they met, including then-Médicins du monde president Bernard Kouchner, and the 'nouveaux philosophes' André Glucksmann and Pascal Bruckner.[78] Socialism was also a potential theme of his planned 1984 seminar at Berkeley (see Chapter 8). Even so, as late as 1984 Foucault said 'in the absence of anything better, I shall support the programme of the Socialists. I recall something (Roland) Barthes once said about having political opinions "lightly held". Politics should not subsume your whole life as if you were a hot rabbit.'[79]

But in October 1979, when he gave the prestigious Tanner lectures at Stanford University, he chose to return to the analyses of *Security, Territory, Population*, giving a two-part analysis that treated, in the first lecture the pastorate, and in the second the twin themes of reason of state and the police. It is telling that he returned to this earlier material, because it would act as a summary and recapitulation of themes explored almost eighteen months before, with some inflexions and shifts of emphasis, and with regard to the police much new material, but also as a prelude to his next lecture course in Paris, *On the Government of the Living*. For all his detours through state practices, economic reform and theory, and diplomatic procedure, he continually returns to a core concern: the reformulation of the history of sexuality towards a history of modern subjectivity. As he tells his audience in California: 'What I am working on now is the problem of individuality – or, I should say, self-identity in relation to the problem of "individualizing power" ' (EW III, 300; DE#291 IV, 136).

5

Return to Confession

In his work on governmentality, especially in the 1978 lectures, Foucault was continually making references to the question of confession, giving important indications of the book he was continually trying to write on Christianity. But as well as the difficulty of the material there were other setbacks. In July 1978 a car hit him near his Paris apartment, and as late as September 1979 he complained that his injuries interfered with his writing concentration on that second volume, even though he was working hard.[1] In October 1979, while lecturing at Stanford, he gave a useful assessment of how this project was developing: 'All those Christian techniques of examination, confession, guidance, obedience, have an aim: to get individuals to work at their own "mortification" in this world', which should not be understood as death, but as 'a renunciation of this world and of oneself' (EW III, 310–11; DE#291 IV, 147–8). Such themes are developed in considerably more detail in the 1980 course *On the Government of the Living*. This course returned explicitly to Christian practices, and provides the most detailed examination of material that might have appeared in the *History of Sexuality*. As Senellart notes, this course is as disconnected from its present as the previous year's course, on neoliberalism, had been connected to it. The theme of that previous course was continued in the 1980 seminar, but made little impact on the course (GL 320/325).[2]

Nonetheless, the course can still be seen as the third of Foucault's courses on 'governmentality', or, as he now increasingly suggests, government. As *The Birth of Biopolitics* makes clear, government can be understood in a range of ways, as government over children, families, a household, of the soul, of communities (BB 3/1–2). While in that course, and its predecessor, the focus was on the exercise of political sovereignty, the broader issues re-emerge in Foucault's final two courses, both under the title of *The Government of Self and Others*. But first, crucially, they are discussed in *On the Government of the Living*. This course looked at the notion of truth-telling [*dire-vrai*], and offered a detailed analysis of Christian modes of confession, introduced by an analysis of *Oedipus Rex*. He gave some important lectures in the United States in October and November 1980 that made use of material prepared for this course, and developed it in important ways. His 1981 course at the Collège, *Subjectivité et vérité* [Subjectivity and Truth], was the first course since 1970–71 devoted to antiquity. The day after that course, which finished on 1 April, he gave the first *Wrong-Doing, Truth-Telling: The Function of Avowal in Justice* lecture in Louvain, which continued until May.

There are various attempts made at an overall synthesis of the project. Foucault describes his work as attempting a 'genealogy of the modern subject' (OHS 33; ABHS 201); that he is examining the 'government of men through the manifestation of the truth in the form of subjectivity' (GL 79/80); and, more specifically, 'how subjects are effectively linked in and by the forms of veridiction in which they engage... political history of veridictions' (WDTT 9/20). All of these provide valuable insights into how the sometimes-disparate material is linked together; they also indicate the shifting nature of his focus from the initial sketches of the project of the history of sexuality. What is revealing is that, by the end of these courses, Foucault seems to have finished with this investigation into early Christian understandings of confession and subjectivity. The focus from then onward, as in *Subjectivité et vérité*, is firmly on pagan antiquity. Even later lectures that touch on these themes draw extensively on the earlier presented material. With regard to Christianity, he clearly thought that he had reached a publishable stage. For example, a chapter entitled 'The Battle for Chastity' (DE#312 IV, 295–308; EW I, 185–97), which discusses John Cassian, was published in 1982, though may date from 1979–80;[3] and the 1980 lecture 'Sexuality and Solitude' (DE#295 IV, 168–78; EW I, 175–84), which touches upon Augustine, appeared in 1981.[4] Now, of course, we can resituate all these texts within the much wider range of material available, especially these lectures courses, both at the Collège and in Louvain.

On the Government of the Living

On the Government of Living was the first course to be presented after a significant change in Foucault's working habits. For years he had been an almost daily visitor to the Bibliothèque Nationale, but in Summer 1979 he had grown so frustrated with its problems that he relocated to the much smaller Dominican Bibliothèque du Saulchoir, situated on the rue de la Glacière.[5] There, on open shelves rather than the closed stacks of the Bibliothèque Nationale, he was able to consult primary texts from antiquity to Christianity, crucial for his emerging research. The course as delivered is rather different from Foucault's retrospective presentation of it in the course summary. For a course that is primarily focused on early Christianity, it spends a lot of time on discussions of pagan antiquity. The first character introduced is Septimus Severus, Roman Emperor in the second to third century CE. The story of Severus is told in Dio Cassius's history of Rome.[6] In his palace he had constructed a chamber where the ceiling was painted with stars. This depiction showed the stars of his destiny, his fate, at the moment, the *kairos*, of his birth. This was the place where he would pass judgement on cases that came before him. And yet there was a part of this painting, the part that showed the future, and especially the hour of his death, which was in a place to which all but he and his closest family were forbidden access (GL 3–4/2–3). For Foucault, this story is almost the exact reverse of the history of Oedipus. Oedipus is the opposite because no one knows his destiny, neither he nor his subjects, and because his destiny is not fixed on the ceiling above him but is tracked beneath his feet in his journeys. Severus lays down the law in a situation where almost his entire destiny is mapped out; Oedipus plays out his destiny in almost complete ignorance (GL 4–5/3). This leads Foucault .to the semi-serious suggestion that 'Anti-Oedipus, of course exists. Dio Cassius had already found him' (GL 5/4). But the example concerns more than this, because it raises the question of the 'need, I was going to say the economy, of knowing that which is governed and how to govern' (GL 6/5).

Foucault's focus in the course is 'the nature of the relations between this ritual of manifestation of truth and the exercise of power' (GL 7/6). The relation between power and truth is examined through the term *alēthourgia* (GL 8/7), which Foucault coins as a rendering of the Greek term *alētheourgēs*. His concern is with hegemony as a mode of governing, a mode of leading or conducting [*conduire*] others and the self. He suggests that there is no practice of hegemony without a practice of *alēthourgia* (GL 8/7). As he tells his audience, the course's intention is to analyse 'the government of men by truth' (GL 12/11). In doing this he says that the relation he is concerned with is not so much power-knowledge, of which he is getting tired, but the transition from power to government, linking to the two previous courses (GL 10–11/9, 13–14/12; see OHS 118); and from knowledge to truth. The overall aim of the course is summed up by a later formula of attempting to 'write a history of the force of truth, a history of the power of truth, a history... of the will to know (GL 98–9/101).

Foucault recognizes he will only provide fragments of this, and some of the initial discussions are indeed somewhat scattered and unstructured, where he links back to previous courses and discussions; and throws out a range of disparate examples. He makes explicit links between the analysis of reason of state in *Security, Territory, Population* and the project in this course (GL 11/9), and with the analysis of liberalism in *The Birth of Biopolitics* (GL 14/12). He underlines his objections to the idea of ideology (GL 12–13/11–12); stresses that he does not want to analyse the practice of *raison d'État* as a 'theory or representation of the state but as an art of government'; and insists he wants to look at liberalism 'not as economic theory or as political doctrine but as a certain manner of governing, a certain rational art of governing' (GL 14/12). He provides a thumbnail sketch of power and truth relations in the shift to the modern epoch, giving examples of *raison d'État* in royal courts in the fifteenth–seventeenth centuries and the hunt against witches in Bodin (GL 11–12/9–11). Only a few minutes later, he then sketches five ways of conceiving the relationship between power and the manifestation of truth – rationality in Botero and *raison d'État*; economic rationality in Quesnay and the Physiocrats; scientific specification in Henri de Saint-Simon; general consciousness in Rosa Luxembourg; and consciousness of the inevitable in Aleksandr Solzhenitsyn (GL 14–17/13–16). The fundamental point of this opening lecture is to suggest that questions of government and truth are linked in crucial ways before the birth of rational governmentality, and that therefore their history can be traced back much further. While *Security, Territory, Population* had traced some of these lineages, here Foucault is suggesting a need to interrogate these questions at a more fundamental level.

Somewhat surprisingly, he chooses to spend the next few lectures in another detailed reading of the case of Oedipus. Foucault had analysed this before, notably in the 1970–71 course *Lectures on the Will to Know*, and then in several visiting lectures in the USA and Brazil. Here it is an example of *alēthourgia*, a way of revealing truth, making several distinctions, such as between slaves and royalty, and spoken, oracular, religious *alēthourgia* and judicial *alēthourgia*, founded on testimony. These lead him to the key focus of the course, procedures of truth-telling, veridiction. What is the focus between the art of governing men and modes of auto-*alēthourgia*? How does Oedipus sit in relation to Creon – the brother of Jocasta, the wife and mother of Oedipus, the deputy for King Laius who gives the throne to Oedipus and is his successor as king – or the oracle Tiresias? The key theme that comes from this reading is the idea of the *tekhnē tekhnis*, the supreme art, the art of arts, the technique of techniques, the mode of governing (GL 50–51/51), of 'power characterized as a *tekhnē*, as a technique, as an art ... of knowing to what extent [*mesure*] the exercise of political power requires, implies something like a *tekhnē*, like a knowledge [*savoir*], a technical knowledge, a know-how, which justifies an apprenticeship, a development of laws, for-mulae, a mode of doing' (GL 51/51). This is not located only in the Oedipus story or texts of pagan antiquity, but can also be found in a famous text by Gregory Nazianzen. Here, it is not simply a case of political governance, but the more individualizing form of 'spiritual direction'. In the text of Gregory, there is a formulation which Fou-cault thinks is characteristic of the direction of conscience until the eighteenth century: '*Tekhnē tekhnis* is the art of directing souls' (GL 51/52). This then is the key theme of the course: 'to study the relation between this *tekhnē tekhnis* as supreme art, that is art of governing men, and *alēthourgia*. To what extent [*mesure*] does the art of gov-erning men entail something like a manifestation of truth?' (GL 51/52).

The question of government is therefore crucial, but increasingly it is the relation of the self, the *autos*, and *alēthourgia* which comes to dominate the wider project (GL 67/67). Indeed, the relation between subjectivity and truth – the title and theme of the next course – is already being explicitly highlighted here (GL 73–4/74–5). This links to a range of questions around witnessing acts of truth. He notes that the exercise of power frequently demands not only submission and obedience, but also demands of truth: 'Why, in this grand economy of power relations, is a regime of truth indexed to subjectiv-ity developed?' (GL 80–1/82). To interrogate this, he focuses on the notion of *l'aveu*, admission or avowal, or confession (GL 80/82). Foucault uses this word frequently, as highlighted above, and at times seems to distinguish it from the more general notion of confession for which he uses the French term *la confession*. He is not always consistent, and the contrast can be overdrawn between the terms. In addition, Foucault gave lectures on this topic in English, for which he used the word 'confession' in place of both French words. Foucault sees confession working as a crucial theme in a range of registers, but his principal topic of examination, in this course, is early Christianity, in order to examine 'the historical constitution of a relation between the government of men and acts of truth, especially reflective acts of truth' (GL 81/82). Foucault outlines two regimes of truth, and the tension between them: 'the regime of faith and the regime of confession [*l'aveu*]' (GL 82/84). What is interesting for Foucault is that confession is both profession of faith and act of avowal (GL 82–3/84).

The Early Church Fathers

This is an important indication of the way that the course will develop, because lots of themes in Christianity are discussed, not just confession of sin. What is interesting in the Church, especially, in the early Church Fathers, is the constitution of a role, the confessor, 'who organizes, regulates, ritualizes *l'aveu*', something that eventually becomes sacraments: 'Christianity is certainly, at base, essentially, the religion of confession' (GL 82/84). These questions develop over time, and become tangled up with the notion of heresy, which Foucault describes as 'entirely foreign to the Greco-Roman world'. Confession, avowal, sits alongside dogmatic faith; and the treatment of heresy is partnered by the penitential confession. He uses this, very schematically at this early stage of the course, to track the break between Catholicism and Protestantism at the time of the Renaissance (GL 83/85). But his key focus is in the break from antiquity whereby Christianity is 'the apparition, in the Hellenistic and Roman world, [of] a regime of truth which is at the same time extremely complex, extremely rich, extremely dense and extremely new' (GL 84/86).

Various figures make key appearances in Foucault's discussion. Especially important are the analyses of Cajetan, Tomaso de Vio (1469–1534).[7] Cajetan was a pre-Council of Trent theorist of confession, from whom Foucault takes the phrase '*actus veritas*, the act of truth' (GL 79/81). Another writer of major importance is Tertullian, who had first been mentioned in a 1977 interview (DE#206, III 313; P/K 211) as the originator of the concept of the flesh, but who was not discussed in *Security, Territory, Population* in the material on the pastorate (GL 104/107; 110 n. 27/112 n. 27). From Tertullian, Foucault now takes several key concepts and practices: he is seen as the inventor or at least the elaborator of 'original sin' (GL 118/122); as crucial to the notion of 'economy of truth' and the development of *metanoia* (GL 130/133).

Metanoia is very important, because Foucault sees this Greek term as the equivalent of the Latin *paenitentia*, just as *exomologēsis* is the related term to *confessio* (GL 150/153–4). This pairing of terms, in the two processes of verbal confession and physical atonement, is of significance for much of Foucault's analysis. Foucault underlines that the process captured by *metanoia – paenitentia* – 'does not designate the ritual, canonical, ecclesiastical penitence'. Instead, 'when we find the word *paenitentia* in texts of this epoch, we must think that it is a matter of conversion and not of penitence' (GL 150/153). There are therefore considerable complications in Foucault's terminology – of French words to translate Latin renderings of Greek concepts; a set of difficulties that are compounded when we try to carry this over into English. While Foucault sometimes uses the French term *aveu* to translate *exomologēsis*, that is *confessio* (GL 150/154), his manuscript notes, '*confession* = *exomologēin*' (GL 172 n. */174 n. *).

Towards the end of the course Foucault first makes the contrast between *exagoreusis* and *exomologēsis*. The latter term had been discussed extensively in previous lectures, where Foucault has suggested that it is almost the Greek term for what the Latin language calls *confessio* (GL 150/154). Even so, some Latin authors, such as Tertullian, continued to use the Greek term (GL 197/202). *Exagoreusis*, though, is new: it is 'the putting oneself into discourse, the perpetual putting of oneself into discourse' (GL 301/307) – 'the final examination of conscience, of its secrets and mysteries in direction and *exagoreusis*' (GL 305/311). *Exomologēsis* is the 'manifestation in truth of being a sinner', but there is 'no longer any dramatic or spectacular element in bearing of gesture or dress' in *exagoreusis*. Rather it is a relation of the self to the self, as subtle [*ténu*], as permanent, as analytic, as detailed as possible (GL 301/307). *Exomologēsis* is a specific event, but *exagoreusis* is closer to a way of life.

These terms are developed in the lectures in the USA later that year, discussed in the next section. But significantly, Foucault's retrospective presentation of the course suggests that the contrast was crucial to its delivery: 'two concepts must be distinguished, each of which corresponds to a particular practice: *exomologēsis* and *exagoreusis*' (GL 317/322). He then outlines the idea of *exomologēsis*, and, through Cassian, stresses the three aspects of the techniques of spiritual direction: 'the mode of dependence with respect to the elder or master, the way of conducting the examination of one's own conscience, and the duty to describe one's mental impulses in a formulation that aims to be exhaustive: the *exagoreusis*' (GL 319/323).

Unconditional obedience, uninterrupted examination, and exhaustive confession form an *ensemble* in which each element implies the other two; the verbal manifestation of the truth hidden in the depths of oneself appears as an indispensable component of the government of men by each other, as it was carried out in monastic and especially Cenobitic institutions beginning in the fourth century. But it needs to be stressed that this manifestation was not for the purpose of establishing one's sovereign mastery of the self over the self; what was expected, rather, was humility and mortification, detachment toward the self and the constitution of a relation with the self that strives toward the destruction of the form of the self. (GL 320/324–5)

This presentation of the relation between *exomologēsis* and *exagoreusis* is misleading as a summary of the course: but as an indication of where Foucault is going, it is of great significance.

Also telling in this course are Foucault's infrequent, often general, but significant references to antiquity. He would, of course, considerably develop these over the next four courses and related writings. The challenge is whether the fairly stark readings here would be sustainable on the basis of more thorough research in the future. For example, his claims that Greek and Roman examinations of consciences are entirely different from Christian, and that as a consequence 'the subjectification of Western man is Christian, not Greco-Roman' (GL 231/236, see 241/246, 247/252–3) would be substantially modified in later analyses. Foucault here moves to a brief reading of antiquity to set out this contrast. His examples are the Pythagoreans, who are traditionally seen as the inventers of the examination of conscience, and the model for others including Christians such as Jean Chrysostom (GL 232–3/237–8).

There are some passages in the delivered course, reinforced by the manuscript, where he is clearly already making extensive use of material from antiquity. For example, there is an intriguing discussion of Seneca (GL 234–7/239–43; 235 n. */239–40 n. §), which would be utilized in the US lectures in the Autumn. He equally makes some comments on how antiquity's techniques are utilized in monasticism, thinking about penitence and monasticism work together (GL 253–4/258–9). Here he makes the telling contrast: Monasticism is a 'life of perfection, or rather it is a life of perfectioning, the way towards a perfect life' (GL 254/260). 'There are, therefore, from the fourth century, a certain number of fundamental techniques of ancient philosophical life transferred into the interior of monastic institutions in Christianity', but this is not to say they are not changed. The technique of direction, in particular, is now inscribed within a 'general *dispositif*' (GL 268–9/274). Foucault's course thus ends as a loosely

connected set of themes. Although he tries to bring the disparate
analyses together in its final moments – from Septimus Severus
through Oedipus to different models of government of individuals in
Christianity and antiquity – he struggles to articulate a clear overall
purpose (GL 303–7/309–13).

It is here that the curious text signed by 'Maurice Florence' becomes
significant. Following an invitation 'in the early 1980s' to contribute
to the *Dictionnaire des philosophes*, a text provided by Foucault was
edited by François Ewald, who wrote its opening lines.[8] It appeared
under a fairly transparent pseudonym. Defert and Ewald describe the
original text as 'a section of the introduction' to 'a first draft of
Volume II of the *History of Sexuality*',[9] but Ewald is also reported to
have dated it to 1980.[10] If both the dating and description are correct,
it may be a fragment from the volume on Christianity. The first indication he would publish on antiquity comes around June 1981, when
he says he anticipates publishing material from the *Subjectivité et
vérité* course (DE#213 IV, 213; EW I, 87).[11] That course is very close
to the material which eventually appeared in Volume III.

The 'Maurice Florence' piece only gives a few clues to its original
provenance. It is a retrospective presentation, covering all his writings
from the *History of Madness* to *Discipline and Punish* – almost
everything preceding the book it is introducing. It shows clear signs
of being concerned with a reconfigured version of the *History of
Sexuality*. But it makes no mention of antiquity, giving instead an
example of 'an exegesis of a sacred text' among other instances of
the relation between subjectification and knowledge (DE#345 IV,
632; EW II, 459–60).

He is now interested in studying:

> the constitution of the subject as an object for himself: the formation
> of procedures by which the subject is led to observe, analyse, interpret,
> and recognize himself as a domain of possible knowledge. In short,
> this concerns the history of 'subjectivity', if what is meant by the
> term is the way in which the subject experiences himself in a game of
> truth where he relates to himself. The question of sex and sexuality
> appeared...to constitute not the only possible example, certainly, but
> at least a rather privileged case. Indeed, it was in this connection that
> through the whole of Christianity, and perhaps beyond, individuals
> were all called on to recognize themselves as subjects of pleasure, of
> desire, of concupiscence, of temptation and were urged to deploy, by
> various means (self-examination, spiritual exercises, *aveu, confession*),
> in regard to themselves and what constitutes the most secret, the most
> individual part of their subjectivity, the game of true and false. (DE#345
> IV, 633; EW II, 461)

These examples squarely situate the text in relation to concerns of the 1979–80 period, both in lectures and the writing Foucault was undertaking alongside them. Additionally, towards the end of the text, Foucault situates his previous studies of the 'mad, the sick, the delinquent subject' as ones which looked at 'the manner in which men are "governed" by each other', and suggests that 'it is a matter of analysing "sexuality" as an historically singular mode of experience in which the subject is objectified for himself and for others, through certain specific procedures of "government"' (DE#345 IV, 636; EW II, 463). While the reconfiguration of his work so that the work on sexuality is the third element recurs in later texts, it is striking that here 'government' is seen as the key interpretative lens. Government had of course been the focus of his Paris courses from 1978 to 1980, and would be again in his final two courses.

The 'history of sexuality' is here conceived as fitting within Foucault's overall project as a 'third segment' of his work, looking at 'relations between the subject and truth or, to be exact, to the study of the modes according to which the subject was able to be inserted as an object in the games of truth' (DE#345 IV, 633; EW II, 461). Truth and subjectivity had appeared as a key theme in *On the Government of the Living*, operating in different ways in distinct parts of Christianity, especially in baptism (see GL 165–84/167–87), in *exomologēsis* and *exagoreusis* (GL 305/310–11). Baptism was supposed to wipe the individuals of sin, and if they committed sin again then it could only be wiped clean through penance, which became almost a second baptism. Subjectivity and truth, of course, would be the key focus of his next course at the Collège, as he turns to antiquity, but it would also be the topic of some lectures elsewhere.[12]

About the Beginning of the Hermeneutic of the Self

Between October and November 1980 Foucault was in the United States, where he gave several lectures in English. First were the Howison lectures at Berkeley, under the title of 'Truth and Subjectivity' on 20 and 21 October.[13] The first lecture treated antiquity, especially Seneca, and the second early Christianity. It was after the first that Foucault met Peter Brown, forging an important intellectual friendship for both men.[14] Foucault repeated these lectures at Dartmouth College on 17 and 24 November, with the separate titles of 'Subjectivity and Truth' and 'Christianity and Confession', including some important variations. These lectures have long been available in English as 'About the Beginning of the Hermeneutics of the Self', edited by Mark Blasius, with several of the Berkeley variants noted. The title comes from a remark Foucault makes in the first Berkeley lecture (OHS 41 n. a). The lectures have only recently been translated into French in the *L'Origine de l'herméneutique de soi* volume, which contains two interviews from this trip,[15] and provides a more systematic and complete set of notes of the variants between the Dartmouth and Berkeley versions. Between these West and East coast lectures, Foucault conducted a seminar at New York University with Richard Sennett, which is preserved in part in the text 'Sexuality and Solitude'. That text, which exists in variant forms, repeats some of the material from the other lectures, though adds some important additional analyses.[16] We also know that Foucault held seminars on 'Sexual Ethics in Late Antiquity and Early Christianity' at Berkeley, and there was also a lecture in November at Princeton University, organized by Blasius. Though entitled 'The Birth of Biopolitics', this was very close to the second of the 'Omnes et Singulatim' lectures of 1979, and much would be reused in 1982 in Vermont.[17]

The 'Hermeneutics of the Self' lectures are revealing because this is the first time Foucault spoke about antiquity in relation to his project on the history of sexuality, or, as it was now becoming, a history of subjectivity or a 'genealogy of the modern subject' (ABHS 201; OHS 33).[18] This preceded his treatment of the antiquity in this project at the Collège de France: a reversal of his usual practice. The stakes of this project are significant, and Foucault is explicit that this is a tactic: 'I have tried to get out from the philosophy of the subject through a genealogy of this subject, by studying the constitution of the subject across history which has led us up to the modern concept of the self' (ABHS 202; OHS 35; see ABHS 225 n. 26; OHS 65–6 n. a).[19] As he said at Berkeley:

> In sum, the aim of my project is to construct a genealogy of the subject. The method is an archaeology of knowledge, and the precise domain of the analysis is what I should call technologies... the articulation of certain techniques and certain kinds of discourse about the subject. (ABHS 223 n. 4; OHS 36–7 n. b.)

Or, as he says in a draft of the New York lecture, there is a 'possibility of writing a history of what we have done which can be at the same time an analysis of what we are; a theoretical analysis that has political meaning'.[20] He links this work to his earlier studies of 'the subject as a speaking, living, working being', and how in institutions like hospitals, asylums and prisons 'certain subjects because objects of knowledge and at the same time objects of domination' (ABHS

203; OHS 36–8). The lectures are also interesting because Foucault begins with a nineteenth-century text of psychiatry, from François Leuret. This is revealing, because it shows that the question here is one of confession, of producing in patients a confession of their madness. It is not enough for them to acknowledge this because they are being forced to – through the use of a cold shower – but they must acknowledge it themselves (ABHS 200–1; OHS 31–3; see also WDTT 1–3/11–14).[21] The current project, explicitly linked to sexuality, is about 'those forms of understanding which the subject creates about himself'. These are what he describes, for the first time in extant materials, as 'techniques or technology of the self' (ABHS 203; OHS 36–8).[22] These techniques of the self need to be studied alongside techniques of domination, but he notes that the government of others is dependent on the self. Here is the beginning of the formulation of the government of self and others that would be the theme of his final lecture courses (ABHS 203–4; OHS 38–9). As he said in these lectures:

> Governing people, in the broad meaning of the word [as they spoke of it in the sixteenth century, of governing children, governing families or governing souls], governing people is not a way to force people to do what the governor wants; it is always a versatile equilibrium, with complementarity and conflicts between techniques which assure coercion and processes through which the self is constructed and modified by himself. (ABHS 203–4 and 224 n. 13; OHS 39 and n. b.)[23]

In the first lecture Foucault suggests that antiquity does not put a major emphasis on self-examination and confession and that where it does, the emphasis is on individuals, their benefit and their self-mastery. Often a master would be employed in order to help with a specific event or situation such as a bereavement or other ordeal. This does not lead to an exhaustive self-examination, nor to a detailed confession of all small details to the master. However Foucault suggests that there are traces of techniques of finding out the truth about the self, and that these take on a greater importance over time, in the Pythagoreans, the Epicureans and the Stoics (ABHS 205–6; OHS 41–2). From this sketch Foucault proposes taking short excerpts from Seneca, from *De ira* and *De tranquillitate animi*, to illustrate the theme. Seneca is important because he was a Stoic writing at the time of the Roman Empire and the beginning of Christianity. The first text illustrates the idea of a self-examination or a confession to oneself, an examination of a single day at its end; the second is about confession to another, particularly on the medical model of consultation

(ABHS 206–9; OHS 42–8). The latter gives rise to the formulation of 'truth as a force', not a correspondence theory of truth, but truth as invested in relations, 'as a force inherent to principles and which has to be developed in a discourse' (ABHS 209; OHS 48–9). Foucault suggests that the individual who confesses to Seneca, his friend Serenus, does not do so as part of a process of individualization, but as 'the constitution of a self' (ABHS 209; OHS 49). In neither of these texts is the confession of something deeply hidden: the self is not discovered, but is 'constituted through the force of truth' (ABHS 210; OHS 50).

The second lecture tries to show that Christianity takes these themes but develops them in a crucially different way, such that our 'modern hermeneutics of the self' depends much more on 'Christian techniques than…Classical ones' (ABHS 211; OHS 65). Christianity is a religion that imposes an obligation of truth, both of believing certain dogmas and in certain texts, but also as a process of confession, where each Christian must tell others their truth, 'to bear witness' against themselves (ABHS 211; OHS 67). It is the second Foucault wants to concentrate on, and to do so not by looking at the period around the Reformation, with 'the sacrament of penance and the canonic confession of sins', but at the early Church in two institutions, 'penitential rites and monastic life' (ABHS 211–12; OHS 67–9). Penance was a status, not an act, a state of being to avoid being expelled from the Church, and to allow a possible reintegration (ABHS 212; OHS 69–70). Key to this status was 'the obligation to manifest the truth', the notion of *exomologēsis*, which was both an act that would close the period of penance, the moment of reintegration, and the various tasks undertaken during the period of penance as a whole. Foucault cites various texts from Tertullian, Jerome, Ambrose, Cyprian, and Pacian to illustrate the analysis. 'The punishment of oneself and the voluntary expression of oneself are bound together' (ABHS 214; OHS 72). As Foucault stresses, Tertullian's Latin translation of the Greek *exomologēsis* is '*publicatio sui*, the Christian had to publish himself', make their status evident, 'a dramatic manifestation of the renunciation to oneself' (ABHS 214; OHS 73).

In monastic institutions something different is at stake. Here there is a continuity from pagan practices, with the monastic life seen as the true philosophical life, and the monastery as a school of philosophy. It is therefore unsurprising that 'there is an obvious transfer of several technologies of the self in Christian spirituality from practices of pagan philosophy' (ABHS 215; OHS 76). Foucault takes John Chrysostom as his example of the continuity. But there are two important differences that come from the specifically Christian model: 'the principle of obedience' to a master and 'the principle of contemplation' of God (ABHS 216; OHS 77–8). The 'peculiar characteristics' of Christian monasticism, here, are elaborated on the basis of John Cassian's *Institutiones* and *Collationes*, and two key points are stressed: the monk examines not only his actions, like the Stoic, but his thoughts, 'the permanent mobility of [the] soul' (ABHS 216; OHS 78); and the crucial moment is the verbalization, the confession itself in words, as the proof, the manifestation of truth (ABHS 219; OHS 82–3). This verbalization is important for multiple reasons, but crucially it has an interpretative function; it is a permanent activity, a kind of running commentary on thoughts; it is designed to dig deep into internal secrets; and it is a process of *metanoia*, conversion, from 'the reign of Satan to the law of God'. The Greek fathers called this 'permanent, exhaustive, and sacrificial verbalization of the thoughts' by the name *exagoreusis* (ABHS 220; OHS 86–7). Foucault therefore suggests two different models of confession in Christianity – *exomologēsis* and *exagoreusis* – though they are linked, in that 'the rule of confession in *exagoreusis*, this rule of permanent verbalization, finds its parallel in the model of martyrdom which haunts *exomologēsis*' (ABHS 221; OHS 87).[24] Foucault notes that medieval confession of sins is 'like a strange mélange of *exagoreusis* and *exomologēsis*' (OHS 107). In the earlier period they are related in other ways, and Foucault quickly sketches the way that *exomologēsis* might be seen as 'the ontological temptation', concerned with the being of the sinner, and *exagoreusis* 'the epistemological temptation of Christianity', concerned with the analysis of their thoughts. It is the second, as an 'epistemological technology of the self', which has come to dominate today. In modern thought, there is an attempt to ground this on a positive sense of the self, 'the politics of ourselves' (ABHS 222–3; OHS 89). But in early Christianity, and this is the radical break with antiquity, there is a *renunciation* of the self, with truth and sacrifice intertwined: 'we have to sacrifice the self in order to discover the truth about oneself, and we have to discover the truth about oneself in order to sacrifice oneself' (ABHS 221; OHS 87–8).

The 'Sexuality and Solitude' lecture at NYU begins in almost exactly the same way to the Berkeley and Dartmouth lectures, with the analysis of Leuret, moving to discussion of objectification/subjectification and the biographical reading of his work. But instead of discussing Seneca and antiquity, Foucault moves straight to Christianity, invoking Peter Brown's challenge to 'understand why it is that sexuality became, in Christian cultures, the seismograph of our subjectivity'. This, however, is accomplished in a rather different way.

Foucault says that the example he and Sennett had used in the seminar was that of the monogamous, faithful and abstemious elephant in a passage from François de Sales (EW I 179; DE#295 IV, 172–3).[25] The key comparison however is between Artemidorus and the fourteenth book of Augustine's *City of God*, with relation to the *Contra Julian*.[26] Artemidorus provided an analysis of dreams that reversed Freud because sexual dreams told of political or social futures; but also crucially interests Foucault because sexual acts were less important for him than the status rather than the sex of the partner. In fact, privileging the male, the only act he sees as significant is penetration, but this is a social role as much as a sexual act in itself. Augustine's text concerns the status of sexual relations before the Fall, in Paradise. Sex now is an affliction, an 'epileptic form', but then it was different because every part of Adam's body was controlled by his soul. The fig leaf, on this reading, was not to cover the sexual parts because they were naked, but because they moved without volition (EW I 180–1; DE#295 IV, 174–5). For Artemidorus, the sexual question is penetration; for Augustine erection; 'not the problem of a relationship to other people, but the problem of the relationship of oneself to oneself, or, more precisely, the relationship between one's will and involuntary assertions'. This is the problem of libido, which requires 'a permanent hermeneutics of oneself . . . sexual ethics imply very strict truth obligations' (EW I 182; DE#295 IV, 176). In a passage from the original manuscript of the lecture, but not delivered, Foucault suggests that 'the techniques were mainly developed in the ascetic milieu and monastic institutions, and those relayed by the Augustinian theory of libido had, I think, a huge influence on Western technologies of the self'.[27] Foucault suggests that it is striking that this literature from the fourth and fifth centuries was concerned, not so much with sexual behaviour, but 'with the stream of thoughts flowing into consciousness, disturbing, by their multiplicity, the necessary unity of contemplation [of God], and secretly conveying images or suggestions from Satan'. This is the reason for the importance of continual scrutiny and commentary on these thoughts by the monk. Real purity was not attained by lying down with 'a young beautiful boy without even touching him, as Socrates did with Alcibiades' . . . but when there are no impure thoughts or images in mind, even in dreams. In this sense, 'the question of sexual ethics has moved from relations to people, and the penetration model, to the relation to oneself and to the erection problem', concerning thoughts and connected movements. But in both, crucially, 'sexuality, subjectivity and truth were strongly linked together' (EW I 182–3; DE#295 IV, 177–8).

These lectures are therefore perhaps most interesting for their clear juxtaposition of the readings of antiquity and the early Church. While Foucault clearly intended this to be a major theme of his published work, with the second and third volumes of the *History of Sexuality* preceding the fourth, in his lecture courses he tended to treat them discretely. The discussions of Christianity in *The Abnormals*, *Security, Territory, Population* and *On the Government of the Living* all precede the detailed work on antiquity in *Subjectivité et vérité* and the courses that followed it. We do not have an available record of how Foucault would have reworked the analysis of Christianity in their light. In a sense what we have in these late 1980 lectures is an indication of how Foucault might have presented *Les Aveux de la chair* at that time, with an introduction on antiquity leading to a substantive analysis of Christianity. He suggests there is a fundamental break between a pagan obligation to know your self and a Christian, monastic precept of confessing your inner thoughts to a superior. The transformation is important in 'the genealogy [Berkeley: constitution] of modern subjectivity' and begins the 'hermeneutics of the self' (ABHS 204; OHS 40 and 40–1 n. a.). Foucault's claim at this point is that Christianity sees the emergence of 'a much more complex technology of the self' than antiquity (ABHS 221; OHS 89; see OH 121). This claim was one he quickly abandoned, realizing it drew too much on secondary accounts and that antiquity needed its own, standalone, treatment (DE#326 IV, 384; EW I, 254). Unsurprisingly, given what he has worked on in detail up to this point, the analysis of Christianity is much more detailed than that of antiquity. His next courses in Paris show, in great detail, how he deepened and reworked that initial reading.

The Problem of Confession

People listening to the lectures *On the Government of the Living* in 1980 in anticipation of *La Chair et le corps* would have been disappointed; and the same is true for us today hoping for the manuscript of *Les Aveux de la chair*. Defert and Senellart both underline that Foucault's dispute with Gallimard in 1975 led to a decision not to publish a book for five years (C 50/62; Senellart in GL 334/335). But Senellart also stresses that in the intervening years Foucault had shifted emphasis from 'the post-Tridentine [post-Council of Trent] Christian pastoral' to an 'entirely different epoch of Christianity, without an explicit link to the problematic of the flesh' (in GL 334/335). Yet what is telling is that 'flesh' was to have been a

significant theme not only in the second volume of the original plan
but also, if its title is an indication, in the fourth volume of the final
one. *On the Government of the Living* only tangentially touches
upon this theme, as Foucault notes that 'the theme of pastoral power
does not entail a technique of direction, even if, later, when this
technique of direction was developed within Christianity, it is placed
within the realm of the pastorate' (GL 249/255).

Looking at the discussion of confession in the first volume of the
History of Sexuality and *The Abnormals* in the light of these later
analyses is revealing. The discussion of the topic of confession in
those texts was somewhat unconvincing, and further work on this
material for *La Chair et le corps* contributed to Foucault abandoning
the original plan and working more historically than thematically.[28]
Foucault initially concentrates on the period after the Council of
Trent, and when he discusses material before this the somewhat
sweeping statements are largely unsubstantiated (for example, A
161/173–4). He trades on a fairly small range of secondary material
for this earlier period, notably Lea's *A History of Auricular Confession*,[29] although the later period – from the sixteenth century on –
seems better researched. In his discussions of the later period he cites
some key texts, including, among others, Milhard, Habert, Charles
Borromée, de Ligouri (A 173–4/186–7, 176–7/189–90, etc.). But as
the editors note, it is not clear that Foucault read the texts themselves,
as almost all the documentation comes from Lea's research.[30] This is
not to suggest Foucault's reading of the mid 1970s (that is, in the
first volume of the *History of Sexuality* and *The Abnormals*) is
without interest. There is some discussion of the development of the
practice and that the architectural device of the confessional is only
found from the sixteenth century (A 168/181).[31] As early as 1975,
linking the then newly published *Discipline and Punish* to the concerns of the later volumes of the *History of Sexuality*, Foucault had
paired 'the political anatomy of bodies, a moral physiology of the
flesh' (A 180/193). Some of Foucault's comments link to earlier
courses at the Collège de France, including those that informed the
writing of *Discipline and Punish* (A 158/170; 180/193). But the discussion seems to be principally in order to contextualize the analysis
of masturbation in subsequent lectures: indeed Foucault suggests that
masturbation occupies a privileged place in the confession of sin (A
179/192–3, 187–8/201–2).[32] As he describes the relation at that time:
'The body is incarnate and flesh is incorporated [*une incarnation du
corps et une incorporation de la chair*]' (A 179/192). We now know
that the manuscript of *La Chair et le corps* was not *entirely* destroyed
in the mid 1970s, because Philippe Chevallier provides a brief

description of an extant manuscript dating from 1978 on confession and concupiscence in the sixteenth and seventeenth centuries.[33] Senellart wonders, with good reason, if this is the work alluded to in the 1983 'On the Genealogy of Ethics' interview, when Foucault mentions having 'more than a draft of a book about sexual ethics in the sixteenth century' (EW I, 255; DE#326 IV, 383).[34] But if this manuscript and draft material does date from 1978, then it is likely to have needed extensive revision before being something Foucault would see as in keeping with his later analyses.

One of the problems of the argument of the mid 1970s is that Foucault thinks that the date of 1215 is crucial (see A 162/174). Canon 21 did initiate annual confession and is a central pillar of the modern Church. Lea has described it as 'perhaps the most important legislative act in the history of the Church'.[35] However it is not at all clear that this moment was particularly important either for the idea of confession in itself or the emphasis on sexuality which Foucault accords to it. As Payer has shown, some quite serious questions can be raised about Foucault's emphasis.[36] One of these is a direct challenge to Foucault's privileging of the edict of the Fourth Lateran Council, suggesting that we need to go further back. The other is that the *Summae confessorum*, the penitential manuals of the subsequent period, tend to concern other sins rather than sexual ones: 'consideration of sexual maters was virtually smothered by treatises on subjects quite unrelated to sex... only a selective reading of the confessional manuals after 1215 could find in them a particular concern with sex...'[37] Payer, while sympathetic to some aspects of Foucault's work, is fairly damning in his summation, suggesting that what Foucault 'claims for the post-Lateran period simply cannot be substantiated', that the claim of three centuries (HS I 33/23) really should be twelve, and that sex should not have 'pride of place'.[38] Yet some time before these lines of Payer's were published, Foucault had realized exactly the problems they point to. He had gone back much further than the early thirteenth century; had realized that the key concerns of the medieval period were not necessarily sex; and that moral conduct generally, that is techniques of the self, and not sexuality particularly, should be his guiding concern. In 1981 he clarifies that the twelfth-century development is only in terms of the form of penance, and its renewable nature (WDTT 102/104). But it is through following the theme of confession that he came to realize all these things. This working through certainly tied Foucault up for many years.

This is not only evident in the works that were either part of, or directly shed light on, the *History of Sexuality*. Confession also plays an important role in some of Foucault's minor works. It helps to explain his interest in the confessional memoirs of Pierre Rivière and Herculine Barbin, and the collection of *lettres de cachet* he presented with Arlette Farge (see Chapter 8). Foucault mentions these three projects as demonstrating the interplay of 'types of *savoir*, forms of normality, and modes of relation to oneself and others' (DE#340 IV, 581; EW I, 202). In a revealing interview given in 1981, at the time of the course in Louvain, Foucault expressed both his interest and his confusion.

> Confession [*l'aveu*] is an instrumental element I constantly come across, and I wonder whether to write the history of confession in itself, as a type of technique with different aspects, or to treat this question in the context of studies of the different domains where it seems to play a role, that is in the domain of sexuality and penal psychiatry. (WDTT 249/256)[39]

This is revealing because of the continual interest in the question of confession, which stretches back at least as far as the 1971–2 course *Théories et institutions pénales*, through the discussion of psychiatric expertise in criminal cases in *The Abnormals* and elsewhere, through work on the 'dangerous individual', to the first volume of the *History of Sexuality* and projected future volumes.

The 1981 Louvain course is an intriguing document, for at least two reasons.[40] First, that it rehearses and synthesizes material across the entirety of his work in the 1970s, alongside the work on Christianity in the 1980 course; but second that it says very little that is dependent on the work in *Subjectivité et vérité*. The second is intriguing, in part, because Foucault gave the inaugural lecture at Louvain the day after he finished the course at the Collège. It is almost as if, realizing he had now embarked on a new historical period that would take his work in novel and challenging directions, he wanted to have one last chance at providing the history of confession he had promised for so long. Although, as will be discussed below, he does discuss antiquity in Louvain, much of this is in relation to much earlier courses, and he quite quickly moves over his more recent analyses (see WDTT 91/93). In general, reading *Wrong Doing, Truth Telling* is revealing, because while much would have been familiar to his Collège de France auditors, and now those of us who now read the published courses, the synthesis and overall presentation is novel. And we must remember that few in his Louvain audience would have had much idea of how this traded on extensive work over several years. In this, and other respects, including the legal focus, this course is not dissimilar to the 'Truth and Juridical Forms' lectures of almost a decade before.

The course moves through a number of stages in its treatment. In the first lecture, Foucault provides a reading of Homer's *Illiad* and Hesiod – material that links back to his first Collège course. The second lecture also makes use of that course in yet another discussion of Oedipus, filtered through the reading in *On the Government of the Living*. In the third to fifth lectures, Foucault also makes extensive use of the 1980 course, and the late 1980 lectures in the United States, as the discussion moves through Seneca, Christianity, monasticism (with special emphasis on Cassian), some allusions to antiquity, and the question of *exagoreusis* and *exomologēsis*. Much of this discussion is cast in the general light of the *tekhnē tekhnis*, which he explains is not simply government in the 'general collective sense of a political art' but additionally 'the government of individuals by one another, the government of souls' (WDTT 63/72). In the final lecture he brings this analysis to touch on medieval and modern material, with a discussion of torture and the inquiry, which owes much to *Théories et institutions pénales*, and then some of the cases studied in *The Abnormals* and 'About the Concept of the "Dangerous Individual"'. These include the Sélestat woman and Henriette Cornier (WDTT 211–12/212). If nothing else, the course clearly demonstrates the enormous breadth of his interests and the substantial resources he had to hand in unpublished work by this stage of his career. Holding these potential disparate examples together is a continual focus on the questions of truth and subjectivity, of how modes of veridiction constitute and mould the self, what he at one point calls 'the obligation to tell truth about oneself' (WDTT 91/93).

These cases are in the most contemporary lecture of the course, but it is important to note that Foucault was conducting a seminar at Louvain alongside the lectures. The focus was on Belgium specifically, and the use of the idea of 'social defence' (see WDTT 248–9/255). The seminar was a project led by Françoise Tulkens, who had been responsible for inviting Foucault to give the course. The proceedings of the seminar, though without a text by Foucault, were finally published in 1988 as *Généalogie de la défense sociale en Belgique (1880–1914)*.[41] As the editors of the course note, 'the lectures would trace a genealogy of the type of subject the doctrine of social defence presupposed, and the seminar would trace a genealogy of the accompanying apparatus: the institutions, practices, and discourses of social defence'.[42]

All these potentially disparate concerns are linked through his description of confession, avowal, as 'an act by which the subject, in an affirmation of what they are, binds themselves to this truth, places themselves in a relation of dependence with regard to another and at the same time modifies the connection that they have to themselves' (WDTT 7/17). There are some very interesting discussions of writing that bring together injunctions from those such as Seneca, Jean Chrysostom and Saint Anthony in Athanasius's *Vita Antonii*. The injunction here is one of writing down everything, 'all of the movements of the soul'. Foucault suggests that 'this was the precise turning point in the techniques of [self], techniques of the self, technologies of the self found in ancient pagan philosophy, the hinge between these techniques and new techniques' (WDTT 143/144), 'the birth of what we might call a hermeneutics of the self in the Western world' (WDTT 147/148, 164/166). There is also an important deepening of the relation between *exomologēsis* and *exagoreusis*. There was *exomologēsis* in penance and *exagoreusis* as an ascetic and spiritual practice in monastic communities. In reality, these two practices – *exomologēsis* of penance and spiritual *exagoreusis* – represented far more two poles between which there was a series of graduated forms, than two institutions or two practices that were perfectly distinct one from the other (WDTT 169–70/172).

It is unclear what Foucault himself thought the status of this material was. It was delivered three years before his death, which would have given him time to publish it if he had so chosen. He is asked in one of the interviews in Louvain if he intends to publish a book on confession, and demurs, suggesting that 'I hesitate to publish on this question because, in one sense, the study of confession [*l'aveu*] is purely instrumental for something else' (WDTT 249/255). But as the editors note, the lectures have the character of a book 'because the text reads like a completed work'.[43] Indeed, they suggest that the text we have, which they have reconstructed from audio and video recordings, as well as the manuscript, may be seen as the closest Foucault got, not to *Les Aveux de la chair*, but to the book promised back in 1976, *Pouvoir de la vérité* (HS I 79 n. 1/-). These lectures, or, in their terms 'this book', 'trace a history of avowal since the Homeric era and explore the power of truth-telling in justice'.[44] Yet Foucault's project has moved on since 1976, and it is telling that in another interview from this trip, he wonders if he 'should not write a history of subjectivity-truth' (WDTT 250/256). Picking up on this suggestion, the editors comment: 'A draft was delivered in these Louvain lectures.'[45]

It is tempting, certainly, to see this course and others as the missing piece in the puzzle, as providing the lost text or the absent link between disparate concerns. Yet despite the differences of emphasis in the intervening years, the relation of Foucault's concerns of the early 1980s back to the material on the inquiry and proof or test in the medieval period is especially interesting (i.e. WDTT 203/203). This is because it shows how work that was produced before the first volume of the *History of Sexuality* is still useful to him, even after he has realized some of its limitations. Although he criticizes the emphasis he had placed on the seventeenth and eighteenth-century campaigns against masturbation as demonstrating a clear break (WDTT 250/257), from the presentation in this lecture course, and discussions elsewhere in his work, it is clear that he was not interested in completely abandoning the earlier plan, or that he felt that all of his previous work had been misjudged. He makes a number of qualifications, and deepens his analysis, but continually returns to previous material. For example, on 22 June 1982 he uses examples of children's masturbation and hysterical women to illustrate the thesis that sexuality has not simply been repressed, and that this was not merely a question of morality but one of pleasure for the parents. This pleasure was one of 'sexual excitement and sexual satisfaction', for the parents themselves, a kind of 'systematization of rape' (DE#336 IV 530–1; FL 375–6). He continues to stress themes which are extremely close to ones delivered on 5 March 1975 on the 'epistemophilic' incest of contact, observation and surveillance and its role in the foundation of the modern family (A 234/249).

Foucault's interest in confession might move from power relations to the production of truth, but it remained at the centre of his concerns.[46] By 1980–1, with *On the Government of the Living* and *Wrong Doing, Truth Telling*, Foucault had done most of the work on early Christianity. We know that a draft of *Les Aveux de la chair* was completed around this time. That unpublished volume, even though it treats a different historical period to *La Chair et le corps*, is perhaps the key to the whole *Sexuality* series. Confession is the crucial element in both the abandoned and unfinished plans. But Foucault remained unhappy with the introductory material to this volume, which he says discussed antiquity. Although he had discussed this period in some detail in earlier lectures, notably in *Lectures on the Will to Know*, he would return to it with unprecedented depth of engagement, beginning with *Subjectivité et vérité*. All of Foucault's future courses treat this period. Antiquity becomes the focus of his on-going 'history of the relations between truth and subjectivity' (GL 297/303).

6

The Pleasures of Antiquity

The work on Christianity in the late 1970s and 1980 had already anticipated some of the themes Foucault would concentrate on for the final years of his life. Crucially, the development of this material led to significant changes to the work being undertaken. The first important change was that the topic matter changed from the late Medieval to the early years of Christianity. Some of this was discussed in Chapter 5 above. As he says in a lecture conducted in Louvain in 1981, he realized that the restrictions he had initially seen in the seventeenth and eighteenth centuries could actually be found in ancient texts – both 'Christian and even older' (WDTT 251/257). But a second, even more significant change developed from the drafting of the material. Foucault later claims that the introduction he drafted at this time rested upon a number of 'clichés' about pagan ethics (i.e. Greece and Rome), which were misleading, based as they were on generalizations in the secondary literature (EW I, 254; DE#326 IV, 384).[1] Turning back still further, he said he wanted to sort out his view of the earlier period before he published this book on Christianity (EW I, 254; DE#326 IV, 384).[2] That, it seems, is what led Foucault into those earlier periods – material on which first started to appear in his lecture course *Subjectivité et vérité* in 1981. Instead of the work on Christianity being the second volume of the *History of Sexuality* series, it was moved further down the plan. Indeed, Foucault says that one of his aims is to chart 'how to establish this division [*partage*], how to undertake the cartography of this "parting of the waters [*partage des eaux*]", as Peter Brown calls it, between what we call Christianity and what we call paganism' (SV 40).[3]

Sexuality, Subjectivity and Truth

Foucault's focus in the course is on what he calls 'arts of life'. In these the self is crucial, though there is also 'the presence of the other, their speech, their authority' (SV 34). The other crucial relation, as well as to the other, is 'the relation to truth' (SV 34). These lectures are intriguing for multiple reasons, not least that in the opening lecture, Foucault discusses the relation between history, subjectivity and truth in a way few of his previous courses had done: with an explicit focus on sexuality (SV 16). He notes that this label is relatively recent, two or three centuries, and that 'sexuality' as a domain is different from his previous studies of 'madness, illness, death and crime' (SV 16). One of the differences between sexuality and these other domains, as he now understands things, is that in these other domains 'the essential [part] of the true discourse is held over the subject, but from the outside, from another'. In sexuality, he suggests, the institutionalization of the truth about a subject is on the basis of 'an obligatory discourse of the subject about themselves'. So it is not from the privileged, external position of a doctor, psychiatrist, or criminologist, but 'through the practice of confession [*d'aveu*, avowal] that the true discourse on sexuality is organized' (SV 17). The course this year, then, will conduct 'a history of the notion of concupiscence [sexual desire, lust], as is has been host of the subjective experience of sexuality, or rather of sex and sexual relations' (SV 17).

This, then, marks an important difference of emphasis from the work of the first volume of the *History of Sexuality*. If, there, the emphasis was on the question of power, and the way specialized medical, psychiatric and criminological discourses had shaped the sexual status of individuals and populations, here the focus is more on the subject and the relation of self to self. This had been, of course, explored in the previous course in Hellenistic and early Christian times. Here the emphasis is squarely on that earlier time period, and Foucault provides both detailed readings of Greek thought and makes a number of explicit comparisons with Christianity. Four themes will be discussed: the reading of Artemidorus' *Oneirocritica*; the status of marriage; the question of life, especially as *bios*; and the shift from *aphrodisia* to flesh, with the emergence of subjectivity.

Artemidorus's *Oneirocritica*

By far the longest discussion of a text in this course concerns Artemidorus' *Oneirocritica*, an analysis of the interpretation of dreams, which Foucault uses to think about subjectivity and truth in relation to *aphrodisia*.[4] He suggests that 'onirocritique is not of course an art of living, onirocritique is not exactly an art of conduct' (SV 51), and it concerns not simply deciphering the truths hidden in dreams, but also of knowing what to do about them. This is a curious text, partly inspired by Stoicism, and one of the reasons why Foucault is so interested is because three chapters are concerned with sex.[5] Foucault even claims that this is, among extant Greek and Roman texts, the 'only document which provides us with a fairly complete picture of the sexual acts, sexual relations – real, possible, imaginable, etc.' (SV 53). This is 'not a literary work…nor a work of moral philosophy' (SV 53). Nor is it 'a legal or mode code', and Foucault suggests that such a thing really does not exist in Greek and Roman thought at all (SV 55).

Foucault also notes that the dreamer is always the 'adult male, the head of the family' (SV 58). The point is not merely the gendered nature of Artemidorus' analysis, but that the head of the family needs to understand his dreams precisely in order to be a good father (SV 58–59). 'It is a book for the father of the family, and of course because of this it is normal that all dreams, sexual or otherwise, are referred to the reality which is social, political and economic life' (SV 59). This is important, because it gives rise to one of the key oppositions Foucault finds. Today, almost anything is read in terms of its sexual undercurrent: 'it is always the social which tends to be a sexual metaphor', and any political success, reversal of fortune and so on is interrogated in terms of the 'sexual truth it hides'. But for Artemidorus, 'one asks of a sexual dream the political, economic, social truth it speaks of' (SV 60).

For Artemidorus, there are three types of sexual dreams: acts that confirm to the law, the *nomos*, acts contrary to the law, and acts against nature, *physis* (SV 61). Foucault notes that there is a tension here, because things that conform to nature but not to the law appear to be missing – in the schema of for/against law and for/against nature there should be four categories, not three (SV 61). Yet it seems that things in accord with nature are either in accord with the law or not. Foucault works through the different figures that might appear in the dream: the man's own wife, which signifies his profession; his concubine (which has a meaning closer to a mistress here), which for Artemidorus makes no essential difference; then visiting an *ergasterion*, a brothel (SV 62–3). That is not a favourable dream, as the small rooms lined up side by side resemble a cemetery, and so this is a sign of death (SV 63). To dream of sex with slaves signifies profit, goods and possessions, it 'indicates that these possessions will become greater and more magnificent' (SV 64). Crucially, this makes no difference if the partner is a male or a female slave, except if the father of the household is not the dominant, active partner. If he is, then it is a sign of taking pleasure in his possessions, but if he is the passive then it signifies *blabē* – 'shame, sexual aggression, state of passivity, state of constraint' (SV 64). Other sexual relations with friends and relations can also be examined for the implications they have – unmarried women are good, especially if rich; married women are bad, as they are under the 'power of their husband'; a man is good if the dreamer is active, but if they are passive then it depends on the age and social standing of the other figure (SV 64–5). Here, Foucault notes, is the only time a woman is indicated as the possible dreamer, when if she 'dreams that she is penetrated by someone, that is obviously an advantage for the woman because it is in her nature to be penetrated' (SV 64).

Those are the relations conforming to law, and to nature. But there are possible sexual relations outside the law, *para nomon*, which Foucault stresses is more 'strangers to the law, rather than contrary to the law' (SV 65). This is the question of incest – between parents and children and between siblings. Between a father and his child is, aside from 'one or two very marginal exceptions', always negative. But between a mother and son 'almost always has a favourable signification' (SV 65). Foucault notes that mother–daughter incest is not even mentioned. The mother–son relation – the son here is the dreamer, not the mother – is favourable because it means the father will die, though he is at pains to stress this is not to Oedipize the story, and suggests that the dominant understanding at the time was positive, and for a range of reasons.[6] Because the mother signifies profession, to dream of sleeping with your mother is a sign of profit, or success in a political career; but she also signifies nature, which can mean health, and the earth, which would mean a good harvest for a farmer. The exception is this dream if you are sick, which signifies a return to the earth-mother, to die. But most connotations are, he underlines, very positive (SV 66).

As well as acts outside the law, there are those outside nature, *para phusin*. This is initially about particular actions or positions. There are natural means for all animals, and Artemidorus works through several of these before suggesting that humans are no different. The natural position is face-to-face, the man on top of the woman. Foucault notes that 'this normalization of a certain type of sexual relation does not date from Christianity' (SV 67). But there are other actions against nature: sex with gods, with animals, with corpses, sex 'which you can have with yourself', and two women together (SV 68).

Foucault is not interested in the first three, but says a little more about the last two. 'Union with yourself' is not, he underlines, masturbation. Masturbation in a dream had been dealt with earlier, and for Artemidorus that signifies having sex with a slave: Foucault underscores that this is the only time in this work that a dream about sex signifies sex (SV 68). Rather, what he means of a dream of sex with yourself is self-penetration: 'this act is against nature because it is impossible' (SV 68). And Foucault notes the strange decision to say that sex between women is against nature, when, for Artemidorus, sex between men – even between a man and child under the age of five, is not. The reason, for Artemidorus, is that sex between women is against nature, described as *perainein*, as it implies a 'relation of penetration', that is an 'imitation of the role of the man and a usurpation of this penetration which is the privilege of man' (SV 68). Foucault therefore underlines that penetration is a crucial issue for Artemidorus. 'The male sexual organ, with its capacity to penetrate, defines the universal and constant naturalness of the sexual act' (SV 69). This is why masturbation, which does not involve penetration, is unimportant. Penetration by artificial means, such as between women, is unnatural (SV 69).

The status of the partner is the other key factor, which is why sexual dreams can say so much about social standing. The sexual relation with the man's wife is the privileged relation; the incestuous relation between a man and his children is totally forbidden. But between these two there are a 'multiplicity of more or less acceptable relations', depending on factors such as age, social status, wealth, active/passive and so on. But, he underlines, this is a set of sexual codes for the father of the family: the 'naturalness (defined by penetration) and the sociality (characterized essentially by the social position of each of the partners, their role in society) of sexuality' (SV 70).

So, concluding the analysis of this text, Foucault notes that pagan ethics and Christian ethics share some similarities and yet also are importantly different. The idea of a sexual ethics is orientated around the male, the father, through familial relations is already there in pagan thought. But the important difference is that 'this sexuality is thought within a kind of continuity with the social relation...an entirely continuous ethics' (SV 71). This is due to status: it is seen as entirely appropriate for a man to have sex with his wife to produce offspring, and 'to take his pleasure with his slave': they are part of the same social role. They are not seen as two different sexualities, alien forms of desire. There is, therefore, a profound difference between 'the Greek experience which they call *aphrodisia* and the

Christian experience of the flesh' (SV 71). Yet this is not due to Christianity alone, and the seeds are found in the heart of ancient philosophy, in Stoicism and Epicureanism. The analysis of how 'this new form of experience in which *aphrodisia* (the pleasures of sex) will be thought in a new way and with a new type of relation to truth' (SV 71).

Foucault is not claiming to find in Artemidorus an 'absolutely shared, transcultural, transhistorical domain, which would be sexuality' (SV 77). Rather he is looking for very specific experience, which the Greeks called *aphrodisia* (SV 77–78). This term is the stake of his analysis, and one which he thinks can be contrasted with two other experiences: 'the Christian experience of the flesh and the modern experience of sexuality' (SV 78). These are 'not three domains of separate objects, but rather three modes of experience, that is three modalities of the relation of the self to the self in the relation [*rapport*] which we have to a certain domain of objects which are related to sex' (SV 78).

Foucault stresses that Artemidorus does not make a negative or positive judgement of sexual acts, not their direct moral value, but rather how to understand the prognostic value of the dream, of what it foretells in terms of social, rather than sexual, relations (SV 78–79). He says that there are two key principles concerning *aphrodisia*. The first is the 'principle of isomorphism': the relation of sexual acts to 'events in social life' (SV 79). The key break in *aphrodisia*, Foucault therefore contends, is not between heterosexuality and homosexuality, but between 'socio-sexual iso- and hetero-morphology' (SV 82). The key is that a man of status in society should have the right kinds of sexual relations. This could be within marriage, or through a relation to a boy or slave, as long as the man is the active partner. If, however, they are reversed, and the master in social relations is the inferior in sexual ones, then this is a relation of hetero-morphology, which is seen as bad (SV 82). Marriage is held up as the valorized, highest form of iso-morphism, but as not the exclusive one for a married man. Extra-marital relations are thus not condemned in themselves, but through their specifics. A relation with a servant meets the standard of iso-morphology, but with the wife of a neighbour is hetero-morphology, and thus adultery. It is more of a juridical definition than a moral one, contends Foucault, or at least a moral one because it is in contradiction with the social relations of the society, a violation of the rights of the neighbour over his wife (SV 83–4). This is, Foucault argues, a very different sense of morality than found in Christianity – the exclusive localization of sexual relations in marriage – and in modern 'sexuality' with its 'biological, anatomo-physiological division of the sexes', which provides the divide between hetero and homo-sexuality (SV 84).

The second principle of *aphrodisia* is the principle of activity, related to the question of nature. Principally here it is the question of penetration, which distinguishes the natural or unnatural status of sexual acts, though this is not simply penetrator-penetrated or active-passive (SV 86). Crucially, penetration is *not* a reciprocal act, it is 'not a process which takes place between two individuals. It is essentially the activity of *a* subject and the activity *of the* subject' (SV 87). As Foucault elaborates, for Artemidorus it is not even a question of what is penetrated – although he prohibits the mouth because of food and language. This non-relational understanding is important, because it creates a unitary subject at the heart of the sexual act. It is only the active partner who is a sexual subject. It is not a question of two elements, but 'the activity of one subject and one alone' (SV 87–8). Where this leaves the question of the partner is unclear. There are three main categories of partners – a woman, a boy, and slaves – a division which is found in other classical texts such as Hippocrates (SV 88–9). But these 'objects of penetration' do not themselves seem to count as subjects in this equation. 'Pleasure is an experience of the subject', and the only subject of *aphrodisia* is the one who is active. This gives rise to an entire ethics which essentially rests on the disqualification of passive pleasure, where 'female pleasure is a void [*gouffre*]' (SV 90).

In this Greek understanding of *aphrodisia* – 'the ethical perception of sexual acts' (SV 92–3) – Foucault claims that marriage is not enormously important for the ethical discussion of sex (SV 93). Marriage is uncomplicated, and so far more important in ethical treatises is the relation between men and boys. The emphasis is not merely because it was tolerated, because if it was simply tolerated then it would be like marriage and there would be little to say (SV 93–4). It is precisely because of its importance and complications that so much is said about it. It is a puzzle, and so is 'a perpetual spur to reflect, think, discuss, speak' (SV 94). One of the key issues is what marks the boy out from women or slaves. Like them he is the object of the sexual act, rather than the subject; but unlike them he will, in time, become a subject, both a social subject and a subject of sexual relations. Thus the relation of the man to the boy is also 'morally valuable... a social relation of pedagogy, exemplification, aid and support' (SV 94). The challenge comes from ensuring that the adult or older man remains the active partner, and knowing when the boy changes status and becomes a social subject. The sexual relation is in part an apprenticeship, teaching how to live, how to be a citizen and so on

(SV 95). Foucault later notes that the crucial moment is when the boy grows a beard and 'when, in principle, he ceases to be a desirable and legitimate object for men and when he becomes, in the world of *aphrodisia*, an active subject' (SV 182).

Foucault is not, of course, interested in these questions merely because of sexual or even ethical concerns. The focus remains on a mode of conduct, a mechanism for governance of the other, a technology of the self, which gives 'the individual the status of a subject', and an obligation to tell-the-truth [*dire vrai*]. 'It is the technology of the self in relation to the other, it is a certain manner of preparing the other to enter the status of a subject' (SV 97). He underlines that the problem of truth is closer to the transmission of truth in the pedagogic relation, rather than that of appropriate pleasures (SV 97). 'The passage from an obligation of truth understood as a pedagogic duty to an obligation of truth as a discovery of the truth of the self', which is not just found in Christianity but in a contemporary of Artemidorus (SV 97). However this gives rise to a concern of Foucault's use of material to derive wider social understandings. Artemidorus has as his focus the question of dreams, and the chapters on sex are only a small part of a large work. Foucault arguably takes the discussion of dreams of sexual acts to be a description of sexual acts in themselves, and this, in turn, as insight into the moral code of *aphrodisia*.

The Status of Marriage

While marriage had not been, Foucault suggests, a major concern in classic Greece, it later became a much more important topic of concern.[7] Its earlier comparative neglect had been, Foucault suggests, because it was seen as an uncomplicated issue: it was certainly not that it was undervalued as a social institution. However, while in the earlier understanding it was seen as only one site of sexual relations – privileged but not exclusive – in some texts of a later period it became the only allowable place. However, the crucial break, 'the grand point of the parting of the waters in the history of reflection on love', is not with Christianity. Foucault contends that 'it is earlier, and Plutarch is its witness' (SV 191). Plutarch is perhaps best known for his series of parallel lives of famous Greek and Roman figures, but the text which is Foucault's focus is the 'Erotikos', also known as the 'Dialogue on Love' or in its Latin title of the 'Amatorius', a text which can be found within his wider *Moralia* (SV 178–201).

In that text Foucault finds an important contrast between the love of boys and the love of women (SV 178). Foucault argues that we know that there were many more texts, no longer extant, which treated this theme (SV 179). The 'love of boys has become a love *aneu kharitos*, a disgraced love' (SV 200). The term *kharis* means something like grace, favour. While the earlier Greeks had thought of the ethic of pleasures only from the point of the one who was active, the man; and the object, woman or boy, was not important (SV 197), here there is a focus on the object of desire. This gives rise to what Foucault calls 'the new economy of sexual pleasures, the new economy of *aphrodisia*...the conjugalization of sexual pleasures, the conjugalization of *aphrodisia*' (SV 150). Conjugalization means, here, the localization of sex within the institution of marriage.

Foucault notes that in classical Greek thought there had been a recognition of tensions between *aphrodisia* and *bios theoretikos*, between a life of pleasures and 'the theoretical life'. Some philosophers had recognized that sexual pleasure was incompatible or at least dangerous for such 'a life which is dedicated, devoted to the search, the understanding [*saisie*] and contemplation of truth' (SV 153). In classical *aphrodisia*, where there was a sexual relation there was no relation to truth, and the instruction of boys in the truth was only found where the sexual act was renounced by the man (SV 169). The person who wishes to lead must control their desire. This is not, Foucault suggests, very common in classical antiquity, with the exception of the relation between Socrates and Alcibiades. Socrates does not consummate his relation with Alcibiades, not because he does not desire him, but because he wants to educate him and therefore must renounce sexual pleasure (SV 268, 292). This is a text to which Foucault will devote much more attention in the subsequent course.

Foucault therefore wants to challenge the idea that before Christianity there was 'a certain golden age of sexual freedom', and notes that in Greece there was also 'a fundamental mistrust with regard to sexual actions' (SV 158). In both *aphrodisia* and the flesh 'sexual activity comes to be considered as incompatible with a relation to the truth'. There are, however, differences, of which the crucial one is that the relation to the truth changes. While in the Greek experience it renders the individual incapable, at least for a while, in having access to the truth; in the Christian model it is more that the truth of sex needs to be discovered (SV 159–60). The question becomes one of asking 'what is the truth of my concupiscence?...the truth of my desire' (SV 160). Thus Christianity 'splits or doubles the problem of the relation of the sexual to truth', and it does so in a way that makes the truth of sexual desire itself an issue (SV 160). It is thus not Christianity that makes sex on the side of the impure, because the Greeks preceded them in this; as they did with the idea that the sexual relation was incompatible with the truth. Foucault suggests that this is a fundamental relation, linking subjectivity to the truth of our desire, and characterizes not merely Christianity but 'our entire civilization and our entire mode of thought' (SV 160). Where the sexual act was located in marriage, it becomes the 'object of analysis of philosophy, the object of analysis of this discourse of truth...object of knowledge [*connaissance*], object of truth' (SV 170). This then is Augustine's inquiry about the relation between truth and desire (SV 170).[8]

This leads to a number of consequences. A crucial question is where this 'new regime of *aphrodisia*, so profoundly linked now to marriage and the man/woman relation' came from (SV 206). Foucault notes that the documentary resources are very fragmented (SV 206) so he relies on the work of historians including Veyne (SV 207) and Claude Vatin (SV 235–6).[9] In the past, marriage was a private, rather than juridical act, it was an agreement between a father and a future husband, but he notes there is a development in Greece and in pre-Roman Egypt, with a public religion sanction of marriage, which eventually becomes a public institution sanctioned by civil institutions (SV 208). Then legal codes start to develop, especially in the early Empire under Augustine, around debauchery, rape, and adultery (SV 208). A long-known moral offence of adultery is turned into a sanctionable offence in the *lex de adulteriis* (SV 208–9). In sum, there is a whole set of practices – literary, socio-cultural, philosophical and legal – which produce this notion of marriage (SV 222).

One of the crucial changes is a break from the idea of the isomorphism of socio-sexual relations. If marriage becomes the privileged site of sexual relations, then it is the site of *aphrodisia*, and other sexual relations are outside of it (SV 260–1). Another transition is that in the classical model it was solely focused on the adult male, but now there is, if not an equality, more of a balance between the two partners in a marriage (SV 261). The relation between the individual and their sexual activity becomes important. Instead of an individual who takes part in certain acts, the individual in part becomes defined by them, a sexual-status (SV 263).

Foucault suggests that while in antiquity adultery by women was seen as immoral but by men was not seen as a major problem, there is a noticeable shift where it is seen as a problem for both. This change, though, is not due to Christianity alone, but can be traced to developments in the first and second centuries CE, in Stoic thought (SV 164–5). In Musonius Rufus, for example, Foucault contends that we find a 'sort of juridical or juridico-moral elevation of the woman to the level of the man...but inversely the lowering of the pleasure of the man to the level of the pleasure of the woman... It is the man who sets the juridical norm of existence, it is the woman who sets the moral norm of pleasure' (SV 165). Sex outside of marriage becomes prohibited, both for men and women, including for the man with women such as his slaves (SV 165–6). Reading Musonius Rufus, Foucault notes that if the woman cannot have relations outside of marriage, with a slave, why should a man be so allowed (SV 266)? This comes from an argument about the control of the self: 'the desire of sexual relations is so intense and so violent that he cannot control it, that he is not master of his self' (SV 267). Inside a marriage, Rufus thinks this is important because the husband must guide, lead the wife, he must 'teach [*pédagogiser*]' her. And how can he do this if he cannot master his own self? It is a relation based not 'on juridical equality but on moral inequality' (SV 267; see HS III, 201–2/150–1).

In addition there is a codification, a 'whole set of prescriptions concerning sexual comportment within marriage' (SV 166). The first is that making children becomes the goal, rather than pleasure (SV 166–7). The second, which is important in Christianity, is the creation of an 'emotional bond [*un lien affectif*] between husband and wife' (SV 167). Other developments concern modesty: sex is only permissible at night and in the dark; and so on (SV 168). Foucault notes that this is still a long way from the 'complex codification' of the Middle Ages, but there are anticipations of this here even in pre-Christian texts (SV 169). The relation of *eros*, which in classical Greek texts was focused on the man and the boy, is now turned to the interior of marriage, to the husband and the wife: 'an eroticization of marriage relations', and, alongside this, a codification of those relations (SV 169).

Modes of Life

Foucault begins the course with the story of the elephant in François de Sales that he had previously discussed in the 'Sexuality and Solitude' lecture (SV 3–6, 9, 17, 39–40, 230). He is interested in the way the elephant is held up as an exemplar of moral behaviour concerning sex and marriage.[10] But the use of the story is also interesting because it leads to some wider discussion of animals in the Greek text of the *Physiologus*, a bestiary dating from around the second century after Christ (SV 6–8, 17–18); of Solinus (SV 8–9); and Aristotle's work on animals, especially the *History of Animals* (SV 10–12). But it is also part of a discussion of the distinction between *zōē* and *bios* in Ancient Greek thought. Now, of course, it is impossible to avoid the uses made of this by Giorgio Agamben, but Foucault makes the distinction in this way.

> You know that, for the Greeks, there are two verbs which we translate by one and the same word: *vivre*, live. You have the word *zēn*, which means: to have the property [*propriété*] of living, the quality of being a living being. Animals certainly live, in this sense of *zēn*. Then you have the word *bioūn* which means lead a life, which is in relation to the manner of living this life, the manner of leading, conducting it, the way [*façon*] which allows it to be qualified as happy or unhappy. *Bios* is something which can be good or bad, while a life which one leads because one is a living being is simply given by nature. *Bios* is qualifiable life, life with accidents, necessities, but it is also life which one can make oneself, to decide oneself. *Bios*... is the course of existence, but a course understood as inseparably linked the possibility of managing, transforming, and directing it... *Bios* is the correlative of the possibility of modifying this life, to modify it in a rational way and as a function of the principles of an art of living. All these arts, all these *tekhnai* for the Greeks, and the Latins after them, are so far developed, these arts of life bearing [*portant*] on *bios*, on this aspect [*partie*] of life which develop [*relève*] a possible technique, a reflective and rational transformation. (SV 36)

Foucault suggests that there are three key elements in the Greek art of life: *mathēsis, meletē, askēsis* – relation to others or instruction [*enseignement*]; meditation or reflection, a relation to the truth; and ascetics, exercise, 'work of the self on the self, relation of the self to the self' (SV 35–6). 'I have spoken of an art of existence, a transformation of being, of the action of the self on the self' (SV 36).

Foucault suggests that the Greek *tekhnai peri bion*, arts of life, can be understood as 'biotechniques', although that term has rather different present connotations (SV 37). In a passage from the manuscript which was not delivered he continues:

> Biopoetics is justified because it is clearly a kind of personal fabrication of its own life... We can thus follow the problem of sexual conduct: the biopoetics where it is a matter of the aesthetic-moral conduct of an individual existence; the biopolitics where it is the normalization of sexual conducts as it is considered politically as a requirement of a population'. (SV 37 n. a.)

But these techniques are not a major theme of the course until quite late. When he does return it is to describe discourses on marriage as *tekhnai peri ton bion*, techniques 'which have life for their object', 'techniques for living' (SV 253).

Tekhnē is not a code of permission and prohibition, it is a certain systematic *ensemble* of actions and a certain mode of action...When the Greeks spoke of *bios*, when they spoke of this *bios* (this life) which must become the object of a *tekhnē*, it is clear that they did not mean 'life' in the biological sense of the term...The Christian division between life in this world and the afterlife means we have lost the Greek sense of the word; but nor it is a social division of 'professions and positions [*statuts*]. (SV 253)

Instead, Foucault draws upon Heraclides Ponticus, who described life as a *panegyris*, a religious festival or assembly. 'Some come there to compete in a struggle, others come there to run a market, others to the spectacle...some are born slaves to glory, others are greedy for wealth, but philosophers, they pursue the truth' (SV 254). There are three groups of people then: politicians who compete and seek glory; the sellers looking for wealth; and the philosophers who enjoy the spectacle. 'Struggle, market, spectacle. Politics, chrematistics, philosophy: these are the three modes of life' (SV 254). But Foucault's concern is not with the division or the interrelation, but rather with the sense of life that is there in all three categories. Just as a *panegyris* is the same festival for all, regardless of their role, so too does life has something shared that transcends the particular life chosen (SV 255).

Foucault goes so far as to claim that 'it appears that the Greeks did not know what subjectivity is, or that they did not have the notion';[11] that there is no straightforwardly equivalent term in Greek, and that the 'closest to what we understand by subjectivity...is this notion of *bios*. *Bios* is Greek subjectivity' (SV 255). He stresses that our notion of subjectivity, and thus the way we think of the Greek *bios*, comes through a Christian framework [*cadre*] (SV 255). The fundamental distinction is that in Christianity there is a relation to the afterlife, a conversion, and an authenticity, 'a profound truth to discover and which constitutes the basis, the foundation [*le socle*], the ground [*le sol*] of our subjectivity' (SV 255). This means that the differences between the Greek and Christian modes are threefold. First, the Greeks thought of *bios* 'in terms of ends that each person set [*se pose*] for themselves' rather than in terms of an afterlife or communal, absolute goals; second, it was not set in terms of 'the possibility or injunction of a conversion, but a continual labour of the self on the self'; and third, not in terms of a truth or hidden authenticity to be discovered, but a continual quest for the right form of existence (SV 256).

Nonetheless, Foucault does not want to mark this as a radical break between ancient and Christian thought. Especially in Stoicism

in the last centuries BCE and the first century CE, there are anticipations of 'the Christian doctrine of the flesh', making it more of a
continuum with small modifications along the way. In this, he suggests, historians have been doing this work for some time (SV 257;
see SV 45). However, he is clear that there is a transition, just not
one that can straightforwardly be situated between ancient and Christian thought. He sketches some very quick contours of this, and that
the key transition is not with the 'appearance of Christianity, but with
a particular internal mutation of Christianity' (SV 258). The techniques of the self, or technologies of subjectivity of classical Antiquity
are slowly transformed into 'new technologies of subjectification,
new *tekhnai peri ton bion*'. The Christian idea of the flesh is 'not a
new code of sexual comportment but constitutes the matrix of a new
experience' (SV 259).

From *Aphrodisia* to Flesh, and the Emergence of Subjectivity

Foucault sees *aphrodisia* as crucial to the (classical) Greek, Hellenistic
and early Roman periods, only to be overturned with the rise of
Christianity. The two key principles he finds characteristic of *aphrodisia* – isomorphism and activity (where only the active subject is
important) – are crucial to periods until around the eighth to the
twelfth century, when 'a very intense codification of sexual activity'
was organized (SV 100). Foucault dates this transition to the 'first
penitentials of the seventh to eighth centuries until the grand organization of the auricular confession of the twelfth century' (SV 101).
This is a crucial part of the Christian, Western, European, modern
civilization.

What is significant here is that there is a transition within Christianity, where all sexual relations are codified:

> codification of acts, codification of relations, codification of thoughts,
> codification of desires and temptations, codification in marriage and
> outside of marriage, codification around the extraordinary, the immense
> family of incests which we defined in the high Middle Ages, codifica-
> tion around the supposed, sought-for, never entirely fixed but always
> pointed [*pointée*] limit of the against-nature, codification which is
> made in the form of religious commandments, that which is made in
> the form of civil legislation, and which is also made in the form of
> medical normativity. It is true that we have developed a formidable
> codifying activity around sexuality. (SV 101)

In this, Foucault is setting up an opposition between *aphrodisia* and
the Christian experience of the 'flesh' (SV 102). In *aphrodisia* he

stresses there are very few absolute restrictions – with the exception of parent-child incest, and 'a sort of taboo, the horror in regard of oral relations [*rapport buccal*]' (SV 102). This is why we need to 'dispel the illusion of code, the juridical mirage' (SV 103) in antiquity. The problem with a lot of historians is that they try to trace the 'preparation' for Christian morality in antiquity, 'a slow growth of ancient, pagan morality towards the rigorous and pure ideal of Christianity', but Foucault wants to reject the idea of 'the transformation of a code or the substitution of one code for another' (SV 103). In antiquity, he suggests, the philosophers, moralists and directors of conscience are not attempting to elaborate [*édifier*] a new code, but to 'modify ethical perception' (SV 103). Foucault suggests that often there is supposed to be a fundamental code, and then the modifications are understood in relation to this – 'I would like to do the reverse, and move from nuance before prohibition, gradation before limit, continuum before transgression' (SV 100).

The two key principles of isomorphism and activity are therefore modified. It is not the case that marriage is underrated until Christianity: on the contrary it is highly valued precisely because of isomorphism. But Christianity breaks with the idea that marriage is only one form of socio-sexual isomorphism, instead replacing it with the 'principle of exclusive localization of the sexual relation in conjugality' (SV 104–5). The principle of activity is also questioned. Instead of pleasure in activity being good and pleasure in passivity being dangerous, 'all pleasure whatever, even that of the active subject, presents by nature the risk and the danger of making the subject relinquish [*échapper*] the mastery which they exercise over themselves' (SV 105). This production of a 'physical, sexual relation which is uniquely conjugal and hedonically neutralized' is akin to the elephant in François de Sales (SV 106). He contends that this transformation of principles makes much more sense than the idea of a substitution of codes (SV 106–7).

For Foucault, then, arts of life should be understood as an 'ensemble of philosophical, moral and medical prescriptions' (SV 274), where techniques or technologies of the self are situated 'between a model of comportment and a system of valorization' (SV 274). These arts are not merely aesthetic; they have important political resonances too. On the one hand he notes the role of the aristocracy in Greece in supporting the 'traditional ethic of *aphrodisia*', but stresses that the power of this class is diminished post-Alexander the Great, and with the rise of the Roman Empire (SV 276–7). There is, therefore, a wider socio-political context to the transformation he has traced. But there is another political sense he finds, when he provides some interesting discussion of the relation between government of the self and the prince in classical Roman accounts. His examples are Suetonius' *Life of the Caesars*; Tacitus, presumably *Agricola* on the British governor; and the *Historia Augustus* (SV 281). The recurrent theme is the relation between political power and sexual activity, and the criticism of political rulers who were not able to govern themselves before governing others (SV 281–4). The topic of Foucault's last courses is, of course, already anticipated here, but so too is there a return to the relation between political power and monstrosity found in *The Abnormals* course (SV 284–5). As Foucault notes: 'A fundamental problem is therefore posed: that of the power of the prince over others and the technology of the self [*soi-même*], of the prince as subject, of the prince as he governs others and has to govern himself' (SV 286). There is therefore an ancient anticipation of what Foucault calls 'governmentality – the government of the self by the self and government of individuals, one by others' (SV 286).

Foucault's key concern here though is the transition between different understandings of the relation between the body, desire and pleasure. He continually underlines that the Greek notion of *aphrodisia* cannot be reduced to what we today call 'sexuality' or the Christians called 'the flesh': 'The Greeks knew neither sexuality nor the flesh...*Aphrodisia* for the Greeks, *venerea* for the Latins, is an activity. It is not a property of nature, it is not a trait of nature, is not a dimension of subjectivity' (SV 287, see 290). The transformations of the techniques in the first and second centuries, especially under Stoicism, is not yet flesh or sexuality. Nonetheless, he claims, 'sexual activity becomes...a permanent dimension of subjectivity, or rather the relation that one has from the self to the self' (SV 288). *Aphrodisia*, which was a relation between the self and others, becomes interiorized so that it becomes a relation of the self to the self, a process of subjectification (SV 288). Yet this process has a parallel development, which Foucault calls the objectification of *aphrodisia*, where the relation is not just an assessment of the self, but work upon the self, 'to become an object for oneself', a move which anticipates the examination of conscience found in the early Church and which was examined in *On the Government of the Living* (SV 289). However, some of the earliest examinations of conscience in Stoics such as Seneca and Marcus Aurelius did not take sex as a privileged object, but instead focused on 'ambition, anger, reactions of behaviour'. It was with spiritual techniques of the fourth and fifth centuries in Christianity that the emphasis shifted (SV 289–90; see WDTT 252/258).

The technologies of the self, for Foucault, disrupt the 'tight unity' of *aphrodisia*, of the link between 'body, soul, pleasure, desire, sensation, body mechanism'; and shift the focus from the pleasure in itself, of the act, to the desire that led to the act (SV 291). Foucault therefore talks of the subjectification and objectification of *aphrodisia* and the birth of desire: 'the dislocation of the unity [*bloc*] of *aphrodisia* and the emergence of desire', the cost being 'separating or the relative neutralization of the act and the pleasure, the body and the pleasure' (SV 292).[12] Once again, Foucault reformulates his project of a 'history of sexuality'. The inquiry should not be 'how and under what conditions has desire been repressed?' (SV 292). Instead we need to interrogate how desires, pleasures and bodies become desire alone, the subject of desire:

> One must show in contrast how desire, long before being repressed, is something which has been little by little extracted and emerged from an economy of pleasures and bodies, how it was effectively extracted, how and in what way, around and about it, it crystallized all the operations and all the positive or negative values concerning sex...Desire is effectively what we could call the historical transcendental from which we can and must think the history of sexuality. The emergence therefore of desire as the principle of subjectification/objectification of sexual acts. (SV 293)

This is followed by a passage that shows how crucial his seeming detours have been for the work:

> It would be a bit inadequate and entirely insufficient, with regard to the scope and complexity of the problems, to want to undertake a history of sexuality in terms of the repression of desire. We must, on the contrary, beginning from the history of technologies of the self which appear to me a relatively fecund point of intelligibility, beginning from a history of governmentalities – governmentality of the self and the other – show how the moment of desire is isolated and exalted, and how is formed, from there, a certain type of relation of the self to the self which itself has undergone a certain number of transformations, since it was seen to be developed, to be organized, to be distributed in a *dispositif* which was that of flesh first, before becoming, much later, that of sexuality. (SV 293)

Around June 1981, when Foucault wrote the course summary, his emphasis had shifted further. Clearly he was continuing to develop ideas, reworking and orientating his research. The course summary notes that the course will be the basis of a forthcoming publication, and that only a 'brief summary' will be needed (SV 299 n. 1; EW I, 87). Indeed, in May 1984, Foucault suggests that he had finished his work on sexuality three years before (DE#354 IV, 704–5; PPC 252). While he would continue to work on the manuscripts until his death, all subsequent lecture material was intended for future projects outside the sexuality work.

Even in June 1981 the course is situated within a broader inquiry into subjectivity-truth relations, concerning self-knowledge and 'techniques of the self'. The Greek injunction of 'know oneself' is situated within this wider enquiry of techniques turned towards the self (SV 299; EW I, 87). This is not an entirely accurate overview of the course, nor is the invocation of Plato's *Alcibiades* as the 'starting point' (SV 299; EW I, 88). Indeed, this retrospective framing of the project, and the analysis of *Alcibiades*, is much closer to the 1982 course *The Hermeneutic of the Subject*. In *Subjectivité et vérité*, *Alcibiades* is only briefly mentioned, whereas in 1982 it is a fundamental text of analysis. However, Foucault does make the telling point – which on the reading developed here is true of this and all his late courses – that this 'project is at the intersection of two themes treated previously: a history of subjectivity and an analysis of the forms of 'governmentality'" (SV 300; EW I, 88). Foucault goes on to link his previous inquiries into 'madness, illness and delinquency', and even the inquiry into the *savoirs* of 'language, labour and life' under the banner of the first; and his most recent lecture courses, as well as work on power, 'confinement and the disciplines' as examples of the second, along with the then forthcoming study, with Arlette Farge, on the *lettres de cachet* (SV 300; EW I, 88).

A contemporary report quotes Foucault as saying 'it is not so much power that interests me...but the history of subjectivity',[13] a claim repeated in the synthetic text he gave to Rabinow and Dreyfus for their book on his work (EW III, 327; DE#306 IV, 223). The opening part of that text, 'Why Study Power: The Question of the Subject', was written in English, and was a talk he gave at the University of South California at a symposium 'Knowledge, Power, History: Interdisciplinary Approaches to the Works of Michel Foucault', held on 29–31 October 1981.[14] The second part, 'How is Power Exercised?' was written in French and was translated by Leslie Sawyer for the book.[15] While undated, Rabinow recalls that it was a slightly older text and Foucault was glad for a place to publish it.[16] In the first part, Foucault makes the move from power to the subject his focus, bringing in Kant, the 'economy of power relations', and linked his work to the Frankfurt school and the Enlightenment. These were themes that point both back and forward, to the various forms of the 'What is Enlightenment?' essay on Kant, and his ongoing concerns with power and subjectivity.[17] In the 1981 course summary, Foucault is already repositioning this overall project within the framework of a broad emphasis on the care of the self. In that, it would be a different way of undertaking the history of subjectivity – the point made at the outset of the course, that this is no longer the imposition of external constraints, but through modes of self-direction; and through a reorientation of the work on governmentality, to look at 'the government of the self by oneself in its articulation with relations with others' (SV 300; EW I, 88). The rest of the summary is a fairly clear and accurate description of the course's content, but the opening pages situate it in relation to past projects, and provide a revealing glimpse into Foucault's aspirations for its future development. However, as Gros notes, this course, like the year before, but unlike many previous ones, 'remains impervious to the immediate political situation'.[18] Yet we know that Foucault was a somewhat detached observer of the 1981 election in France and was more actively involved in campaigns around the Vietnamese 'boat people' and the declaration of martial law in Poland (C 57, 59–61/71–2, 74–6).[19] The latter would be the key to his disillusion with the Mitterrand government.[20] But perhaps the most intriguing political intervention was one in which his name was largely erased: a document prepared for a meeting of the 'free defence' movement of lawyers and others in May 1980. A crucial clause of this short document reads: 'It is not because there are laws, it is not because I have rights, that I am entitled to defend myself: it is to the extent that I defend myself that my rights exist and that the law respects me.'[21]

The Hermeneutic of the Subject

Immediately after *Subjectivité et vérité* Foucault began his lectures at Louvain, which were treated in Chapter 5, given their closer thematic relation to *On the Government of the Living*. Aside from some interviews conducted on that visit, sources for the development of Foucault's thought between the close of these two lecture courses and *The Hermeneutic of the Subject* in early 1982 are limited. We know, however, that in this period Foucault was working in earnest on the manuscript of a book under the title of *L'Usage des plaisirs*, developing ideas first explored in *Subjectivité et vérité*,[22] and also on another new book, with the working title of *Le Souci de soi*. On 19 April 1983 he said the latter book would be appearing with Éditions du

Seuil, not Gallimard.[23] While these are the titles of what was eventually published as volumes two and three of *The History of Sexuality*, at this time the contents did not align in the same way.

The exact division of material will be discussed in the next chapter, but it is important to note this here because *The Hermeneutic of the Subject* course presents material which was intended to be part of a book under the working title of *Le Souci de soi*, which was then thought of as separate from *The History of Sexuality* (EW I, 255; DE#326 IV, 383). Foucault later used the same title for a volume in that series, but it then had a different focus, roughly corresponding to the second half of what was drafted as *L'Usage des plaisirs* in 1983. Relatively little of the 1982 course's detailed analyses find their way into work Foucault published in his lifetime. The course is Foucault's longest, because he abandons running a separate seminar and so lectures for two hours each week.

Like its Collège de France predecessor, *The Hermeneutics of the Subject* continues the broader project of the relation between subjectivity and truth (HSu 3–4/2, 201/209–10, 243 n. */253 n. *). As Foucault specifies, the focus is the 'question of the relation between truth-telling and the government of the subject' (HSu 220/230). This key theme only tangentially relates to the *aphrodisia*/flesh/sexuality relation explored in the previous course, and the focus shifts to a complementary analysis of what he calls 'care of the self', *le souci de soi* or *le souci de soi-même*. This is the idea that we should concern ourselves with ourselves, that is, we should take care of ourselves. The term this translates is found in Greek as *epimeleia heautou*, and in Latin as *cura sui*. Foucault's key point is that the famous injunction from Delphi to 'know yourself', *gnōthi seauton*, is part of a wider project of taking care of the self (HSu 4–5/2–3). He later stresses that this is not to diminish the importance of *gnōthi seauton* or to suggest it is merely subordinate, but to stress the two are 'entangled', a 'dynamic entanglement' (HSu 67/68–9). *Gnōthi seauton* has tended to overshadow *epimeleia heautou*: his point is to redress the balance (HSu 473/491).

Foucault demonstrates that the idea of the care of the self can be found in numerous Greek and Latin works, including the portrayal of Socrates in the *Apology*, the dialogue *Alcibiades*, as well as in later thinkers such as Epicurus and Epictetus, and in Stoic thought, including figures such as Seneca and Marcus Aurelius. It can also be found in texts such as Philo of Alexandria's *On the Contemplative Life*, Plotinus' *Enneads*, and works by St Basil of Caesarea and Gregory of Nyssa. In the course summary, Socrates and Gregory are used as bookends (HSu 473–4/492), in the course itself he slightly extends this, mentioning the 'lengthy genealogy I am trying to recount from the *Alcibiades* to Saint Augustine' (HSu 181/188). What this means is that the notion of the care of the self is used as a means of explaining a wide range of texts and historical periods. The care of the self is thus something which Foucault thinks runs through all Greek, Hellenistic and Roman philosophy, and Christian spirituality. It is a way of being that is developed over the course of a millennium, from the fifth century BCE to the fifth CE (HSu 13/11–12). It goes through numerous 'changes and transformations' (HSu 173/180), of course, and has implications even today, which Foucault discusses in some interviews. Yet most of the course is devoted to a similar time period to *Subjectivité et vérité*. This is the Hellenistic period of late Antiquity until the second century of our current era, essentially the early Roman Empire until the Flavian dynasty.

Foucault suggests that studying the culture of the self is essential in order to shed light on the history of subjectivity and the history of the relationship between the subject and the truth. This relation, which is in some sense the crucial concern of the *History of Sexuality* series, is important for a number of reasons. First, Foucault suggests in a few places that the way to get around the problematic notion of the subject was to write a genealogy of that very concept. The hermeneutics of the title is not simply a cataloguing of different modes of the subject, nor is it merely an historical inquiry, but it is a part of the 'genealogy of the modern subject' (ABHS 201; OHS 33), the 'historical ontology of ourselves' which Foucault announced in a late interview (EW I, 262; DE#326 IV, 393). It is an examination into the constitution of the subject, what he calls 'a history of the different modes by which, in our culture, human beings are made subjects' (EW III, 326; DE#306 IV, 223). Second, Foucault thinks it is politically important because it is at the heart of understanding the notion of governing. Government, of the self and of others, the management of an individual life and the management of a city (HSu 81/83) is a central theme to this course. It clearly links to earlier concerns with the body and the social body or population and is crucial in understanding his interest in Christianity. The relation of spirituality, the monastic life, and asceticism to group notions of the flock and pastoral power are referred to continually throughout this course (see, for example HSu 172/178, 240–3/250–3, 345–7/363–5), even though their full elaboration was elsewhere.

Alcibiades

While most of the course is on a different period, Foucault begins with an analysis of a dialogue from classical Greece, generally attributed to Plato, *Alcibiades*. He returns to it regularly through the course. While the focus is on *Alcibiades*, Foucault begins his reading of Plato with three passages from the *Apology* (HSu 7–8/5–7). His point is that Socrates is frequently telling his interlocutors that they should concern themselves with themselves – their virtue, physical well-being and soul, rather than external things like 'wealth, reputation and honour' (HSu 491/473). He notes that there are earlier antecedents, such as the Spartan claim that the reason that they employed Helots to take care of their lands was so they could take care of themselves (HSu 32–3/31).[24] Foucault notes, however, that for Spartans this was not a philosophical question, but marked a privilege that was 'political, economic and social' (HSu 33/31). Socrates is building on this history in the *Alcibiades* dialogue.

The dialogue is of disputed authorship, though Foucault is not concerned with this, suggesting that the key issue is not who wrote it, but when (HSu 33/32, 43/43).[25] Socrates is in dialogue with a beautiful and somewhat impetuous young man, and advises him to take care of himself, suggesting that this is both necessary to prepare him for a political career – a career in the *polis* – and something that should not be left too late. He must take care of himself before he can take care of others. Socrates sees his role as a pedagogical one, tutoring and guiding. In doing so, Socrates also relinquishes his own desire for Alcibiades, recognizing that this would get in the way of his tutoring role, though Foucault notes that Alcibiades is now past the 'famous critical age' after which boys became men and were off limits as objects of sexual desire (HSu 34/32–33). There are two key questions – what is the self with which he should be concerned, and how should it be taken care of (HSu 39–40/38–9; 51–2/51–2, 436/454)? Ultimately the two questions are connected: care of the self requires knowing yourself, the nature of your soul (HSu 66/67, 400–1/419).

After this initial discussion the focus moves forward to the Hellenistic period and that of the early Empire. Part of the reason Foucault is interested in this dialogue, it is later revealed, is because of the Neoplatonists of the second century CE, who suggested that the text was fundamental and should be placed at the very beginning of the Platonic dialogues (HSu 163–7/170–3). Different parts of the course thus work both a prelude to the work in *Subjectivité et vérité*, and a parallel inquiry, citing some of the same texts, but with a different project at stake, that of writing a history of ancient practices, technologies of the self, of the care of the self. Foucault provides multiple examples, often in some detail, to illustrate his arguments. I will discuss just two important themes: the situation of this work in relation to the question of government, exemplified by his discussion of Stoicism; and the links to the wider work on Christianity and subjectivity.

The Multiple Forms of Government and the Exercises of Stoicism

Foucault at times consciously situates the work he is undertaking here within the wider frame of his project, pointing at the relation between taking care of the self, being governed, and being able to govern others. Part of the point of the Alcibiades story is that he needs to take care of himself before he is fit to play a leading role in the *polis*. Foucault is therefore trying to interrogate the relation between ethics and politics, not in relation to deriving rules from political action, but political rules from ethical precepts – govern the self first, then others. Foucault later notes there is a shift, where care of the self is not seen as preparatory for care of others, but as an end in itself (HSu 108/111–12). As he suggests near the beginning of the course: 'Governing', 'being governed', and 'taking care of the self [*s'occupier de soi*]' form a sequence, a series, whose long and complex history extends up to the establishment of pastoral power in the Christian Church in the third and fourth centuries (HSu 44/45).

Foucault later suggests that the idea of government of others can be traced until the sixteenth century, when it is replaced by *raison d' État* (HSu 239/250). This sequence does not merely link *The Hermeneutic of the Subject* to *On the Government of the Living*, but back to *Security, Territory, Population* too, as well as pointing forward to his final two courses, both of which bore the title *The Government of Self and Others*. This theme is already beginning to emerge in these lectures, as is that of *parrēsia*, free-speech.[26] 'The philosopher, then, loudly promotes himself as the only person capable of governing men, of governing those who govern men, and of in this way constituting a general practice of government at every possible level: government of self, government of others' (HSu 131/135). In making these broad links, Foucault situates his earlier work on power within the more general theory of governmentality. This is because we must understand governmentality 'as a strategic field of power relations in the broadest and not merely political sense of the term...a strategic field of power relations in their mobility, transformability, and reversibility'. This, in turn, 'must refer to an ethics of the subject defined by the relationship of self to self' (HSu 241–2/252). To the earlier sequence of governing, being governed and care of the self, Foucault then adds elements: 'power relations – governmentality – the government of the self and of others – the relationship of self to self, constitute a chain, a thread'. These enable the connection of 'the question of politics and the question of ethics' (HSu 242/252), and more broadly link almost all of the themes of Foucault's courses and his books of this period.

Gros notes that while Foucault's promise to elaborate the relation of the care of the self to the question of the Prince (HSu 191/199) is unfulfilled in the course, he did write material on this theme, which is preserved in his notes and finds its way, in part, into *The Care of the Self* in 1984.[27] This course addresses this theme in only a limited way, largely through a reading of Marcus Aurelius (HSu 191–4/199–202).[28] He was of course both the author of the work we know as *Meditations* and Roman Emperor, but also exchanged letters with Marcus Cornelius Fronto that give a valuable insight into his life and preparation for rule. Foucault notes that this correspondence has been neglected (HSu 151–2/157), but suggests the relation between a future emperor and his rhetoric teacher is one where 'our modern categories of friendship and love are no doubt wholly inadequate' (HSu 478/497–8; see 153/158–9). Foucault reads much of the correspondence, and indeed the *Meditations*, as comprising a series of reflections on the key themes he had sketched earlier in the course concerning 'the body; the family circle and household; love. Dietetics, economics and erotics' (HSu 156/161). These are examples of what he describes as exercises, *askēsis*. Foucault is quick to mention the importance of Hadot's work on Marcus Aurelius for his own reading – 'it wouldn't have occurred to me on my own' (HSu 280/292).[29] He is particularly struck by the 'morning examination' in book V of the *Meditations*, which is not reflective on what has already been, but projective: 'the only time in this practice of the self that there is an exercise really turned towards the future as such...a near and immediate future' (HSu 461/481). The key term is the notion of *askēsis*, a practice or exercise, akin to the physical training of an athlete. One aspect of these are discourses, *logoi*, that we should carry with us in preparation for events and situations – these are likened to a *pharmakon*, a medicine or drug, or a surgeon's kit by Marcus Aurelius (HSu 480/499). As Foucault remarked in an interview with the magazine *Gai pied* in 1981, 'asceticism as the renunciation of pleasure has bad connotations. But ascesis is something else: it's the work that one performs on oneself in order to transform oneself or make the self appear which, happily, one never attains' (DE#293 IV, 165; EW I, 137).[30] While in the interview Foucault links it to the possibility of a 'homosexual ascesis', the reading of *askēsis* in the course is developed through a discussion of Musonius Rufus's text *Peri askēseōs*, though he notes earlier precedents (HSu 301–2/315–6; see 408–9/426–8).

Foucault suggests *askēsis* is 'a practice of truth...not a way of subjecting the subject to the law; it is a way of binding him to the truth' (HSu 303/317). In this treatment of Stoicism we can see the continuity with *Subjectivité et vérité*, but while he is re-treading the same historical ground there is a different thematic emphasis. Instead of how subjectivity and truth link to the problematic of sexuality, here the concern is with the relation to the self. Indeed, he calls this period 'a genuine golden age in the history of care of the self' (HSu 79/81). One of the key things he tracks, among various transformations, is the generalization of the injunction to care for the self. This now applies to all, regardless of social status; the changing of the purpose – it is not now so that one may better govern others, but better care for the self as a final goal; and that care of the self no longer has knowledge of the self as the key: that remains, but within a wider framework (HSu 80–1/83–4). In all these, the developments of this period shift the emphasis from an earlier period, of which the *Alcibiades* stands as the exemplar. In these later developments 'care of the self' 'was freed from its privileged connection with pedagogy, how it was freed from its political purpose...The care of the self thus took the form of a general and unconditional principle' (HSu 237/247). The notion of the test, the proof [*l'épreuve*], which had been so important in the initial triptych of Paris courses, re-emerges here as a crucial theme, especially in the sense of testing oneself, rather than, as it had been before, as a mode of being tested. It, along with abstinence, is a fundamental ascetic practice: 'life as a test' (HSu 411–5, 419/430–3, 438). This theme is transformed from a high to a basic ideas in Christianity, where 'every Christian will be called upon to regard life as nothing but a test' (HSu 428/446).

Towards Christianity and Subjectivity

It is clear, reading this course in the light of *On the Government of the Living*, how much Foucault is anticipating linking these analyses to ones he has already made – both in lectures and unpublished writings. While he continually says that he will address Christian, or as he sometimes specifies, the 'ascetic-monastic' model, in more detail, this is rarely delivered in this course (HSu 244–5/255). Foucault promises that he will develop the theme of the care of the self in relation to 'the transition from pagan philosophical ascesis to Christian asceticism in the fourth and fifth centuries' (HSu 32/30), but this is unfortunately not fulfilled either in this course or subsequent ones.[31] It is regrettable that his lectures do not really provide a good example of the Christian material recast in the light of the far more subtle and detailed reading of antiquity he developed in the early 1980s. Nonetheless, it seems that many of the analyses made around 1980 would hold, and that it is their introduction, and comparative aspects, that would be most affected by the later work.

One thing that is continually stressed is that to understand how Christianity emerged – both historically and more specifically in relation to its position within the *History of Sexuality* – we need to understand how it built upon and transformed pagan relations to the self, rather than simply the transformation from *aphrodisia* to the flesh (see HSu 174/180–1, 202–6/211–14, 316–17/333). Here, the emphasis is more on the shift between classical conceptions, and the Hellenistic period. As in the previous year's course, this is where a number of crucial shifts occur. One example is the *tekhnē tou biou*: 'the art, the reflected method for conducting one's life, the technique of life…the art of living' (HSu 171/177–8). This interest in the art of life pre-dates Foucault's late notion of an 'aesthetics of existence'.[32] Foucault suggests that from at least the Cynics this is the dominant mode of philosophy. 'Making one's life the object of a *tekhnē*, making one's life a work [*œuvre*] – a beautiful and good work (as everything produced by a good and reasonable *tekhnē* should be) – necessarily entails the freedom and choice of the person employing this *tekhnē*' (HSu 405/424). In particular, Foucault suggests that ancient freedom is crucial, because it is 'one of the dividing lines between these philosophical exercises and the Christian exercise', which stressed the *regula vitae*, the rules of a 'well-ordered' life (HSu 405/424). But a critical shift comes earlier. In antiquity, Foucault suggests that the *tekhnē tou biou* required the *epimeleia heautou*. That is to say, the art of life required care of the self. In the Hellenistic period, by contrast, 'the care of the self is no longer a necessary and indispensable element of the *tekhnē tou biou* (the technique of life)', but the reverse, where *tekhnē tou biou* 'falls entirely within the now autonomized framework of the care of the self' (HSu 429/447–8, see 465/485). The care of the self becomes a general and absolute condition, rather than limited to those who wished to govern others. This is, Foucault contends, 'a relatively important event in the history of Western subjectivity' (HSu 430/449). As Foucault noted earlier in the course:

Whoever wishes to study the history of subjectivity – or rather, the history of the relations between the subject and truth – will have to try to uncover the very long and very slow transformation of a *dispositif* of subjectivity, defined by the spirituality of knowledge [*savoir*] and the practice of truth by the subject, into this other apparatus of subjectivity which is our own and which is, I think, governed by the

question of the subject's knowledge [*connaissance*] of himself and of
the subject's obedience to the law. (HSu 304–5/319)

But it is not just in relation to subjectivity, because Foucault, in
implicit dialogue with Husserl and Heidegger, suggests that Western
objectivity is also related to this question, of how 'the world became
the correlate of a *tekhnē*' (HSu 466/486, see Gros, HSu 469–70
n. 27/489 n. 27). Indeed, the course is remarkable for being one of
the very few places where Foucault discusses his relation to Heidegger.
Foucault is asked by one of his auditors about the role of Lacanian
concepts in his thinking of the issues of truth and subjectivity. Foucault
suggests that in the twentieth century there have not been many
people who have raised questions of truth, the subject and the relation between the two. For him, there are only two: Heidegger and
Lacan. As he thinks people will have guessed, it is starting from
Heidegger that he has tried to think through these issues (HSu 180–
2/187–9; see DE#354 IV, 703–4; PPC 250).[33] In particular Foucault
is taking up Heidegger's question of how a particular understanding
of *tekhnē* and the concomitant knowledge of the object was central
to understanding how being came to be forgotten. For Foucault it is
important to ask how this notion of *tekhnē* is related to the formation
of the Western subject, and the relations of freedom, constraint,
truth and error that are associated with it.[34] This should act as a
valuable corrective to those who suggest that it is difficult to give a
Heideggerian reading of Foucault's central concern of the 1980s, with
subjectivity, truth and ethics.[35] Aside from a few very general comments in the course's conclusion, Foucault does not elaborate on this,
though the final lines and an undelivered manuscript line hint at how
this links to his interest in the question of the Enlightenment (HSu
467/487 and n. *), a topic he will return to at the beginning of the
1983 course.

Technologies of the Self

Foucault developed some of these themes in lectures in Toronto in
May–June 1982 on the care of the self from antiquity to Christian-
ity,[36] and developed these themes in six seminars on the theme of
'Technologies of the Self' at University of Vermont in October and
November. On the latter trip he was interviewed and also gave an
updated version of the second of the 'Omnes et Singulatim' lectures
from 1979, this time under the title of 'The Political Technology of
Individuals'.[37] This phrase 'political technology' is used to distinguish

the work in the lecture – which draws on his work in the 1978 and 1979 courses on governmentality – from the work of the seminar, which studied 'ethical techniques of the self...technologies of the self' (EW III, 404; DE#364 IV, 814). The materials were gathered into the book published in 1988, alongside some pieces by other seminar participants.[38] The transcripts are the most interesting material.

Foucault begins with a discussion of how he reached this point, saying that he has realized the relation between behaviour and truth is a key theme, and that as a consequence the work has become 'a rather odd project: not the evolution of sexual behaviour but the projection of a history of the link between the obligation to tell the truth and the prohibitions against sexuality' (EW I, 224; DE#363 IV, 784). In an interview earlier that year he had put it in a related way:

> I don't try to write an archaeology of sexual fantasies. I try to make an archaeology of discourse about sexuality, which is really the relationship between what we do, what we are obliged to do, what we are allowed to do, what we are forbidden to do in the field of sexuality, and what we are allowed, forbidden or obliged to say about our sexual behaviour...It's not a problem of fantasy; it's a problem of verbalization. (EW I, 125–6; DE#336 IV, 530)

At Vermont, trading on the course title from Paris, he described the project as a 'hermeneutics of technologies of the self' (EW I, 224; DE#363 IV, 784), and clarifies that there are multiple ways we can understand technologies: technologies of production, of sign systems, of power and finally, of the self. He says that his work has treated mainly the third and the fourth, though they rarely exist entirely in isolation. His stress now, compared to the work of the 1970s, which 'perhaps insisted too much on the technology of domination and power', is on the last (EW I, 225; DE#363 IV, 785).

Just as in the (much longer) Louvain lectures from eighteen months before, what Foucault provides in these seminar transcripts is a fascinating synthetic treatment of his work over the previous few years around this theme, drawing upon the previous three Paris courses. He schematizes his two concerns as 'two different contexts which are historically contiguous: (1) Greco-Roman philosophy in the first two centuries AD of the early Roman Empire and (2) Christian spirituality and the monastic principles developed in the fourth and fifth centuries of the late Roman Empire' (EW I, 225–6; DE#363 IV, 786). The key theme is the care of the self, *epimeleai heautou*, which had emerged as a focus of *The Hermeneutic of the Subject* lectures.

Foucault works through Plato's *Apology* and the *Alcibiades*, Epicurus, the Stoics, Seneca and writing the self, the correspondence between Marcus Aurelius and Fronto, Plutarch, Philo of Alexandria, dream interpretation, John Cassian, Gregory of Nyssa, Tertullian, and Augustine.

Much of this is now familiar from his Paris courses. It is a heavily compressed summary of material, but reads extremely well. But at the time, few would have had the access to those Paris lectures – either in his Vermont audiences of 1982 or the wider Anglophone readership in 1988. Now, in the light of the courses' publication and translation, we can both see where concepts and readings were first developed, how his confidence in claims increased, and how links were made. What is especially interesting in the Vermont seminars is that he presents the treatment in broadly chronological order. While the courses had worked backwards from the early Church in 1980, to the Empire and Hellenistic Greece in 1981 and 1982, and to Plato in 1982, here he reverses the order. We therefore see something of how he might have presented things in the *History of Sexuality* as conceived, though the work here is seen as a parallel project to that on sexuality.

Like the volume's editors, Defert notes that the transcripts from this seminar were not edited by Foucault before his death, but he adds that Foucault had intended to edit the material 'into a book on techniques of the self'. Defert describes the plan for the book as linking ethics and politics, and comprising material on 'Alcibiades, or the idea of care of self and political life; Epictetus, listening, writing, and the practice of the self; self and others' (C 61/78). The only part of this which appeared in Foucault's lifetime was the essay 'Writing the Self', published in 1983 in a special issue of the journal *Corps écrit* on the theme of *L'autoportrait* (DE#329 IV, 415–30; EW I, 207–22). This essay draws extensively on material presented in the 1982 course, especially the lecture of 3 March on practices of 'personal and individual writing' (HSu 341/359), and discusses Athanasius's *Vita Antonii*, Plutarch's *Peri euthumias*, Pliny and Cicero's letters, Seneca's letters to Lucilius and Marcus Aurelius's correspondence with Fronto.

This was not the only book Foucault planned at this point. Around the time of the Vermont seminars, in late 1982, Foucault also proposed a study under the title of *Le gouvernement de soi et des autres* to Éditions du Seuil (C 61/78). This would, of course, be the title of his last two courses in Paris. The proposed book would have appeared in the series *Des travaux*, edited by Foucault, Veyne and François Wahl.[39] These two books were intended to be outside the *History of*

Sexuality because at this point – late 1982 and early 1983 – Foucault thought he had at last almost finished.

> This long work of the self on the self, this labour that all the authors describe as long and arduous, does not aim to split the subject, but to bind him to himself, to nothing else, to no one but himself, in a form in which the unconditional character and self-finality of the relationship of the self to the self is affirmed.[40]

7

The Two Historical Plans of the *History of Sexuality*

The March 1983 Draft

From the research given preliminary expression in three courses – *On the Government of the Living*, *Subjectivité et vérité*, and *The Hermeneutic of the Subject* – and related materials, Foucault thought he could produce a number of book-length publications. We know that the volume he drafted on Christianity around 1979–80, *Les Aveux de la chair*, was put aside for a time while he worked on antiquity. But he did publish a discussion of Jean Cassian from this entitled 'The Battle for Chastity' in May 1982, in a collection edited by Philippe Ariès on 'Western Sexuality', a piece he described in the following way:

> This text is an extract from the third volume of my *History of Sexuality*. After having consulted Philippe Ariès on the general orientation of the current collection, I feel that its approach fits with the other papers. We both think that the prevailing notion of Christian sexual ethics needs serious revision and that, moreover, the central value of the question of masturbation has an entirely different origin than the doctors of the eighteenth and nineteenth centuries. (DE#312, IV, 295; EW I, 185–6 n. *)[1]

Foucault clearly thought he was close to completion of a volume on antiquity, because this volume on Christianity is described as the *third* of the series, rather than the second. By March 1983 he had a draft of that proposed second volume, entitled *L'Usage des plaisirs*.[2] In discussions with Rabinow and Dreyfus in April he outlines the plan for future publications. *The History of Sexuality* was now envisaged as a much more chronologically *historical* study, tracing the subject of sexuality back to antiquity. *Les Aveux de la chair* would look at Christianity in the first to fifth centuries, including such topics as John Cassian, monasticism, Augustine, and Christian hermeneutics of the self. Foucault suggests that this period sees a shift in ethical practices from a small elite to a larger society, which can be traced as a development in relation to Christianity (EW I, 254; DE#326 IV, 383).

At this time, Foucault's draft of *L'Usage des plaisirs* – now conceived as the second volume – had the following structure:

Preface
Introduction: Problem
    Method
    Objective
Part I: The Use of Pleasures
I: Concepts and Principles
– Aphrodisia
– Chresis
– Measure and Moment
– Mastery of the Self
II: An Example: Onirocritique
– Method
– Analyse
– The Dream and the Act
Part II: Practices of Temperance
I: Dietics
II: Economics
III: Erotics
Part III: The Culture of the Self
I: Development and Context
– Concern Yourself with Yourself
– The Political Game
– The Matrimonial Role
II: Techniques
– The Conversion of the Self
– The Vigilance of the Self
Part IV: The Demands of Austerity
I: The Body
– Galien
– Are they Good, are they Bad?
– The Regime of Pleasures
II: The Wife
– The Conjugal Link
– Sexual and Conjugal Relations
– The Pleasures of Marriage

III: Boys
– Plutarque
– Lucian
– Erotic Fiction[3]

In the discussions at this time, Foucault also talks of a third book in progress:

> *Le Souci de soi*, a book separate from the sex series, [which] is com-
> posed of different papers about the self – for instance a commentary
> on Plato's *Alcibiades*...about the role of reading and writing in con-
> stituting the self, maybe the problem of the medical experience of the
> self, and so on...(EW I, 255; DE#326 IV, 383)

Foucault published parts of all three of these books as envisioned in early 1983 – 'The Battle for Chastity' from *Les Aveux de la chair* in 1982; 'Rêver de ses plaisirs' from *L'Usage des plaisirs*; and 'Self-Writing' from *Le Souci de soi*, both in 1983. He also published a fragment of a 1982–83 draft of the introduction in *The Foucault Reader*, which, like the 'Maurice Florence' text, provides an overview of Foucault's career, situating the work on sexuality in a much longer chronology and schema of work, as well as including links to what might appear to be side-projects such as those on Pierre Rivière, Alexina B (Herculine Barbin), governmentality and the *lettres de cachet*.[4] He mentions the original, thematic plan of the *History of Sexuality* as 'my planned study of children, women and "perverts" as sexual subjects', but notes that while there were three possible ways of analysing this – as 'a domain of *savoir*, a system of rules, and a model for relations to the self' – he ended up concentrating on the last, at the expense of the plan (DE#340, IV, 583; EW I, 204).

He tries to explain some of the reasons for the delay, and the abandonment of that original plan: 'I found myself confronted with a choice which was a long time in unravelling: a choice between fidelity to the chronological outline which I had originally imagined, and a different line of inquiry in which the modes of relation to the self took precedence' (DE#340 IV, 583; EW I, 204). In April 1983 he claims that he drafted the book three times – a version on sex, a version on 'the self and techniques of the self' without sex, and then a final version that kept 'the equilibrium between one and the other' (EW I, 254; DE#326 IV, 384). This comment applies to the *L'Usage des plaisirs* draft, which at the time included material that eventually appeared in Volumes II and III. In terms of the shift from the original plan, it also appears that fatigue was a major factor: in 1984, in two separate pieces, Foucault admits that he was bored (DE#350 IV, 668; PPC 255; DE#357 IV, 730; PPC 47). In one of the same interviews he suggests that had he merely been an academic he probably could have gone ahead with this original project, 'knowing in advance what I wanted to do and where I hoped to arrive', but because he was also an intellectual, he was subject to change, to have his own thought altered by the process of study (DE#350 IV, 675; PPC 263–4). It is this willingness to have not merely the method but also the very subject of inquiry dictated to by the material uncovered that sets Foucault apart from many of his contemporaries.

Foucault continues: 'I ended up placing the work's emphasis on what was to have been simply the point of departure or historical background; rather than placing myself at the threshold of the formation of the experience of sexuality, I tried to analyse the formation of a certain mode of relation to the self in the experience of the flesh' (DE#340 IV, 584; EW I, 205). That work on the flesh, *la chair*, was to be examined in the projected volume on Christianity. But in order to study that, Foucault notes that he needed make a dramatic change in the period under consideration. 'In pursuing my analysis of the forms of relation to the self, in and of themselves, I found myself spanning eras in a way that took me farther and farther from the chronological outline I had first decided on...' (DE#340 IV, 583; EW I 204). The period to be investigated was the period in late antiquity when the 'principal elements of the Christian ethic of the flesh were being formulated' (DE#340 IV, 584; EW I 205), not only in Christian thinkers, but in ones that preceded them. Naturally this took Foucault into completely unknown territory for him, but he felt it was 'best to sacrifice a definite programme to a promising line of approach', and that books were worth writing because they taught the author things he had not previously known (DE#340 IV, 584; EW I, 205). The volume being introduced is that book, on late antiquity. But here, it is a singular 'volume' (DE#340 IV, 578; EW I, 199 n. *), not two volumes (the actually published Volumes II and III). As he noted in 1984 when the books came out:

> It is true that when I wrote the first volume of *The History of Sexuality* seven or eight years ago, I absolutely had intended to write historical studies on sexuality starting with the sixteenth century and to analyse the evolution of this knowledge up to the nineteenth century. And while I was doing this project, I noticed it was not working out. An important problem remained: why had we made sexuality into a moral experience? So I locked myself up, abandoned the works [*les travaux*] I had written on the seventeenth century, and started to work my way back – first to the fifth century in order to look at the beginnings of

the Christian experience, then to the period immediately preceding it, the end of Antiquity. Finally I finished three years ago with the study of sexuality in the fifth and fourth centuries BC. (DE#354 IV, 704–5; PPC 252; see DE#357 IV, 730; PPC 48)

This is the basis for the formulations which began to appear in his lectures of the early 1980s, tracked in Chapter 5. His comment of 'three years ago' must mean that he completed the bulk of the research on sexuality, as opposed to techniques of the self, in 1981, after *Subjectivité et vérité*, though we know he was redrafting for a long time afterwards. In the early 1983 introduction he formulates the project in this way: 'rather than a chapter in the history of mores, rather than a search for the origin of the moral law, this work aspires to be a study of the genealogy of the moral subject [*sujet moral*] and of the practices through which it constitutes itself'.[5]

The August–September 1983 Redraft

In April, Foucault returned to Berkeley as Regents' Lecturer, giving a lecture entitled 'The Culture of the Self' on 12 April 1983. The lecture covers a great deal of content, beginning with Lucian, moving through Kant, summarizing work on the care of the self from Plato's *Apology* to Gregory of Nyssa, touching on the Spartans, the Stoics and *Alcibiades*, and concluding with some comments on writing the self. There is little especially new in the lecture, though there are some revealing follow-up discussions.[6] It also led to one of the most personal recollections of meeting Foucault, from an undergraduate student.[7] In an interview to the campus newspaper's weekly magazine Foucault confessed that he had hoped to complete the two volumes he was working on (the ones on antiquity and Christianity) before the trip, but had failed to do so, and was now 'working like a dog every morning' trying to finish them.[8]

However, later in 1983, he changed his mind about the arrangement of material. He took the manuscript of *L'Usage des plaisirs* and divided it in two, into the actually published second and third volumes. Confusingly, as well as keeping the title of the longer version as the title of Volume II, he used the title of the book 'separate from the sex series' as the title of the third volume, even though its contents were now very different. The 1983 *L'Usage des plaisirs* manuscript becomes two books: *L'Usage des plaisirs* [*The Use of Pleasures*] and *Le Souci de soi* [*The Care of the Self*]. Defert notes that this decision was made in August 1983, and that the redrafting was done by

September (C 63/80).[9] But the division of material was not quite a simple one of a manuscript cut in half. While a section on the concepts and principles around 'The Use of Pleasures' appears in Volume II – now discussing *Aphrodisia, Khrēsis, Enkrateia*, Freedom and Truth – the analysis of onirocritique appears in Volume III. The part on 'Practices of Temperance' is reworked for discussion in Volume II. 'The Culture of the Self' appears in Volume III, though split into two sections, as do the divisions of 'The Requirements of Austerity'. The original plan makes a clearer comparison between the three-part analysis of classical Greece and Rome. It receives its first expression in *The Hermeneutic of the Subject*, where Foucault sketches three themes to be treated, the relation of care of the self to, respectively medicine and the body, with the question of dietetics; social activity especially in the household, the *oikos*, and the Greek notion of the 'economic'; and the love relationship, the erotic (HSu 58–9/59–60): Dietetics-Economics-Erotics. This returns in his analysis of Marcus Aurelius and Fronto (HSu 156/161). This division structures the original plan and Volumes II and III: Parts 2–4 of *The Use of Pleasures* as actually published are entitled 'Dietetics', 'Economics' and 'Erotics', and Parts 4–6 of *The Care of the Self*, where the parts are entitled 'Body', 'Wife', 'Boys'.[10]

One implication of this division of March 1983's drafted second volume into September 1983's Volumes II and III was that the book on Christianity was moved down to become the fourth volume. It was left unpublished at his death. But it is not the only such book. *Le Souci de soi*, as first announced, was never published either. Foucault is torn between two parallel projects, often using the same material but for different purposes. One is a history of ancient ways of thinking about what we now call sexuality – for which the key terms are *aphrodisia* and the flesh – in relation to various techniques of the self; and the other is a history of those techniques themselves, many of which are not concerned with sexuality. And for a while that was indeed Foucault's plan, as he outlined to Dreyfus and Rabinow.[11] That a book appeared with the title *Le Souci de soi* should not confuse us.[12] We know something of what it, as originally conceived, would have included – a reading of Plato's *Alcibiades*, the chapter on 'Self-Writing' published in February 1983, and discussions of medicine, etc.[13] In the 'Self-Writing' essay Foucault himself describes it as part of 'a series of studies on "the arts of the self", on the aesthetics of existence and the government of the self and others in Greco-Roman culture in the first two centuries of the empire' (DE#329 IV, 415; EW I, 207).[14] There are traces of this material in Chapters II and III of the book he published under the title *The Care of the Self*, but not sufficient material to include all the things he had planned. There is, for example, no extended discussion of *Alcibiades*, which was a major theme in *The Hermeneutic of the Subject* course. Nor is there the material on writing or reading, or the extended discussion of Seneca or Plutarch which might be expected, given that Foucault suggested they led him to this work (EW I, 254–5; DE#326 IV, 383). All of these are touched upon in greater detail in *The Hermeneutic of the Subject*. That course is orientated very explicitly towards the question of the care of the self, but is much closer to what Foucault originally envisioned *Le Souci de soi* would do than the actually published book of that title is. As Gros suggests, this course is in some sense an elaboration of Part II of the published book.[15]

However, the course is only part of what Foucault produced on this topic, and Gros discusses four additional dossiers of material, beyond the course manuscript, that contain a number of folders and drafts on these themes. The dossiers are entitled '"Alcibiades, Epictetus", "Government of the self and others", "Culture of the self – rough draft", [and] "The Others"'. The last two are drafts of material that would appear in *The Care of the Self*, but the first two contain 'a series of thematic studies ("listening, reading, writing", "critique", "government of the self and others", "age, pedagogy, medicine", "retirement", "social relations", "direction", "battle", etc.)'[16] He describes these dossiers as containing 'entire pages of finished writing dealing with points of which there is still no definitive record...Certainly, Foucault did not have time to give an account of all of his research on ancient techniques of the self in the three months of the course...Foucault's last years, from 1980 to 1984, really were in any case a period of amazing conceptual acceleration, of a sudden proliferation of problematics'.[17]

The Published History of Sexuality

While Foucault published three pieces drawn from the work completed under the March 1983 plan, only one appeared in the actually published volumes on sexuality. The 1983 essay 'Rêver de ses plaisirs. Sur l' "Onirocritique" d'Artémidore' is an early version of the three sections of Chapter I of *The Care of the Self*.[18] The text was apparently based on a lecture in Grenoble on 18 May 1982, though it would have been a long lecture if all the material was delivered.[19] There are changes of various kinds between the 1983 version and the final 1984 one in the book, though most are minor. The 1983 text has no notes, and even the references to book and section of *Onirocritica* are missing.[20] The most significant change comes at the end: two short paragraphs in the book (HS III, 50–1/36) replace a longer one in the article (DE#332 IV, 487–8). The earlier version is quite conditional in its claims and cautious in wider lessons to be learned. The passage in the book is less circumspect – 'here one easily recognizes the principal characteristics of the moral [*morale*] experience of the *aphrodisia* in the form in which it had appeared in the texts of the classical age'.[21] Foucault then moves to how later texts provide not 'breaks [*ruptures*], radical changes, [the] emergence of a new form of experience of pleasures' but 'noticeable inflections' and a modification 'in the way moral [*morale*] thought defines the relation of the subject to his sexual activity' (HS III, 50–1/36). In addition, it is likely that part of the reason the material from the article was removed from the book is because its key focus – the notion of *khrēsis*, *usage*, use – is discussed in Chapter I.2 of the second volume. When Foucault delivered the lecture and likely still at the time he delivered the text to be published as an article, the draft manuscript was one where the discussion of *Onirocritica* immediately followed the section on 'Concepts and Principles' within a larger part on 'The Use of Pleasures'. This rearrangement of material would seem to explain some of the changes between the 1983 essay and the final book version.

There was considerable debate even as the books were about to go to press, with Foucault having to be persuaded that this was the best plan, instead of the publication of *Les Aveux de la chair* first or all three parts together in a single volume.[22] What it meant, of course, is that Foucault's discussion of the plans at different times often accord very badly with what actually transpired. Indeed, the interview with Dreyfus and Rabinow was reworked by Foucault before its French publication a year later.[23] Here he changed the outline to: 'A book on the problematization of sexual activity in classical Greek thought concerned with dietetics, economics and erotics, *L'Usage des plaisirs*; then a re-elaboration of the same themes in the first centuries of the Empire, *Le Souci de Soi*; then a problematization of sexual activity in Christianity from the fourth-fifth century, *Les Aveux de la chair*' (DE#344 IV, 611). This is the plan found on the unpaginated insert slipped into early copies of *L'Usage des plaisirs* and *Le Souci de soi*, which discusses the reasons for the change and lists the final order.[24]

Volume 1 La Volonté de savoir
Volume 2 L'Usage des plaisirs
Volume 3 Le Souci de soi
Volume 4 Les Aveux de la chair (forthcoming)

Here, *Les Aveux de la chair* is described as a book that 'will treat the experience of the flesh in the first centuries of Christianity, and the role played by hermeneutics and the purifying decipherment of desire'.[25] Speaking of himself in the third person, Foucault suggests that 'to speak of sexuality as a singular historical experience implied undertaking the genealogy of the desiring subject and to return not only to the beginnings of the Christian tradition but also to ancient philosophy'.[26] Even more explicit, he states that he 'went back from the modern era, beyond Christianity until antiquity'.[27] Following his lecture courses, we can see this in practice. He worked backwards, as historians regularly do, even though the books were presented in forward order: 'one reason for the delay in the appearance of these books is that the order in which they are coming out is the opposite of that in which they were written' (DE#354 IV, 697; PPC 242).

The Use of Pleasures

In November 1983 Foucault published a new version of the introduction to the series in *Le Débat* (DE#338). With only a small number of changes, most of which are no more than minor amendments that could have been done on page proofs – a few deleted words, the odd additional clause or short sentence, the addition of a footnote, changes to punctuation, sentences linked or broken etc. – this was the version that began *The Use of Pleasures* as finally published.

In the introduction, Foucault begins by recognizing that the series has appeared later than 'anticipated, and in an entirely different form' (HS II 9/3). He notes that the project is to trace the emergence of 'sexuality', as a term and description of a practice – effectively the *dispositif* of sexuality introduced in the first volume back in 1976. Foucault suggests that such an inquiry required work along three axes: '(1) the formation of *savoirs* that refer to it, (2) the system of power that regulates its practice, (3) the forms within which individuals can and must recognize themselves as subjects of this sexuality' (HS II 10–11/4).[28] The first two drew on the tactics of his earlier work on medicine, psychiatry, punishment and discipline, but the last required a different approach. The emergence of 'sexuality', as distinct from the Christian idea of the 'flesh', could not, Foucault contends, be understood from the perspective of the eighteenth century, but required a genealogy of the 'man of desire' (HS II 11–12/4–5). This reorientation could not simply be resolved by 'a quick historical survey of the theme of desire' alongside the original plan, but rather led to a reorganization of 'the whole study around the slow formation, in antiquity, of a hermeneutics of the self' (HS II 13/6). This would be an element within a wider 'history of truth' that Foucault suggests has been his wider project all along, and he thanks his auditors at the Collège de France who 'followed the advances and detours' of this work (HS II 14/6–7). He recognizes the limitations of his grasp of Greek and Latin,[29] and thanks a number of people who have been useful – Brown, Hadot, Dreyfus and Rabinow, François Wahl, Veyne. He even thanks his patient editor at Gallimard, Pierre Nora: the spat of the mid 1970s at least somewhat forgiven (HS II 14–15/7–8). Foucault ends the first section of the introduction by suggesting that while the materials studied are historical, they are not the work of an historian. They are he argues, attempts to think differently, an "ascesis', *askēsis*, an exercise of oneself in the activity of thought', a shift of theme and chronology that had 'a certain theoretical benefit' (HS II 16/8). This benefit is in two registers. The first comes from asking why sexual behaviour becomes an object of moral concern, not by simply looking at prohibitions, and from recognizing that 'the interdiction is one thing, the moral problematization is another'. The second is to see how these sexual codes and problematization were part of a wider set of practices that he calls '"arts of existence" ... "techniques of the self"'. This is where the two parallel projects of Foucault's final years intersect: 'the study of the problematization of sexual behaviour in antiquity could be regarded as a chapter – or one of the first chapters – of that general history of the "techniques of the self" ' (HS II 19/10–11).

One of the striking things about the introduction is its explicit bringing together of the archaeological and genealogical modes of analysis (HS II 19/11–12). One crucial passage is substantially different in the final version compared to the November 1983 draft (DE#338 IV, 546):

But since this analysis of the man of desire is located at the intersection of an archaeology of problematizations and a genealogy of practices of the self, I would like to pause, before beginning, on those two notions – that is, to account for the forms of 'problematization' that I chose to examine, to indicate what is to be understood by 'practices of the self', and to explain how I was led, though certain paradoxes and difficulties, to replace a history of systems of morality based, hypothetically, on prohibitions, with a history of ethical problematizations based on practices of the self. (HS II 21/13)

Instead of a still strangely dominant reading in Anglophone debates, where archaeology is replaced by genealogy, and in turn by problematization, here we have a clear statement of their relation. In an April 1983 discussion he is categorical: 'I never stopped doing archaeology; I never stopped doing genealogy. Genealogy defines the target and the finality of the work. Archaeology indicates the field which I deal with in order to make a genealogy.'[30] Or in a 1984 interview: 'I set out from a problem expressed in the terms current today and I try to work out its genealogy. Genealogy means that I begin my analysis from a question posed in the present' (DE#350 IV, 674; PPC 262). Another common way of characterizing Foucault is a shift from knowledge to power to ethics, but again these latter terms are supplements, not replacements.

The second and third parts of the introduction then elaborate on these two themes, 'Forms of Problematization' and 'Morality and Practices of the Self'. In the light of the lecture material discussed in Chapter 6, and the discussions earlier in this chapter, there is little that is especially new. But it is striking how neatly things now fit into place in Foucault's schema. There is something of a tendency to criticize commonly held positions, which it appears are actually ones Foucault himself subscribed to before undertaking the detailed work. Rather than the description of antiquity as a background to Christianity – which in the draft introduction Foucault said he abandoned and that led him to the detailed work of many years on pagan thought – we now have tantalizing allusions to Christian thought read more subtly in the light of the much deeper analysis of antiquity. There are also some striking contrasts between texts from these earlier periods and the nineteenth century (i.e. HS II 27–8/18).

Yet the historical material is always at the service of the wider project, an examination of the 'mode of subjectification [*mode d'assujettissement*]', the 'ethical work [*travail éthique*]' individuals perform on themselves (HS II 38/27), or the '"ascetics" or "practices of the self"' (HS II 40/28). This notion of *assujettissement* is a crucial notion for this transformative process, defined by Foucault as 'the way in which an individual establishes their relation to the rule and recognizes themselves as obliged to put it into practice' (HS II 38/27). His first approximation is that while codes of behaviour appear later – not in early Christian thought but in their medieval development – Greek and Graeco-Roman antiquity was more concerned with 'practices of the self and *askēsis*' (HS II 42/30). Foucault is explicit that what he is examining is 'a morals [*morale*] for men: a morals thought, written, and taught by men, and addressed to men – to free men, obviously'. Women feature only as objects or partners, not as sexual subjects in their own right (HS II 33/22). For men these questions relate to four areas: the body, the wife, boys and truth (HS II 35/24, 45/32), which are the topics of Parts III–V of the book – on Dietetics, Economics, Erotics and 'La véritable amour', 'The true love'.

A detailed reading of each of these sections will have to be foregone, due to space considerations and the richness of Foucault's analysis. It is striking how relatively little of Volume II had been previewed in Collège de France lectures. The closest is *Subjectivité et vérité*, but much of that course treats the period of the Empire discussed in Volume III, and makes comparisons to the material destined for Volume IV, *Les Aveux de la chair*. Volume II is largely on classical, Hellenic, Greece, which Foucault only rarely discussed in his lecture courses. Where he did, such as the reading of Plato's *Alcibiades*, the focus was different and the analysis was destined for a different book.

The most important section of Volume II is the first, which discusses some of the key concepts – *Aphrodisia; Khrēsis, Enkrateia,* Freedom and Truth. Here Foucault discusses a range of texts, principally by Xenophon, Plato, and Aristotle. The first of the concepts is, Foucault suggests, the closest thing the Greeks had to either the modern 'sexuality' or the Christian 'flesh'. *Aphrodisia* was translated into Latin as *venerea*, and the closest modern approximation is *plaisirs*, pleasures (HS II 49–50/35).[31] 'The *aphrodisia* are the acts, gestures, and contacts that produce a certain form of pleasure' (HS II 55/40). For the Greeks, Foucault suggests, the 'object of moral reflection' was not the act, the desire or even the pleasure, but 'the dynamics that joined all three in circular fashion... it was this dynamic relationship that constituted what might be called the texture of the ethical experience of the *aphrodisia*' (HS II 59–60/43). Clarifying his earlier remarks about this being a morals for men, he shows how this division is about male activity and female passivity, and that this marks a distinction between antiquity's *aphrodisia*; Christianity where 'flesh' applied to both men and women; and modern 'sexuality' which had a 'great caesura between male and female' (HS II 64–5/46–7).

Khrēsis is the 'use [*usage*]' of the book's title; it 'allows one to perceive the type of subjectification that the practice of pleasures had to undergo in order to be morally valorized' (HS II 52/37), about enjoying pleasure in appropriate ways. It is these 'conditions and modalities of a "use"', rather than a code, which defines Greek *aphrodisia* (HS II 72/53), and is defined by considerations such as its relation to need, being at the opportune time, the *kairos*, and the question of status (HS II 73–82/54–61). These lead to two other key concepts: *Enkrateia* is mastery, 'which defines the attitude that was required with respect to oneself in order to make oneself into an ethical [*moral*] subject' (HS II 52/37); and *sōphrosynē*, temperance or moderation, wisdom, 'which characterized the ethical subject in his fulfilment' (HS II 52/37). These terms are close, and sometimes used interchangeably, but 'stop short of being exact synonyms', because *sōphrosynē* is a more general precept, whereas *enkrateia* is a 'more active form of self-mastery, which enables one to resist or struggle, and to achieve domination in the area of desires and pleasures'. Following Helen North, Foucault suggests that Aristotle's *Nicomachean Ethics* provides the first systematic distinction (HS II 87/64).[32] As he later clarifies, this technique of self-mastery as *enkrateia* is derived from the verb *kratein* and related to *arkhein* – exercise power over, rule over, govern. It is at the root of government of the self as well as over others (HS II 94–5/70–1, 102–3/75–6), and for this, as with other pursuits, required training, exercise, *askēsis* (HS II 97/72). Before one can attend to or lead others, one must take care of the self, *epimeleia heautou* (HS II 98/73). *Sōphrosynē* is understood as a freedom, not in the sense of independence or free will, but to be free of the authority of pleasures, 'not to be their slave' (HS II 108/79). Again this links to the governance of others: 'The most kingly man was king of himself (*basilikos, basileuōn heautou*)', where 'his self-rule moderated his rule over others' and he was distinguished from the tyrant (HS II 110/81).

While these virtues were important to women, temperance was of a virile character, predominantly understood as male, where social and sexual virility went together (HS II 112–13/82–3). Thus the active nature of these virtues becomes important, with the consequence that 'intemperance derives from a passivity that relates it to femininity' (HS II 114/84). This is of fundamental importance for a Greek model of thinking that took 'the opposition between activity and passivity' as essential. Foucault clarifies that this active/passive distinction neither maps onto our contemporary distinction 'between hetero- and homosexuality; nor was it confined to the opposition between active and passive homosexuality' (HS II 115/85). Rather it was to do with simply yielding to pleasures, not being in control of them, being passive with regard to them (HS II 115–16/85–6). And this 'freedom-power combination that characterized the mode of being of the moderate [*tempérant*] man could not be conceived without a relation to truth', the care of the self relates to the injunction 'know thyself': becoming an ethical subject also required the constitution of the self as a 'subject of knowledge [*connaissance*]' (HS II 116–17/86). This relation to truth 'did not lead to a hermeneutics of desire, as would be the case in Christian spirituality', but rather to 'an aesthetics of existence' (HS II 120/89).[33]

At the end of this survey of these key concepts, Foucault notes that it 'is only a rough sketch for preliminary purposes' (HS II 123/91).

It is in detailed analysis of relations to the body, marriage and boys that the detail and depth of his readings becomes apparent. The themes of dietetics, economics and erotics again structure the book (HS II 126/93). Foucault's general point in terms of dietetics is to situate their discussions of sex within a wider context. He makes the point that 'the moral reflection of the Greeks on sexual behaviour did not seek to justify interdictions, but to stylize a freedom' (HS II 129/97). What this meant was that while they often recommended abstinence, limitation and regulation, they did not require it, and these counsels could be found in various aspects of life, not only sex, as part of a general 'management of health and the life of the body' (HS II 130/98). This included, in addition, exercise, food and drink, and sleep: 'regimen was a whole art of living' (HS II 133/101). Indeed, Foucault thinks it is notable that within this 'regime of pleasures' there is limited attention to sexual relations compared to the other aspects (HS II 151/114). As such, even this volume discusses in some detail what might be called technologies of the self, always offered as guidance in the written texts we have preserved, rather than strict moral codifications. This was the same for the regime of *aphrodisia*, although temperance was advised, it was not on the basis that acts were bad, or in principle disqualified, but rather from the impact such activities had on the body (HS II 153/117). There is some discussion of the physical nature of the sexual act, an analysis that draws upon *Subjectivité et vérité*. As he later summarizes: 'The physical regimen of the *aphrodisia* was a health precaution; at the same time, it was an exercise – an *askēsis* – of existence' (HS II 166/126).

Bridging the analysis of dietetics and the part on economics, Foucault suggests that 'the physical regimen of pleasures and the economy it required were part of a whole art of the self' (HS II 183/139). The notion of economics here, then, bears only limited relation to what we understand by that term today. It is about the management of the household, the *oikos*. As such, this is where Foucault discusses ancient Greek texts on marriage, mistresses, the treatment of slaves, household budgets and its situation within a wider *polis*. The man's marital status did not impose obligations of fidelity, and he could have affairs, visit prostitutes, love boys, and his slaves. But it did prevent him from another marriage, or sexual relations with the wife of another: 'the wife belonged to the husband, the husband belonged only to himself' (HS II 192/147). The obligation of the man comes from 'being the head of a family, having authority, exercising a power whose locus of application was in the "house", and fulfilling obligations there that affected his reputation as a citizen' (HS II 197/151). Although he discusses texts by Plato and Isocrates, and the Aristotelian *Economics* (probably written by one of his school), Foucault's key focus is Xeno-phon's *Oeconomicus*, which he describes as containing 'the most fully developed treatise on married life that classical Greece has left us', but this within a wider study of how to manage an estate [*patrimonie*] (HS II 198/152). Much of the question of marriage is related to that wider management task, and as Foucault notes, the text is very detailed on that question, but 'quite discrete on the question of sexual relations' (HS II 207/159). Foucault only hints at the analysis to come in future volumes when he discusses the codification of this question in Christianity and the 'sin of the flesh', and, before this, in Plutarch (HS II 238–9/183–4). Yet again the wider question of governing is important: 'an art of governing, governing oneself and governing a wife' (HS II 215/165).

The section on Erotics concentrates on the love of boys. Foucault is at pains to stress that 'the Greeks did not see love for one's sex and love for the other sex as opposites, as two exclusive choices, two radically different types of behaviour' (HS II 243/187). Instead, the themes of temperance and self-mastery were more important. Modern terms such as homosexuality and bisexuality are not helpful in making sense of this, and nor is the idea of tolerance of this behaviour (HS II 243–4/187–8). Foucault's question is why there was so much atten-tion paid to this theme, when it was not a matter of condemnation or prohibition. Why did this practice produce such 'an extraordinary complex moral problematization'? (HS II 251/193). This question is difficult to resolve in part, because while we know many texts were written, only a few are preserved, and so speeches in Platonic dia-logues take on a significant burden, along with Xenophon's *Sympo-sium* and Demosthenes' *Erotikos*. Two themes emerge – the question of social status and active/passive roles. Passivity tended to be con-demned, but when accompanied by being the inferior in social status or age could be acceptable. The link between love and education or training is significant, and the disparity in partners was significant (HS II 251–4/193–5). Equally important was that the object of desire would become, in time, a sexual subject themselves, and the moment of transition needed to be observed and respected. 'As we know, the first beard was believed to be that fateful mark, and it was said that the razor that shaved it must sever the ties of love' (HS II 259/199).[34] At that time a relation of *eros* could transform into one of *philia*, friendship (HS II 261/201).

Foucault notes that 'the young man – between the end of child-hood and the age when he attained manly status – constituted a deli-cate and difficult factor for Greek morals [*morale*] and Greek thought' (HS II 277/213). The issue is not about the Greek love of boys in itself, but the nature of the 'courtship practice, moral reflection and...philosophical asceticism' that developed around it (HS II 278/214). This is where Foucault introduces the theme of isomorphism – developed in *Subjectivité et vérité* in the reading of Artemidorus – between social and sexual relations (HS II 279/215). Here, Foucault draws on a wider range of classical texts to support the points about status and their relation to sexual activity and passivity. This is part of the reason for the emergence of texts around the love of boys: women, prostitutes and slaves were deemed to be inferior socially, and so could be passive sexually. Boys, because they would become subjects exercising 'power and responsibilities' themselves were in a more complicated position (HS II 286/220–1).

Foucault links the three themes of dietetics, economics and erotics through their relation to governance of the self and others. In the first, concerning the body, it was a question of self-mastery; in the home it was about the mastery of the power exercised over the wife; in the *Erotikos* it was a matter of the boy's achievement of 'self-mastery in not yielding to others', of resisting the power of others (HS II 276/212). Somewhat schematically: governance of the self, governance of others, resistance to governance. These were concerns of only 'the smallest minority of the population, made up of free, adult males', but it produced for them 'an aesthetics of existence, the considered art of a freedom perceived as a power game' (HS II 326/253). In the final substantive section of the book he examines these themes in relation to truth, again bemoaning the lack of texts and cautioning against generalizing too much from Socratic–Platonic sources (HS II 296/230). Nonetheless, he finds it important that in Plato, love 'is a relation to truth' (HS II 309/239). In bringing in truth, Foucault is linking this study to a range of his earlier concerns, and anticipating the work on confession to come in a future volume. Indeed, Foucault notes that, somewhat surprisingly given there is little condemnation or prohibition, in Greek discussions of the love of boys there is the beginning of a more abstemious sexual ethics: 'the requirement of a symmetry and a reciprocity in the love relationship; the necessity of a long-term and arduous struggle with oneself; the gradual purification of a love that is addressed only to being itself, in its truth; and man's interrogation of himself as a subject of desire' (HS II 317/245). This will undergo profound changes over time, but the roots of these developments can be found here. And this sits in relation to wider concerns about the techniques of the self. These, for Foucault, are elements within a history of ethics, rather than a history of codes, the former being understood 'as the elaboration of a form of relation to self that enables an individual to fashion himself into a subject of moral conduct'. To understand 'the transformations of moral experience' the history of ethics is more decisive (HS II 324/251). Being exposed to the truth, especially in a relationship that joins *eros* to pedagogy; to knowing the truth about oneself; to telling the truth to a spiritual counsellor. *The Use of Pleasures* may make direct use of very little material from Foucault's lecture courses, but it links in multiple ways to their recurrent themes.

This volume is also revealing for the indications of the contrasts he intends to draw with Christianity, where he suggests 'two opposite yet complementary practices' are developed: 'a codification of sexual acts...and the development of a hermeneutics of desire and procedures of self-decipherment' (HS II 124/92). A fundamental shift, it is suggested, is in the attention paid to women and marriage, rather than the love of boys. There are also glimpses of how the analysis of the second and third volumes links to concerns of the first: 'And we can see a new shift of the focus of problematization (this time from women to the body) in the interest that was shown, starting in the seventeenth and eighteenth centuries, in the sexuality of children, and, generally speaking, in the relationships between sexual behaviour, normality and health' (HS II 327/253). This passage comes right at the end of the second volume, and is followed by a brief paragraph on Augustine and Christianity, and then one that links to the concerns of Volume III, suggesting that many significant changes that precede Christianity can be found 'in the reflection of the moralists, philosophers, and doctors of the first two centuries of our era' (HS II 327/254). Follow those paragraphs backwards and there is a clear sense of how the *History of Sexuality*, as Foucault finally conceived it, might be read. Not only would Volume IV complete the series; the analyses of Volume I would appear in a new light following Volume IV. As he said in April 1983:

> When Christianity, the Church, organized a set of techniques concerning confession, penance and so on, it used and integrated those techniques of the self in an institutional context in which those techniques of the self, which were autonomous in Antiquity, became part of a disciplinary structure; and I think that afterwards, in the pedagogical institutions from the sixteenth century, the relationship to oneself has always been organized, or at least proposed to people, by those institutions.[35]

The Care of the Self

Volume III followed only one month after the publication of Volume II, with Foucault receiving a copy only five days before he died. Given this proximity, it is unsurprising that it follows smoothly from the end of Volume II, delivering on the promise. It is indeed 'a re-elaboration of the same themes' as Volume II, 'in the first centuries of the Empire' (DE#344 IV, 611). Accordingly, the structure is very similar: the bulk of the book is devoted to Parts IV to VI which are entitled 'The Body', 'The Wife' and 'Boys', and mirror the Dietetics, Economics, Erotics parts of Volume II. These three sections are preceded by a reading of Artemidorus, and two important parts that are closest to *Le Souci de soi* as conceived in early 1983, 'The Culture of the Self' and 'Self and Others'. There is no introduction: the much-redrafted introduction to Volume II serves to introduce both volumes. The conclusion is only a few pages. Foucault had anticipated Volume IV following soon after, so as with the second he ended the third more with an opening, transitional section than a closing one. Volume III is thus the least self-contained of Foucault's works, being so dependent on what came before and what was anticipated to follow. In addition, much of this volume is dependent on material presented in lectures – indeed, it is the closest of all of Foucault's books.

As such, the discussion here can be briefer for several parts of the book. The first is the reading of Artemidorus' *Onirocritica*, trading on the analysis in *Subjectivité et vérité* (see Chapter 6) and the 1982 Grenoble lecture, or at least its published form (DE#332). But while in the 1981 lectures this text had to bear the burden of revealing *aphrodisia*, now, coming after the extensive analysis of classical Greece in Volume II, it is situated in a much richer context and its reading is more specific. Foucault sees it as something of a synthesis: rather than initiating a new moment or even as anticipating one, its importance is in providing 'indications concerning current modes of valuation and generally accepted attitudes' (HS III 17/9). Foucault also cautions against using the text 'as a direct commentary on the value and legitimacy of sexual acts'. It is not a code of conduct, but is revealing of 'an ethics of the subject' (HS III 27/16). Most of the elements of the lecture course's reading are, however, retained, even if the presentation is more polished and systematic. It is a text, he suggests where dominant modes of sexual behaviour are presented: the man as the object of analysis and the subject of sexual relations; marriage as an important framework because of the socio-sexual isomorphism, but where relations with mistresses, slaves, prostitutes and boys can all be acceptable, as long as the last respected 'age and status' (HS III 49/35). Nonetheless, a few traces of a code can be found, with prohibitions on oral sex, between women, women usurping the male role, and some kinds of incest. These are far from being the kind of thing labelled as 'flesh' or 'sexuality', and this text still bears the 'principal characteristics of the moral experience of the *aphrodisia*' as had been analysed in Volume II (HS III 50/36). The reading thus functions as a kind of postscript to that volume. What marks an inflection rather than a break are a series of texts, which concern 'the way in which moral [*morale*] thought defines the relation of the subject to his sexual activity' (HS III 51/36).

Part II of the book, on 'The Culture of the Self', also draws heavily on the 1981 course, suggesting that in these early centuries of the present era there was 'a more intense problematization of the *aphrodisia*'. This can be found in a range of Stoic and other thinkers, from whom Christian authors borrowed extensively, often without attribution (HS III 55–6/39). Foucault considers, but dismisses, a wider socio-political reason for this. While there were restrictions, for example in the time of Caesar Augustus, they were sporadic and the writers he uses do not recommend public intervention, but rather private change: 'not a tightening of the code that defined prohibited acts, but of an intensification of the relation to oneself by which one constituted oneself as the subject of one's acts' (HS III 57–8/40–1). It is here that the project on sexuality most closely links to the project of techniques of the self, and *The Care of the Self* as published most closely relates to *Le Souci de soi* as originally conceived. But this chapter is only really in place to provide that wider situation of the work: the full elaboration was to be elsewhere, of which the 1981 *Subjectivité et vérité* course and especially the 1982 lectures in Paris and Vermont give us the best extant substitute. Nonetheless, Foucault does spend some time here rehearsing the key themes. He mentions the wider art of existence characterized by the *tekhnē tou biou*, of which the *heautou epimeleisthai* dominated (HS III 60–1/43). Many of his examples are draw from *The Hermeneutic of the Subject* course – Plato's *Apology* and, briefly, the *Alcibiades*; Plutarch's story about the Spartans; the Epicureans, Epictetus, Seneca, Musonius Rufus and Marcus Aurelius.

This period, the first two centuries of the present era and the beginning of the Empire, 'can be seen as the summit of a curve: a kind of golden age in the culture of the self', although, as before, Foucault cautions that this applied only to a very select social group (HS III 62–3/45). However, and this is a crucial point, the instruction in this care of the self was not directed just at youth, as Socrates had proposed: Seneca and Plutarch provide guidance for men (HS III 68/49). A second crucial point is that the *epimeleia*, the care, was a word not just used to look after the self, but others – a man over a household, a ruler over his subjects, a doctor over a patient. In all of these, as well as concerning the self, '*epimeleia* implies a labour' (HS III 70/50).

The medical parallel is important (HS III 75–81/54–8); so too is the relation between self-knowledge and care (HS III 81–9/58–64). Care of the self was diffused through a range of social associations – not just formal institutions, but 'customary relations of kinship, friendship and obligation' (HS III 73–4/52–3). In these practices, and their circulation, Foucault finds developments in the 'morals of pleasure [*la morale des plaisirs*]'. Not a 'tightening of interdictions', but shifts in 'the manner in which the individual needed to form himself as a moral subject' (HS III 93/67). Breaking with his customary language of power, *pouvoir*, Foucault suggests that 'sexual pleasure as an ethical substance continues to be of the order of force [*de l'ordre de force*]', and it is against this force that the individual must struggle and resist, where they must 'subjectify themselves [*s'assujettisse*] to a certain art of living which defines the aesthetic and ethical criteria of existence' (HS III 93/67). These criteria appear more and more general or universal, and self-knowledge and the relation to truth becomes more important, yet ultimately this *askēsis* is still 'the rule of the individual over himself'. Evil, the law and the 'deciphering of desire' are still a way off, though the beginnings of those transformations can, Foucault suggests, already be seen (HS III 93–4/67–8).

These themes are continued in Part III, which briefly surveys two transformations that Foucault thinks impact on the culture of the self: marriage and politics. The importance of marriage and the couple, and new political roles offer a challenge to the male ethics discussed in earlier parts and the second volume. As Foucault notes, this part, in particular the chapter on marriage, is dependent on previous research (HS III 97/71), especially the work of Veyne, Vatin and Sarah Pomeroy.[36] While marriage had been discussed in the 1981 course, the function of this part seems to be to situate the chapters to come within a wider socio-political context. Marriage is interesting because of its multiple role: as an institution that is important to the family and the city; as the means by which a household is generally structured; and as a basis of a 'shared existence, a personal bond' (HS III 107/78). It is that last role that Foucault thinks is becoming increasingly important, and a means by which a man 'had to regulate his conduct', as involved in a 'governmental function of training, education, and guidance', and 'to form himself as an ethical subject within the relation of conjugality' (HS III 110–1/80).

In terms of the political, Foucault is trying to situate these changes within the decline of the city-state and the emergence of the Empire, while recognizing that a 'centralized imperialism', organized on a hierarchical model, is not yet there. He suggests that it is really a product of the third century. Rather, the early Empire is better understood as 'the organization of a complex space...a space in which the centres of power were multiple; in which the activities, the tensions, the conflicts were numerous; in which they developed in several dimensions; and in which the equilibria were obtained through a variety of transactions' (HS III 114/82–3). As he later suggests, at this time, 'anyone who exercises power has to place himself in a field of complex relations where he occupies a transition point' (HS III 122/88). Marcus Aurelius is of course a key witness: he provides 'the clearest formulation of an experience of political power that, on the one hand, takes the form of an occupation separate from status and, on the other, requires the careful practice of personal virtues' (HS III 123–4/89). The point here, as with marriage trans-formations, is to think about how earlier models, notably self-mastery, were transformed:

> [Self-mastery] had implied a close connection between the superiority one exercised over oneself, that which one exercised in the context of the household, and that which one exercised in the field of an agonistic society...Henceforth one was in a world where these relations could no longer operate in the same way: the relation of superiority exercised in the household and over the wife had to be associated with certain forms of reciprocity and equality. As for the agonistic game by which one sought to manifest and ensure one's superiority over others, it had to be integrated into a far more extensive and complex field of power relations. Consequently, the principle of superiority over the self as the ethical core, the general form of 'heautocratism', needed to be restruc-tured. (HS III 130–1/94–5)

There is, Foucault goes on to suggest, a certain dissociation in the relation between self and others. What was previously so closely linked – 'the three types of authority (over oneself, over the house-hold, and over others)' – is transformed, without disappearing, all at root due to a crisis, not quite of the subject, but 'a crisis of subjec-tivation [*subjectivation*]' (HS III 131/95). This theme – the part is entitled 'Self and Others' – was a theme for future research, some of which was conducted in the final two courses in Paris (see Chapter 8). But even there the political is underplayed, and these few pages on the power structure of the early Empire remain a tantalizing fragment. It is interesting to speculate how Foucault's famous decen-tred analysis of power – first found in his analyses of Ancient Greece in *Lectures on the Will to Know*, and then recast later as the emer-gence of modern discipline beyond central sovereignty – would have made sense of this period. He does describe it as 'the complex network of power' (HS III 127/92), but given that this is a time of, albeit imperfect, multiple and geographically uneven, progressive concentration, it would require a somewhat different approach. At the very least, it makes the historically specific nature of his earlier analyses all the clearer.

While the parallel part of Volume II had privileged food and drink, and the physical act, Part IV of Volume III on 'The Body' is more interested in medicine and the overall environment.[37] There is, for example, an interesting discussion of the medical perception of milieu and temporality (HS III 138–9/101–2). The broad 'concern for the body, health, environment, and circumstances' is the framework for the medical understanding of sexual pleasures (HS III 141/104). Foucault reads Galen here in some detail, discussing 'the physiology of sexual acts' (HS III 145/106), and their relation to 'epilepsy and convulsions' and venereal disease (HS III 149–50/109–10). Later he broadens the analysis to include other authors, discussion of sperm and semen, and conditions such as priapism and satyriasis. At this time, 'beyond the particular sphere of their pathology, sexual acts are placed... at the junction of a complex pathogeny' (HS III 158/116). While the sexual act is 'not evil [*mal*]', it does 'manifest a permanent focus of possible ills [*maux possibles*]' (HS III 191/142). Given all these concerns, Foucault suggests that sexual acts are increasingly placed within 'an extremely careful regimen', but that this is not about which acts should be engaged in or with whom. Instead there are four registers: 'the best moment [*moment utile*] for procreation, the age of the subject, the time frame [*moment*] (the season or the hour of the day), and individual temperament' (HS III 167–8/124–5). Rather than restriction, it is rather 'a whole government of the *aphrodisia*' – a phrase that is used to describe procreation, but holds for the analysis as a whole (HS III 172/127). While the focus is the body, Foucault shows how the physicians related the analysis to the soul (HS III 179/133). He notes, too, that masturbation here – entirely contrary to the focus it will take beginning with Christian monasticism – is rarely mentioned and then generally as natural and positive (HS III 188–9/140).

In Part V Foucault turns his attention to the question of marriage and the household, providing more textual evidence to discuss the claims he had made in Chapter 1 of Part III. He suggests that while in classical Greece marriage had been situated more squarely within the affairs of the *polis*, even subordinated to it, now it was examined more as a subject in its own right. 'In sum, the art of conducting oneself in marriage would appear to be defined less by a technique of government and more by a stylistics of the individual bond' (HS III 199/148). This has a consequence in terms of the analysis of the conjugal relationship, 'a doctrine of sexual monopoly, and in an aesthetics of shared pleasures' (HS III 200/149). Sexual pleasure increasingly becomes restricted to within marriage, certainly for women still, but now also for men, which Foucault calls the '"conjugalization" of sexual relations' (HS III 222/166–7). Marriage is seen as 'the only legitimate context for sexual union [*conjonction*] and the use of the *aphrodisia*' (HS III 227/170). Adultery was 'juridically condemned and morally reproved', both because of the injury done to the husband of the woman, but also, now, the injury done to the wife of the man (HS III 227–31/171–3). Much of the analysis here is drawing on material presented in the *Subjectivité et vérité* course, particularly the readings of Stoic thinkers such as Musonius Rufus and Epictetus. Now, though, the contrasts with classical Greece are drawn more clearly, based on the extensive references and detail provided in Volume II. In particular, Foucault notes that while keeping sexual relations within marriage was praised in Plato, Aristotle and Isocrates, there it was because it exhibited self-mastery. Now it was part of a wider moral programme that helped provide the basis for a later '"juridification" of conjugal relations and sexual practice' (HS III 246/184). In this claim, and elsewhere, there are some hints of how this links to the analysis of Christianity to come (i.e. HS III 241/180–1, 245/183).

Similar claims can be made of Part VI, on boys, where Foucault discusses Plutarch's *Erotikos* – also analysed in the 1981 course – and situates it in relation to earlier texts and hints at future directions. He reads it alongside a dialogue attributed to Lucian – only mentioned in the course summary in 1981 (SV 304) – and, more briefly, four lectures by Maximus of Tyre. Plutarch and Pseudo-Lucian, Foucault suggests, 'attest both to the legitimacy that is still granted to the love of boys and to its increasingly decline as a living theme of a stylistics of existence' (HS III 255/192). However, in the reading of Plutarch he shows how there are two kinds of love, one directed towards *aphrodisia*, the other towards souls; and two objects of love: women and boys (HS III 279/210). But the love of boys is argued to lack *kharis*, which was discussed in 1981 as grace or favour, and here is glossed (following Daphnaeus and Sappho) as 'the consent that a woman willingly gives a man, a consent that can appear only with nubility' (HS III 274/206). This deficiency is important, and means that boys are increasingly excluded from a schema in which 'love is revitalized by the reciprocity of pleasure' (HS III 279/210). Indeed, the increasing disqualification of the love of boys is seen as dependent on the concentration of sexual relations within marriage Foucault had traced in the previous part (HS III 247/185). In the final chapter of this part, Foucault provides a brief discussion of the emergence of virginity as a theme in some Greek romances or novels, including *Chaerus and Callirhoe* and *Leucippe and Clitophon*. Virginity is not just a preliminary state before marriage, but 'a choice, a style of life, a lofty form of existence' chosen by the man in a way that reciprocates a longer expectation of this state for the woman (HS III /230). The chastity is not just outside of the relation, but internal to it as well, until 'love and virginity find their fulfilment in marriage' (HS III 307/231).

How this links to the work of the early Church Fathers, particular John Cassian, is left largely open. The Conclusion to the book makes only some initial gestures in that direction. Summarizing, Foucault notes that austerity is becoming a major theme in the early Empire. Abstention and virginity are praised; sexual relations outside of marriage frowned upon; the love of boys is increasingly disqualified. He asks a sequence of rhetorical questions concerning the extent to which this anticipates Christianity; briefly previews debates in Catholicism and Protestantism about this very point; and summarizes possible relations between pagan ethics and Christian codes (HS III 311–3/235–7). Yet rather than develop these lines of inquiry here, he instead points backwards and suggests related themes can even be found in classical Greece of the fourth century BCE (HS III 314/237). While serving effectively to link the analysis here to that of Volume II, Volume III therefore ends on rather a flat note. Foucault merely indicates that the style of sexual conduct in moral, medical and philosophical texts is different both from the classical period and from Christianity. The final lines suggest some of the themes that need to be discussed – 'other modalities of the relation to self'; finitude, the Fall and evil; subjectifiction, obedience, law and the will of god; 'a type of work on oneself that implies a decipherment of the soul and a purificatory hermeneutics of the desires; and a mode of ethical fulfilment that tends towards self-renunciation' (HS III /239–40). There are similarities with the themes discussed in this volume, but deriving 'from a profoundly altered ethics and from a different way of constituting oneself as the ethical subject of one's sexual behaviour' (HS III 317/240). This comparing is cut off mid analysis, given that Volumes II, III and IV were intended to be read as a whole. Whether the work on antiquity was the introduction to a book on Christianity, as Foucault suggests it was in the early 1980s; or comprised a single large volume in March 1983; or the actually published two volumes of 1984; this work was always intended to be followed by a discussion of the flesh, concupiscence and confession. It is clear from these two volumes how reticent Foucault is to make bold proclamations;

how documented his points are; how he continually refuses to make explicit links to the present; and how his own voice is largely hidden behind the ancient texts. As mentioned above, he is explicit in his debt to recent scholarship by his contemporaries. They are, in many ways, his most conventional works.[38] All the indications are that Volume IV would have continued in that vein.

One intriguing possibility is how this work on Christianity would help to close the apparent gap between Foucault's works of the mid 1970s and the last two books of the *History of Sexuality*. The analysis in this study has tried to emphasis the continuity of his concerns and the way shifts are associated with developments and following problems, noting above that, as the series was reconfigured, Volume I's analyses may follow Volume IV's. A comment in a 1983 discussion at Berkeley is explicit about the link.

> There have been, at certain times, links between techniques of the care of the self and disciplinary techniques. For instance, in the monasteries... monastic institutions of the Middle Ages, and particularly the Benedictine institutions, you find very interesting relationships between the care of the self and the discipline. As you know, the Benedictine monastic institutions derive directly from the Roman legion, from the Roman army. And it is an organization, the monastic institution which took as a model the Roman legion, with the ten men, and the Decurion, and so on... And they have tried to use both this disciplinary model and the techniques of the self... Spirituality which has nothing to do with the army... You could see also in the nineteenth century, how in some... or even in, let's take the Jesuit pedagogical institutions of the seventeenth and eighteenth century – you can see also a very interesting relationship, a link, between the care of the self and the disciplinary techniques. The great colleges, in the French meaning of the word 'college', public institutions for boys in the eighteenth century: it's very interesting to see the relation between the two.[39]

Defert recalls that in April 1984, between illnesses and stays in hospital, Foucault reread Kafka's *Journal* and got 'back to work on the manuscript of *Les Aveux de la chair*' (C 64/81). Aside from a possible fragment of its introduction (see Chapter 5), the key text we have from this manuscript remains 'The Battle for Chastity', published in 1982 and discussing John Cassian. The text develops themes from the 1980 lectures, and like much of the published Volumes II and III is a superficially flat reading of texts, patiently constructing and elucidating their arguments. Chastity is a goal to be pursued, since fornication is 'innate, natural, corporeal in origin, and needing to be

as totally destroyed as the vices of the soul, such as avarice and pride',
and if sufficiently mortified 'lets us live in our bodies while releasing
us from the flesh': 'Depart from this flesh while dwelling in the body'
(DE#312 IV, 298; EW I, 188).[40] This formulation is important,
because it gives us an insight into what Foucault meant with the
original title of the second volume, announced in 1976: *La Chair et
le corps*, *The Flesh and the Body*. Cassian is important, Foucault
contends, because his analysis is without the categories of the medieval 'catalogue of faults' or its 'great codification of sins' (DE#312
IV, 296, 300; EW I, 185, 189). How much this text differs from the
intended volume is unknown. We do know that the texts which he
published from Volumes II and III – 'L'Usage des plaisirs et techniques
de soi' and 'Rêver de ses plaisirs' – were only lightly modified in their
final form, but 'The Battle for Chastity' dates from a few years before
and precedes the new arrangement of the historical plan made in late
1983.

Defert recounts that Foucault was working on the manuscript of
the book on Christianity in Vendeuvre as late as May 1984, saying
that for him 'it was a sort of ritual to finish his books in Vendeuvre...he loved that house'.

> In the last months of his life, he took back the typescript of *Les Aveux
> de la chair*. He expected to finish it. He knew his life was going to be
> short...So he started to work in the last months on *Les Aveux de la
> chair*...I've not been able to read the manuscripts, it was too emo-
> tional. He started to rewrite the manuscript, because the typescript was
> not good enough. But according to his nephew [Henri-Paul Fruchaud],
> who has spent more time on the typescript, he took the typescript and
> rewrote on it. It was more advanced than I thought myself.[41]

In an interview conducted on 29 May, usually taken to be his last,
Foucault stated he was still at work: 'I am in the process of rereading
the manuscripts dealing with the beginning of Christianity which I
wrote for this history of morality' (DE#354 IV, 697; PPC 242).[42] At
this time he told people he had one or two months' work left to do,
expecting publication in October.[43] The history of this book on Christianity – from the projected second volume in the mid 1970s, to the
planned third volume in the early 1980s, to the forthcoming fourth
volume of 1983–4 – is one of a constant deferral: this is the book
that Foucault never published, in any of its positions across the three
plans. Defert recalls that shortly after his death he and the family
decided that the manuscripts were not secure in Foucault's apartment
because too many people had keys, so he took them to be locked in

a bank deposit box, rather than Gallimard's safe.[44] Because of the prohibition on posthumous publications, the manuscript and other material remained there for almost thirty years. It has now been sold to the Bibliothèque Nationale de France but is not yet available to researchers. While *Les Aveux de la chair* is likely to be published eventually, for now it remains something of a holy grail for Foucault scholars.

8

Speaking Truth to Power

While the *History of Sexuality* remains incomplete, before his death Foucault was already thinking about other topics. He had clearly not completely abandoned the idea of a book on practices of the self, even though he had used the title of the originally planned volume for other material. In an interview from January 1984 he discussed possible future work on contemporary questions in modern political theory concerning the relationship between care of the self and politics (DE#356 IV, 722; EW I, 294). It is possible that some of this 'care of the self' material would have found its way into what Defert and Ewald describe as 'a series of more general studies on governmentality...planned with Éditions de Seuil under the title *Le Gouvernement de soi et des autres* [The Government of Self and Others]'.[1] The title was that used by Foucault's last two courses at the Collège de France, the second of which bore the subtitle *The Courage of Truth*. In addition, in 1983 Foucault told Dreyfus and Rabinow that he had 'more than a draft of a book about sexual ethics in the sixteenth century, in which also the problem of the techniques of the self, self-examination, the cure of souls, is very important, both in the Protestant and Catholic churches' (EW I, 255; DE#326 IV, 383).[2] In the original transcript, Foucault is asked if this is the next step, rather than the Middle Ages. He replies that the Middle Ages had 'very strict and formal juridification', and that consequently technologies of the self are not so important. Yet in another remark cut from the published version, Foucault also notes that in relation to the Middle Ages, where there was an equilibrium between regulations concerning food and sex, he has 'a lot of pages about those techniques of the self'.[3] It would seem, after many years going further and further back, that he still thought he could return to the original period of Christianity he had been concerned with.[4] It is also possible that he might have returned to still earlier concerns. He had clearly not abandoned an interest in these topics, when, for example, in a 1982 interview he discusses masturbation and hysteria (EW I, 126–7; DE#336 IV, 530–1).

However, little of this material is currently available, aside from the two Paris courses, a lecture given in Grenoble, and one shorter course making use of the same material at Berkeley. The last part of this book therefore discusses those lectures and interviews from this period.

Lettres de cachet

Before turning to those final lecture courses on *parrēsia*, it is important to consider a book Foucault published in 1982 in collaboration with the historian Arlette Farge entitled *Le désordre des familles* [*The Disorder of Families*]. This was probably the longest-term project with which Foucault was involved, dating back to the *History of Madness* in the late 1950s and early 1960s. Its topic concerned *lettres de cachet*, letters bearing the King's seal. These letters could serve a variety of purposes, but the one that initially attracts Foucault's attention is that they could allow imprisonment, frequently in the Bastille.[5] As he explains in 1973:

> The *lettre de cachet* was not a law or a decree but an order from the king that concerned a person individually, compelling him to do something. One could even force someone to marry through a *lettre de cachet*. In most cases, though, it was an instrument of punishment. One could exile someone by means of a *lettre de cachet*, strip him of certain functions, imprison him. It was one of the major instruments of power of the absolute monarchy...(DE#139, II, 601; EW III, 65)

Foucault signed a contract for a book entitled *Les Embastillés* for Pierre Nora's *Archives* collection with Gallimard in the mid 1960s though never delivered it; in April 1973 he did more research on the topic at the Arsenal library, and was again working in the Bastille archive in the early 1980s.[6] Foucault regularly returns to these letters in his lectures, and tried, unsuccessfully, to write the introduction to Volume I of the *History of Sexuality* using their contents (C 49/61). This research eventually led to *Le désordre des familles*. Part of the reason for this long process is that Foucault was using research assistants to help. In the mid 1970s this was Christiane Martin (A 34/37), but she died before completing this work.[7] Eventually it was completed by Eliane Allo.[8] In the late 1970s the project took on a new energy, with the 'Lives of Infamous Men' project (see Chapter 3), but it was encountering the work of Farge that would be most significant. Foucault cites her work in *Discipline and Punish*,[9] and she was involved in the 1978 discussion in *L'impossible prison*. The mutual recognition continued in her book on life in Parisian streets, in which she pays tribute to the influence of Foucault's work.[10] In 1980 Farge received a package of transcripts from Foucault in the mail, accompanied by a note asking for her advice. After being persuaded by her that they needed a commentary, he invited her to collaborate with him on the project.[11]

The letters were an 'expression of the direct will of the sovereign, without the guarantee of a ministerial signature'.[12] There was debate about these letters during the *ancien régime*, because they were seen to be the exercise of unaccountable power, and the Declaration of the Rights of Man brought them to an end: it stated that due process of law was the only means by which someone could be deprived of their liberty.[13] Yet Foucault and Farge do not solely read the letters in this way. You could imagine an analysis that plays on the idea of cutting off the king's hand. But in their work they recognize that even though the letters were sealed by the king, he did not initiate many of the requests.

> He did so in certain instances, for affairs of state; but most of these letters – tens of thousands of *lettre de cachet* sent by the monarchy – were actually solicited by various individuals: husbands outraged by their wives, fathers dissatisfied with their children, families wanting to get rid an individual, religious communities disturbed by someone, parishes unhappy with their priests. So the *lettre de cachet* presented itself – in its aspect as terrible instrument of royal despotism – as a kind of counterpower, a power that came from below, enabling groups, communities, families, or individuals to exercise power over someone. They were instruments of a control that was voluntary in a sense, a control from below which society and the community exercised on itself. Hence, the *lettre de cachet* was a way of regulating the everyday morality of social life, a way for the group or groups – family, religious, parochial, regional, and local – to provide for their own police control and ensure their own order. (DE#139 II, 601; EW III, 65–6)

It is this more everyday use that Foucault and Farge analyse in the published book, 'less the rage of the sovereign than the passions of

the common people' (DF 10).[14] The letters were, as Farge describes,
'a sanitation mechanism for the capital'.[15] Crucially such letters
bypassed the need for a public trial or procedure, and so helped to
keep family secrets. They interweave their commentary with long
excerpts from the letters. There are four parts: a brief introduction;
sections on marital discord; on children and parents; and a closing
essay on addressing the king. Of the two main sections, the one on
marriage is mainly Farge's work; and the one on children mainly
Foucault's.[16] Some of the materials Foucault collected did not find
their way into this volume, but were used by Farge in her contribution to the multi-volume *Histoire de la vie privée* a few years later.[17]
Foucault and Farge are explicit about collapsing the distinction
between disciplines: 'The idea that History is dedicated to the "accu-
racy of the archive" and philosophy to the "architecture of ideas",
seems nonsense to us. We have not worked in that way' (DF 9). In a
1982 interview on the work, Farge explains that, 'without of course
avoiding the careful analysis of the archives, it is about fitting them
into a theoretical *ensemble*'; Foucault adds that it was always a
project in the 'history of thought' (DE#322 IV, 351).

The work is framed as a means of understanding 'the concrete
functioning of a mechanism of power', but not of 'an anonymous,
oppressive and mysterious "Power"; but as a complex fabric of relations between multiple partners' (DF 347). It is the relation between
the family institution and a 'grand administrative apparatus [*appareil*]' (DF 347). Reflecting on the project in 1984, Foucault noted that
the work allowed them to see 'how the State and private life were in
tension, clashed and at the same time fit together [*interféraient, entre-
choquaient, et en meme temps s'emboîtaient*]' (DE#348 IV, 653). As
such, while its historical focus is many centuries apart, the themes
are not dissimilar to those of his final lectures. It is one of Foucault's
least known works, but given the years between inception and completion the topic was clearly of major interest to him.

The Government of Self and Others

In the 1982 Grenoble lecture on *parrēsia* Foucault begins with a
discussion of Christianity, and contrasts the uses of the term in Christian thought with that of antiquity. The discussion of antiquity begins
with discussions of Euripides, Plato's *Laws* and *Gorgias*, Quintilian's
work on rhetoric, and Isocrates, before moving to the question of
spiritual direction, or what he calls the 'pragmatics of discourse',
which he illustrates with, among others, Arrian, Seneca, Epictetus,

Plutarch and Galen.[18] The material is not especially new to contemporary readers of Foucault but little of this had appeared in his Collège de France lectures at this time. The lecture's themes would be elaborated in the 1983 course, *The Government of the Self and Others*.

Foucault begins the course with some methodological reflections, and then moves to a reading of Kant's 'What is Enlightenment?' essay. While he had discussed this in a 1978 lecture, a piece on Georges Canguilhem (DE#29 III, 431–3), and briefly in a 1979 book review (DE#266 III, 783; EW III, 443), the analysis here would provide the basis for multiple versions, with an extract from the 1983 lecture published in 1984 (DE#351 IV, 679–688), as an essay which reworks its themes (DE#339 IV 562–78; EW I 303–19), and discussions in various other places. The most important theme that emerges in the 1983–84 analysis is the relation of the question to the present: 'What is my present [*actualité*]? What is the meaning of this present? And what am I doing when I speak of this present?' Such questions are the basis for the claim of a future project: 'a genealogy, not so much of the notion of modernity, but of modernity as a question' (GSO 15/14). Kant, for Foucault, founds two parallel directions for philosophy. One is the critical project, which 'defines the conditions under which a true knowledge is possible... an analytic of truth'. The other is this inquiry into the present, 'the present field of possible experience'. It is this, understood as 'an ontology of the present, of present reality, an ontology of modernity, an ontology of ourselves', of which Foucault, tracing a chronology from 'Hegel to the Frankfurt School by way of Nietzsche, Max Weber and so on', wants to see himself as part (GSO 22/20–1).[19]

Following this reading, Foucault rehearses claims about how this work displaces some of his previous analyses. His work has, he suggests, moved from knowledge to veridiction, power to governmentality, and a theory of the subject to techniques of the self (GSO 41–2). Governmentality is still very much the term. As he says in one of his last interviews: 'Governmentality implies the relationship of the self to itself, and I intend this concept of "governmentality" to cover the ensemble of practices that constitute, define, organize, and instrumentalize the strategies that individuals in their freedom can use in dealing with each other' (DE#356 IV, 728; EW I, 300). But this turn to others is, at least for the Greeks, dependent on the relation to others: 'Care for others should not be put before the care of oneself. The care of the self is ethically prior in that the relationship with oneself is ontologically prior' (DE#356 IV, 715; EW I, 287). As he says earlier in that same interview: 'what is ethics, if not the practice of freedom, the conscious [*réflechie*] practice of freedom?...Freedom is the ontological condition of ethics. But ethics is the considered [*réflechie*] form taken by freedom' (DE#356 IV, 711–12; EW I, 284). While crucial, this ontological inquiry is historical, rather than fundamental. His works are contributions to the history of thought, which 'means not simply the history of ideas or representations, but also an attempt to answer this question: how is a particular body of knowledge [*savoir*] able to be constituted? How can thought, insofar as it is related to truth, have a history?' (DE#350 IV, 668; PPC 256).

Despite the March 1983 draft of *L'Usage des plaisirs* being completed the same month that the course finished, *The Government of the Self and Others* bears little relation to the *History of Sexuality* in terms of content and questions. There are historical parallels though, because the focus is on *parrēsia* in antiquity, and in an early lecture he sketches the classical texts which develop the notion, the Hellenistic developments and finally the use of the concept in Christian spirituality (GSO 46/46). In that sense, what is conceived here is an analogous project to the work on sexuality, in terms of the three broad time periods covered and some of the same authors.

Parrēsia is free-speech or free-spokenness – *franc-parler*. It is a virtue or quality that not everyone has; a duty which is required in some instances; and a technique which can be attained and perfected. It is especially important for those who would direct others (GSO 42–3/43). Truth-telling is inherently risky; there will be consequences for the one that speaks this way (GSO 56/56). He goes on to describe as 'a certain way of speaking...a way of telling the truth...that lays one open to a risk by the very fact that one tells the truth' (GSO 63–4/66). There are two other crucial elements: it 'is a way of opening up the risk linked to truth-telling by constituting oneself as a kind of partner of oneself when one speaks, by binding oneself to the statement [*l'énoncé*] of the truth and to the enunciation of the truth'; and it 'is a way of binding oneself to oneself, in the statement [*l'énoncé*] of the truth, to freely bind oneself and in the form of a courageous act...the free courage by which one binds oneself in the act of telling the truth'. Summarizing, '*parrēsia* is the ethics of truth-telling as an action which is risky and free' (GSO 63–4/66). It is thus not just free-speaking, but truth-speaking, veridicity [*véridicité*], and the one who uses it is 'the truthful man [*l'homme véridique*]' (GSO 64/66). A key theme to be explored, then, is the relation between freedom and truth: not how the truth constrains freedom, but how 'the obligation of truth' is 'at the same time the exercise of freedom, and the dangerous exercise of freedom' (GSO 64/67). As such, the aim of the course is to 'undertake, the history, the genealogy, etc., of what could

be called political discourse...a history of the discourse of governmentality which would follow the thread of this dramatics of true
discourse, which would try to locate [*repérer*] some of the major
forms of the dramatics of true discourse' (GSO 66–7/69). The point
of the analysis is as a particular way of approaching the question of
'the government of self and others' (GSO 71/75).

The authors Foucault covers in this course are very wide-ranging,
and he is increasingly comfortable with this historical period. They
include Plato, Plutarch, Galien, Polybius, Thucydides, Isocrates,
Lucian and even links as far forward as *raison d'État* in the sixteenth
century (GSO 67/70). A great deal of the course is devoted to Euripides, especially *Ion*, but also *The Phoenician Women, Hippolytus* and
The Bacchae. Foucault relates this to his familiar example of Sopho-
cles' *Oedipus*, another play about 'truth-telling, of the unveiling
[*dévoilement*] of the truth, of the dramatics of truth-telling, or, if you
like, of *aléthourgia*' (GSO 78/83). Towards the end of the reading
Foucault makes use of Georges Dumézil's work in his analysis (GSO
113–6/122–5).[20] Analysing Foucault's discussion of *Ion* as a whole is
impossible here, but one key point is important. *Parrēsia* is not simply
being a citizen, and not the mere exercise of power:

> It is a form of speech [*parole*] which will exercise power in the frame-
> work of the city, but of course in non-tyrannical conditions, that is to
> say, allowing the freedom of other speeches, the freedom of those who
> also wish to be in the front rank, and who may be in the front rank
> in this sort of agonistic game typical of political life in Greece and
> especially in Athens. It is then a speech from above, but which leaves
> the freedom of other speeches, and allows freedom to those who have
> to obey, or leaves them free at least insofar as they will only obey if
> they can be persuaded. (GSO 98/104)

Later he talks of the relation of other forms of political speech: 'The
rational discourse [*discours*] enabling one to govern me and the discourse of the weak reproaching the strong for his injustice' (GSO
126/135). This becomes especially important, he suggests, in Imperial
Rome, because the discourse is now over the Empire as a whole,
rather than a single city. And the two forms reinforce each other,
because the ruler, as much as he may rely on *logos*, needs the voice
of the weaker guide who will 'if necessary have to take the risk of
turning to him and telling him what injustice he has committed' (GSO
127/136).

In *Ion* (602–3) *parrēsia* is associated with '*polei kai logo khrēsthai*'.
Foucault explains: '*Polei khrēsthai* means to take charge of the city,
to take its affairs in hand. *Logo khrēsthai* means to make use of

discourse, but of rational discourse, the discourse of truth' (GSO 144/157). Then, following Polybius, he shows how *parrēsia* is associated with *politeia*, the constitution; *isēgoria*, 'the right to speak, the statutory right to speak' (GSO 145/157); and with *dunasteia*, a term which becomes oligarchy, but at this time 'is the exercise of power, or the game through which power is actually exercised in a democracy...the formation, exercise, limitation, and also guarantee given to the ascendancy exercised by some citizens over others' (GSO 146/158).[21] Foucault suggests that while these issues of *politeia* and *dunasteria* are distinct, he is concerned with the shift made between the political and politics – *le politique* and *la politique*. *Parrēsia* 'serves as the hinge between *politeia* and *dunasteria*, between the problem of the law and the constitution, and the problem of the political game' (GSO 147/159). Around the mid-point of the course Foucault tries to schematize the relations of *parrēsia*. He talks of a 'constitutive rectangle'. This rectangle has four corners – constitutional, political game, truth and courage. The first concerns democracy, and guarantees of equality and freedom – the formal condition. The second is ascendancy or superiority – the *de facto* condition. The third is truth-telling, 'the need for a rational *logos*', the truth condition. The last is courage in the struggle, the moral condition. 'This rectangle...is what constitutes *parrēsia*' (GSO 157–8/173–4).

Foucault continually returns the theme of *parrēsia* to political concerns, or the relation of speech to the *polis*. This can be in multiple registers. Out of his reading of Plutarch, he suggests that it can be necessary, dangerous and risk powerlessness at the same time; it can function in democracy and autocratic regimes; and as well as being a public act, might be a way of speaking to an individual, to their soul – the soul of the Prince; and the emergent role of the philosopher in this practice (GSO 177–8/193–4). The third is especially interesting, because this links to the wider question of the government of souls, a question of political pedagogy (GSO 180/196; 282/306). Foucault keeps multiplying the examples, including a long discussion of Plato, both of several dialogues including a return to the *Alcibiades*, and the letters, especially Letter VII on the relation to Dionysius. He is interested, among other things, with the relation between philosophy and power (GSO 272/294), noting that Marcus Aurelius, roughly 600 years after Plato, was the 'philosopher sovereign, the philosopher emperor...a man who has to exercise power in a political unit which extends way beyond the unit of the city' (GSO 273/295–6).

Foucault's comment in an early lecture that the lectures will be 'a bit discontinuous' seems appropriate (GSO 42/42). There is much fascinating material here, but the overall project can be hard to discern. As course editor Frédéric Gros notes: 'In 1983, more than in previous years, one feels that Foucault is aware of work in progress: sometimes he feels his way, or marks time, at other times he quickly sketches and tries out syntheses. There is often the very strong impression of being present at the gestation of a line of research, and the tone is never dogmatic.'[22] The lack of a course summary does not help, since with the benefit of a couple of months' hindsight these were often revealing of what Foucault thought he had accomplished or where he wished to go, though there are a couple of places where he provides a survey of the course until that point (GSO 275–7/299–301; 312–14/340–2). Foucault also remarks about the difficulty of providing textual analysis in a lecture context, noting how hard it is to do when his audience does not have access to the texts (GSO 192 n. */209 n. *). There are later attempts to provide some material as photocopies, but plenty of logistical challenges in terms of the number of copies made in relation to audience size, and in the final lecture he reverses the analysis between the two lectures – the conclusion precedes a final textual analysis – because the copies were not ready. Passing references to Jacques Derrida and Karl Popper are somewhat throwaway or allusive (GSO 234–5/253–4).[23] In the second hour of the final lecture Foucault offers some hints of how this analysis may connect to his long-standing interest in confession, beginning a thousand-year history where 'the true transformation of the soul must take place through a rhetoric of confession [*aveu*] in a judicial setting where telling the truth about oneself and being published by someone else will lead to one's transformation from unjust to just'. However, he immediately cautions against using either Christian confession or penal practice as a lens by which to read the ancient texts: we cannot 'allow our view to be obscured by two anachronistic schemas' (GSO 332/361). This is a valuable caution: Foucault's histories are histories of the present; but the present – or more recent pasts – cannot necessarily help us to read history. This was a point made in the introduction to *Discipline and Punish* (DP 39–40/30–1). As much as possible, textually and contextually, we need to approach those arguments on their own terms. Such a position stands in some tension with the reading of Kant advanced at the beginning of the course, in which modern philosophy is understood to be an engagement with the present, rather than a reflection on the past.

While the course does relate its concerns to government, the title of the course is somewhat misleading, and the focus on *parrēsia* is the key aim. Yet, unlike 1982 in Grenoble and the 1984 Paris course this is a specifically political *parrēsia*.[24] There are even moments where the manuscript situates the very detailed textual analysis within a wider project which Foucault chooses not to deliver. Take, for example, the passage at the end of a lecture where he makes reference to the 'the history or genealogy of truth-telling in the political field' (GSO 236 n. */255 n. *). Later, towards the end of the course, he does become more specific, suggesting that we need an historical and not merely formal analysis of 'the ontology or ontologies of the discourse of truth'. Such an analysis would work in three registers, interrogating the mode of being specific to the discourse; the mode of being this discourse 'confers on the reality it talks about'; and the mode of being it imposes on 'the subject who employs it'. Foucault multiples the implications of this in a very dense passage, which is unfortunately not elaborated. He suggests that every discourse be understood as a practice, especially if it is a discourse of truth; that all truth be understood in relation to veridiction; that each ontology 'be analysed as a fiction', that 'the history of thought must always be the history of singular inventions' (GSO 285–6/309–10). These comments help to understand Foucault's notion of an historical ontology, but remain somewhat underdeveloped.[25]

Later that year, Foucault distilled the key themes of the course into the lectures he delivered at Berkeley between 10 October and 31 November as part of a seminar on 'Discourse and Truth'. These were published first as a pamphlet with the subtitle 'The Problematization of ΠΑΡΡΗΣΙΑ' and then later as the unauthorized book *Fearless Speech*.[26] While that was a valuable source of Foucault's ideas on his last major topic, it has now largely been superseded by the publication of the last two Paris courses. The first half is a summary of the 1983 course, there is a reading of *parrēsia* in Aristotle which is new, and in the last lectures he introduces themes that would find their fullest expression in Paris in 1984, notably concerning Plato's *Laches*, Diogenes and other Cynics. The final lecture is a synthesis of his work on techniques of the self more generally, touching on *askēsis*, Seneca's *De Ira* and *De tranquillate animi*.

Alongside this course at Berkeley, Foucault also ran a smaller informal weekly group which met at Paul Rabinow's house close to campus. Participants included Dario Biocca, Arturo Escobar, Keith Gandal, Kent Gerard, David Horn, Stephen Kotkin, Cathy Kudlick, David Levin, Mark Maslan, and Jonathan Simon.[27] Others, such as Jerry Wakefield, spent time with Foucault but outside the organized group. For future work they settled on the topic of the early twentieth century, tracing governmental mechanisms in the First World War and interwar period.[28] Due to Foucault's death the next year this never came to fruition, but Keith Gandal's project outline on 'New

Arts of Government in the Great War and Post-War Period' seeks to
continue that work, studying how mechanisms of wartime governance continued into peacetime. The proposal puts forward the idea
of 'waging' peace, suggesting that 'peace became a new object for
government', having become recognized as a problem during the
Great War.[29] The idea was that this would discuss the USA, USSR,
Italy and France. It seems that at Berkeley Foucault had found the
interdisciplinary, collaborative environment he had been seeking for
so long, though he did not live to begin his own work. Nonetheless,
Gandal, Kotkin and Horn all published books which develop the
project, each of which acknowledge Foucault's inspiration.[30] The
intended focus closely relates to themes of the *'Society Must Be
Defended'* course, and while that work continued in the late 1970s
lectures on governmentality, plans were underway for a return to
Berkeley in 1984 for a seminar on governmentality. This would have
focused on the seventeenth century and early twentieth century, especially the 1920s, and Rabinow recalls the key question being 'was
there a socialist form of governmentality?'[31] Equally, at the Collège
de France his research was returning to the questions of law and
punishment. Gandal says Foucault and his colleagues there were
planning projects on '"the anthropology of punishment": one concerning "recent changes... in social thresholds of tolerance in regards
to criminality and the severity of penal practice" (or the social factors
that determine "fluctuations in the need to punish"), and another
considering "the relations between medical and psychiatric knowledge and penal justice" and "how to adjust today's penal institutions
and medical practice"'.[32]

The Courage of Truth

At the beginning of his final course, which begins three weeks late
due to illness, Foucault remarks that he wants to discuss some matters
in order to bring to an end 'this several years long Greco-Latin "trip"'
and then return to some more 'contemporary problems' (CT 3/2). It
initially appears as if he is restating themes from the previous year,
though through an analysis of some different texts, especially Plato's
Apology, *Phaedo* and *Laches*, and some texts from the Cynics. He
suggests that his overall project – 'the ancient history of practices of
telling the truth about oneself' (CT 9/8) – had been somewhat dis-
tracted before by an insistence on the political, but this now comes
to the fore and is a major theme of this course. The political emphasis

in 1983 had, he suggests, allowed the analysis to be a contribution
not just to work on the subject and truth, but also the role relations
of power play in that question. These three themes – truth, power,
subject – as reconceived, dominate Foucault's work. Repeating claims
from the previous course, he suggests that 'connecting together modes
of veridiction, techniques of governmentality, and practices of the self
is basically what I have always been trying to do' (CT 10/8; see GSO
42/42).[33]

He notes that he has seen that the importance of the other person
in a truth-telling relationship, 'the other person who listens and
enjoins one to speak, and who speaks himself' emerges much earlier
than 'the institutionalization of the confession at the start of the
thirteenth century, [than] the organization and installation of a pastoral power with the Roman church' (CT 6/5). While there are some
important indications of how this work would have been developed
in relation to medieval Christianity (CT 28–9/29), and the final hour
of the last lecture begins to discuss Judaism, the New Testament and
the Church Fathers (CT 296–309/325–38), the focus of the course is
on the Greeks. Foucault notes that there are 'four major modalities
of truth-telling in Greek culture (the truth-telling of prophecy, wisdom,
tekhnē, and *parrēsia*)' (CT 63–4/67). While his emphasis here is on
the last, elements of the others can be found in previous courses,
tracking as far back as *Lectures on the Will to Know*. There are many
remarkable readings in this course of which space precludes more
than a cursory examination.

In his reading of Plato's *Apology* and *Phaedo*, and especially
Socrates' final words telling Crito to sacrifice a cock to Asclepius to
pay a debt, Foucault makes use of an essay by Georges Dumézil.[34]
The traditional understanding is that because Asclepius is the god
who cures, the debt paid is because Socrates has been cured of something in dying, which many interpretations, including that of
Nietzsche, suggest is his life. His soul has been rid of its mortal body.
This has been the dominant reading for more than two thousand
years, although it has some problems, as Nietzsche recognized,
because it does not fit with Socrates' life as it was lived. Various
attempts to explain this have been proposed, but Foucault is persuaded by Dumézil's suggestion. This is that the cure, which Crito
must repay, is for the disease of which he was cured in discussion
with Socrates, namely the common opinion, 'to choose, resolve, and
make up his mind through opinion founded on the relation of self to
truth' (CT 96/105). The debt though is shared: 'we owe a cock to
Asclepius'.[35] Socrates, along with his followers, including Crito, has
been cured by the use of *parrēsia*, 'a truth-telling whose final objective

and constant concern was to teach men to take care of themselves' (CT 102/110). Foucault's reading – and of course Dumézil's, which is in the form of a fictional dialogue, and one which juxtaposes the reading of Plato with one of Nostradamus – is much more complicated than this. Nonetheless this insistence on the care of others, not in a simple political sense, but as a preparatory measure for their own care of the self, is a key theme in Foucault's reading of Plato. And Foucault thinks it is therapeutic for him too: 'As a philosophy professor one really must have lectured at least once in one's life on Socrates and the death of Socrates. It's done. *Salvate animam meam*' (CT 143/153).

Foucault is also making gestures towards the need for collaborative work or a seminar to take some of these ideas forward (CT 30 n. */30–31 n. *). He equally suggests that he is throwing out ideas for others to develop: 'I am not able at present to lecture to you properly on this theme of the true life; maybe it will happen one day, maybe never. I would like merely to give you just some sketches and outlines. Anyone interested in this problem can study it more closely' (CT 151/163). His discussion of the four themes of the cynic life – 'the unconcealed life, the independent life, the straight life, and the sovereign life, master of itself' (CT 231/251) – opens up a range of questions in terms of how this links to the wider project of technologies of the self. He equally raises the project of 'a book on cynicism as a moral category in Western culture', and asks his auditors how they would go about it if they were able to work as a group (CT 163/177). The project might 'conceive of the history of Cynicism, not, once again, as a doctrine, but much more as an attitude and way of being' (CT 164/178). He raises various works which have been written on the idea, including ones he has read and feels able to comment upon, and the very recent publication of Peter Sloterdijk's *Critique of Cynical Reason*, which he has not read but which he has 'been given some, let's say, divergent views on the book's interest' (CT 165/179).[36]

In the two hours of the final lecture, Foucault tries to bring things together. He discusses *parrēsia* in relation to the Cynics, but also wants to explain 'the evolution of the term *parrēsia* in Christian authors of the first centuries' (CT 281/307; see 177/191–2). Such a promise is only fulfilled in part. He says later in that lecture:

> Maybe I will try to explain these themes a little next year – but I cannot guarantee it, I confess that I still don't know and have not yet decided. Maybe I will try to pursue this history of the arts of living, of

philosophy as a form of life, of asceticism in its relation to the truth, precisely, after ancient philosophy, in Christianity. (CT 290/316)

He goes on to suggest that the analysis of 'the change from pagan asceticism to Christian asceticism', which he is sketching here, 'may have to be completely reworked, re-examined from every angle, and begun again quite differently' (CT 290/316–17). This is not a comment about the transition between Volume III and the unpublished Volume IV of the *History of Sexuality*, but about this parallel project on techniques of the self, which had been the common thread to the last three courses in Paris. Less than three months after speaking these words Foucault was dead. It was his last lecture and the last public event of which there is a record.[37] His final words are 'I had things to say to you about the general framework of these analyses. But, well, it is too late. So, thank you' (CT 309/338). This is a reference to the end of the lecture and the time on the clock, but as Defert has noted, it now has another implication (C 64/81).[38]

Life, Work, Interrupted

Foucault's career breaks off with largely completed projects unpublished, and his final courses and late interviews provide multiple indications of future directions.[39] Between 1974 and 1984 Foucault published four authored, one co-authored and two edited books: *Discipline and Punish*, three volumes of the *History of Sexuality*, *Le désordre des familles*, *Politiques de l'habitat*, and *Herculine Barbin*. This is an impressive portfolio by any standards, but he wrote and spoke on a far greater range of concerns, and what was published went through multiple transformations. Since his death we have gained the riches of *Dits et écrits*; thirteen Paris lecture courses, of which nine come from the last decade; courses and lectures at Berkeley, Louvain, Vermont and elsewhere; and a myriad of other texts and pieces of evidence. All of these provide a much more detailed and nuanced account of his intellectual projects, which I have tried to do justice to here.

In particular, in the light of these materials it is now much clearer how Foucault's long-standing interest in the question of confession remains a recurrent and important theme throughout his work of this period. Confession was a theme in the 1971–2 course *Théories et institutions pénales*, was significant in the use of psychiatric expertise in criminal cases, through to his emerging interest in Christian practices, traced back from the early modern period through the Middle Ages to the early Church Fathers. This concern with confession shifts, along with Foucault's major theoretical interests, from a mechanism of power and its relation to knowledge to an intersection between the production of truth and subjectivity.

The history of subjectivity, or a genealogy of the subject, is perhaps Foucault's major concern in this decade. He frequently invokes this description of his work, sometimes clarifying it as a question of the relation between the subject and truth. Rather than the older reading that the subject 'returns' in Foucault's late work, we are now clearly able to see that Foucault tried to work out how to circumvent the problem of the subject through its historical interrogation. This is both the individual subject and the collective one of population, and Foucault's interest in the question of government, or governmentality, is one of the means by which he pursues this theme. Even the work on neoliberalism is in part an attempt to track the emergence of *Homo oeconomicus*. The work on government runs from at least '*Society Must Be Defended*' through *Security, Territory, Population* and *The Birth of Biopolitics* to *On the Government of the Living*, but also extends through to his final two courses, under the title of *The Government of Self and Others*. As he said in 1981, the project of governmentality should be understood as interrogating 'the government of the self by oneself in its articulation with relations with others' (SV 300; EW I, 88). Recall too the suggestion in *The Hermeneutic of the Subject* course that '"Governing", "being governed", and "taking care of the self" form a sequence, a series' (HSu 44/45), which he intends to trace from antiquity to the emergence of pastoral power in the third and fourth centuries of our present era. On that reading, it is clear that the work on governmentality of the mid–late 1970s was in no sense an abandonment of Foucault's overarching project, but a very productive new approach to it, which was generative of future interests and approaches.

This is not to say that there is no material discussed in these lectures that might appear tangential to his dominant concerns, nor to argue that he is entirely clear about where he is going or what he is trying to do. The long-standing struggle to write a book on Christianity – the announced second volume of the 1976 plan, through to a reconfigured subject matter in the early 1980s, to the projected third volume of early 1983, and the fourth volume of the final 1984 plan – is testament to the challenges he faced in interrogating this material. In addition there are several moments where he talks about his difficulties in reconciling what appear to be two conflicting projects in the last volumes of the *History of Sexuality* – a study of sexual behaviour in antiquity and the question of techniques of the self. The collision of those two projects occurs most clearly in *The Care of the Self* – a title originally given to a planned book outside the sexuality series, comprising different material, but which becomes a title of a book in the series, and which bears some traces of the alternative, parallel project.

Another major thread of continuity is Foucault's enthusiasm for collaborative work. His political activism generally took a collaborative form – not just in the *Groupe d'information sur les prisons* but also in groups on health and asylums, which will be analysed in *Foucault: The Birth of Power*. His involvement with the French branch of Solidarity and countless appeals, petitions and press conferences on a range of concerns continued until his death. His earliest seminars at the Collège de France led to the *I, Pierre Rivière* collection and, as Chapter 1 showed, colleagues like Jean-Pierre Peter did archival work which Foucault utilized in later courses. His involvement with CERFI led in time to the *Généalogie des équipements de normalisation*, *Politiques de l'habitat*, and *Les machines à guérir* volumes. To complete the long-planned work on the *lettres de cachet* he collaborated with Arlette Farge. His time at Louvain in 1981, Vermont in 1982 and above all at Berkeley throughout this period led to planned and posthumous collaborative volumes. The Berkeley project on 'New Arts of Government in the Great War and Post-War Period' would have been one of the ways he hoped to explore the question of a governmentality of socialism. This was a topic that seems to have particularly motivated his interest: it was something he was also discussing with colleagues in Paris late in his life.

Above all, though, this was a decade where he was working on the *History of Sexuality* project. Initially begun back in 1974, though with traces from at least a decade earlier, this was something that he worked on right until his death. It goes through a number of crucial transformations, which I have tried to track in detail here. Many promised volumes were part-drafted, trialled in lecture courses, abandoned, and at least part-destroyed. As the project takes on its historical, as opposed to the earlier thematic, form in the early 1980s Foucault begins to publish excerpts in books and journals, but the reorganization of material continued. Only in the last months of his life did he finally publish additional volumes of the series of which the first volume had appeared in late 1976.

Those two volumes, his last published books, *The Use of Pleasures* and *The Care of the Self*, were once seemingly disconnected from his previous concerns. Now they can be seen in the context of a developing set of interests and questions, tracked through shorter publications and his lectures. As Chapter 7 showed, the final form the books took was fixed very late in the process. We are in a privileged position with these books, because successive drafts of the material still exist in the archive. With the exception of a very early form of *The Archaeology of Knowledge*, given by Foucault to Defert to read,[40] Foucault destroyed the preliminary material of his other books. With *The Use of Pleasures* and *The Care of the Self* it seems he did not have a chance to discard the manuscripts. As analysed in Chapter 7, in four large box files archived at the Bibliothèque Nationale there are multiple drafts of the chapters within these volumes. The first box includes several drafts of the introduction and opening chapter, dating back to a period when the two volumes were conceived as one single text on antiquity, and then move through successive drafts of the remaining chapters.

Foucault wrote his manuscripts by hand, and so each new draft was begun again: a laborious process that polished and tightened the prose expression as well as the structural arrangement. At certain points Foucault gave the texts to Collège de France typists, who presented him with a version he would again rework. Occasionally they marked up the manuscript with question marks for illegible words – something with which I have much sympathy. Foucault would take these typewritten texts and write over them, sometimes cutting the page into pieces and pasting sections onto new sheets, writing linking passages before again handing these to typists to produce the next version. Unlike modern word-processing, we can see the material nature of the texts and the physical traces of their development and transformation. Foucault's well-known 1971 description of genealogy as operating 'on a field of entangled and confused parchments that have been scratched over and rewritten many times' applies as much to his own writing as his sources. I have tried in my work here to follow his injunction that the approach to such material must be 'grey, meticulous and patiently documentary' (DE#84 II, 136; EW II, 369).

The privileged insight the manuscripts give into his working practices has until recently been available only to archival researchers – at the Bibliothèque Nationale, the Bancroft Library at Berkeley and IMEC. Now though we have facsimile editions of some early manuscripts, lectures and preparatory reading notes.[41] But to date the most important insights into his thought processes and working practices beyond the publications of his lifetime have come from his lecture courses, principally but not exclusively those delivered at the Collège de France. In terms of tracking his preoccupations, the courses offer a privileged view, but they in no way stand in place of missing works. They are not books by Foucault, but the record of thought in process. Some of the projects he indicated for potential futures are, in his words, 'overviews [*survols*]; they are notes for possible work' (CT 174/189). Foucault has given many suggestions for how such work might be done, both in content and approach.

It is important to recognize that while he continually reworked and rethought earlier formulations, he did not move through clearly demarcated stages, and tended to supplement, rather than replace, earlier methodological developments. Just as archaeology is not replaced by genealogy, but complemented by it, so too with his work on power and discipline in relation to truth and subjectivity. As he notes in a very late interview: 'Power is not discipline; discipline is a possible procedure of power.' He nonetheless recognizes that his own analyses have been limited, specific and non-totalizing: 'Consequently these analyses can in no way, to my mind, be equated with a general analytics of every possible power relation.'[42] We would do well to remember that when discussing, criticizing, and, perhaps most productively, using Foucault.

The nature of this documentary evidence also gives cause for caution. The way we understand Foucault's work has radically transformed in the more than thirty years since his death. There is no reason to suppose that what remains to be published will diminish those insights anytime soon. As such, it would be unwise to pretend this book is more than an interim account. The Bibliothèque Nationale has, as yet, only made a limited amount of the 37,000 pages of materials sold to them by Defert available to researchers.[43] Before being sold, some of these pages were made available to the editors of the Collège de France lectures, whose work has been invaluable to mine here. It will take some time before the entirety of this material is catalogued, made fully available to researchers, perhaps published, and analysed. Beyond the Collège de France courses, whose publication was completed in mid 2015, a series of volumes by Foucault, entitled Philosophie du présent and including unpublished material, is in process with Vrin. So far the volumes have largely been editions of lectures that were either available in English or in unauthorized French versions (OHS, QC): the next volume will be a critical edition of the 1983 Berkeley lectures on *parrēsia*. Yet other material exists in either recorded or written form in accessible archives, and much of the Bibliothèque Nationale material, including the manuscript of the fourth volume of the *History of Sexuality*, is being held back for possible publication.

The nature of those future publications may add further nuance and detail to the picture established here. No account can, at this stage, be definitive, and future research will doubtless be undertaken. It is to be hoped that this study will prove beneficial to that work. In the light of the available material, especially the insights given by the Collège de France courses, this book has provided an overview and synthetic account of the concerns, projects and outputs of Foucault's last decade.

Notes

Abbreviations

1 See Richard A. Lynch, 'Michel Foucault's Shorter Works in English', in Christopher Falzon, Timothy O'Leary and Jana Sawicki (eds.), *A Companion to Foucault*, Oxford: Blackwell, 2013, pp. 562–92.
2 See Alain Beaulieu, 'The Foucault Archives at Berkeley', *Foucault Studies*, 10, 2010: 144–54.

Introduction

1 Interview with Daniel Defert, 25 March 1990, cited in James Miller, *The Passion of Michel Foucault*, London: HarperCollins, 1993, pp. 240–1.
2 Claude Mauriac, *Le temps accompli*, Paris: Grasset, 1991, p. 43, recounts how Daniel Defert showed him this letter one month after Foucault's death, and that he was opposed to what Max Brod did for Franz Kafka.
3 Plans for this were underway at least as early as 1986. See Pierre Nora, 'Il avait un besoin formidable d'être aimé', *L'Evénement de jeudi*, 18–24 September 1986, p. 83. Defert says he and Foucault had discussed it even before his death: Florian Bardou, 'Daniel Defert: Michel Foucault n'a jamais cessé d'être present', http://yagg.com/2014/06/23/daniel-defert-michel-foucault-na-jamais-cesse-detre-present/
4 On the edition, see Daniel Defert, 'Je crois au temps...', *Review Recto/Verso*, 1, 2007: 1–7.
5 See Stuart Elden, 'Toolkit: The Uncollected Foucault', *Foucault Studies*, 20, 2015.

6 The lack of a full English translation is unfortunate. The 3-volume *Essential Works* collection picks only a selection of texts, many of which had been translated before in other collections, and discards the chronological presentation for a thematic one.

7 *Théories et institutions pénales: Cours au Collège de France (1971–1972)*, ed. Bernard E. Harcourt, Paris: Gallimard/Seuil, 2015.

8 Gérard Petitjean, 'Les Grands Prêtres de l'université française', *Le nouvel observateur*, 7 April 1975: 52–7.

9 Petitjean, 'Les Grands Prêtres de l'université française', p. 55.

10 See Stuart Elden, *Speaking Against Number: Heidegger, Language and the Politics of Calculation*, Edinburgh: Edinburgh University Press, 2006. While there is much discussion of the lecture courses, perhaps the best account of them as a whole is Guillaume Bellon, *Une parole inquiète: Barthes et Foucault au Collège de France*, Grenoble: Ellug, 2012.

11 Cited in Nora, 'Il avait un besoin formidable d'être aimé', p. 83.

12 Accordingly, there are references to secondary literature when they help with information or support points, but not simply to note discussions or developments of Foucault's ideas. Major works I have found helpful include Hubert L. Dreyfus and Paul Rabinow, *Michel Foucault: Beyond Structuralism and Hermeneutics*, Chicago: University of Chicago Press, 2nd edn, 1983; Gilles Deleuze, *Foucault*, Paris: Minuit, 1986, trans. Séan Hand as *Foucault*, London: Athlone, 1988 (hereafter French and English are cited separated by /); Clare O'Farrell, *Michel Foucault*, London: Sage, 2005; Mark Kelly, *The Political Philosophy of Michel Foucault*, London: Routledge, 2008; Colin Koopman, *Genealogy as Critique: Foucault and the Problems of Modernity*, Bloomington: Indiana University Press, 2013. I have previously treated more thematic and theoretical concerns in *Mapping the Present: Heidegger, Foucault and the Project of a Spatial History*, London: Continuum, 2001.

13 My inspiration here is Theodore Kisiel's *The Genesis of Heidegger's Being and Time*, Berkeley: University of California Press, 1993, which traces how and why Heidegger came to write *Being and Time* in the way he did, and why he left it unfinished.

14 Stuart Elden, *Foucault: The Birth of Power*, Cambridge: Polity, forthcoming 2017.

15 *Leçons sur la volonté de savoir: Cours au Collège de France, 1970–1971*, suivi de *Le savoir d'Œdipe*, ed. Daniel Defert, Paris: Gallimard/Seuil, 2011; trans. Graham Burchell as *Lectures on the Will to Know: Lectures at the Collège de France 1970–1*, London: Palgrave Macmillan, 2013; *Théories et institutions pénales*; SP.

1 Pervert, Hysteric, Child

1 'Condamnation à mort d'un aliéné homicide', *Annales d'hygiène publique et de médecine légale*, 1 (15), 1836: 128–205.

2 *Moi, Pierre Rivière, ayant égorgé ma mère, ma sœur et mon frère: Un cas de parricide au XIXe siècle*, Paris: Gallimard, 1973. For a much fuller account, see *Foucault: The Birth of Power*.

3 Jean-Pierre Peter, 'Le Corps du délit', *Nouvelle revue de psychoanalyse*, 3, 1971: 71–108; 'Ogres d'archives: Textes presents par Jean-Pierre Peter', *Nouvelle revue de psychoanalyse*, 6, 1972: 249–67.

4 Peter, 'Le Corps du délit', pp. 103, 106, 107.

5 Peter, 'Le Corps du délit', pp. 104, 105.

6 Peter, 'Le Corps du délit', p. 104.

7 He also mentions the latter two in the foreword to *Moi, Pierre Rivière*, p. 14.

8 Peter, 'Le Corps du délit', p. 91.

9 Respectively, 'Ogres d'archives', pp. 249–50, pp. 251–58 and pp. 259–67.

10 'Examen médico-légal d'un cas extraordinaire d'infanticide', *Annales d'hygiène publique et de médecine légale*, 8 (1), 1832: 397–411; reprinted in C. C. H. Marc, *De la folie*, Paris: J.-B. Baillière, 2 vols., 1840, vol. II, pp. 130–46. This is a translation of a text that first appeared in Johann Heinrich Kopp, *Jahrbuch der Staatsartzneikunde*, vol. IX, Frankfurt, Hermann, 1817.

11 Étienne-Jean Georget, *Examen médical des procès criminels des nommés Léger, Feldtmann, Lecouffe, Jean-Pierre et Papavoine*...Paris: Migneret, 1825, pp. 2–16.

12 Alfred Jarry, *Ubu Roi*, Paris: Fasquelle Editeurs, 1921.

13 A fuller discussion can be found in *Foucault: The Birth of Power*.

14 See also his 1973 comments on the inquiry as 'a process of government, a technique of administration, a modality of management...a specific manner of exercising power' (DE#139 III, 584; EW III, 48).

15 Peter, 'Ogres d'archives', pp. 251–58.

16 It is unfortunate that Foucault and his seminar colleagues did not present this case as they had that of Pierre Rivière. The documents he used are summarized in Marc, *De la folie*, vol. II, pp. 71–116. For additional references, see A 125 n. 4/135 n. 4.

17 Many of the points made in this course are developed in much more detail in Jacques Donzelot, *La Police des familles*, Paris: Les Éditions de Minuit, 2005 [1977].

18 Foucault makes use of the analysis in Michel de Certeau, *La Possession de Loudun*, Paris: Gallimard/Juillard, 1970.

19 This can be compared to the discussion of Pasteur's insight into the spread of contagion in the hospital.

20 Arnold I. Davidson, p. xx.

21 See DP 326–7/279–80 and the bulk of the analysis in SP.

22 See Lagrange, pp. 256 n. 14/257 n. 14. Of course, as discussed earlier, Foucault frequently examines crimes *against* children (i.e. A 94–7/102–4, 101–25/109–34).

23 Henrico [Heinrich] Kaan, *Psychopathia sexualis*, Lipsiae: Leopoldum Voss, 1844.

24 Foucault seems to find Charles Jouy's name amusing: the surname sounds like the word 'come'.

25 On the influence of Canguilhem, see Dominique Lecourt, *Marxism and Epistemology: Bachelard, Canguilhem, Foucault*, trans. Ben Brewster, London: NLB, 1975; Gary Gutting, *Michel Foucault's Archaeology of Scientific Reason*, Cambridge: Cambridge University Press, 1994; Pierre Macherey, *De Canguilhem à Foucault la force des norms*, Paris: La Fabrique, 2009.

26 Georges Canguilhem, *Le Normal et le pathologique*, Paris: PUF, 1966, p. 180; *On the Normal and the Pathological*, trans. Carolyn R. Fawcett, New York: Zone Books, 1989, p. 243.

27 A similar argument regarding race is made in SMBD 52–3/61–2, 231–2/259–60.

2   The War of Races and Population

1 See also DE#195, III, 206; P/K 164; DE#200, III, 268; PPC 123; Thierry Voeltzel, *Vingt ans et après*, Paris: Verticales, 2014 [1978], p. 149.

2 'Entretien inédit entre Michel Foucault et quatre militants de la LCR, membres de la rubrique culturelle du journal quotidien Rouge (July 1977)', *Question Marx?* 2014.

3 Foucault says second book, but this is not the second volume as understood in English, because of a different division of material. He means Part II of Vol. I.

4 Interview with Daniel Defert, 12 April 2015.

5 See the discussion of these questions by geographers in *Hérodote*, 6, 1977: 12–23; translated in SKP, along with some contemporary responses from Anglophone geographers.

6 See Ann Laura Stoler, *Race and the Education of Desire: Foucault's History of Sexuality and the Colonial Order of Things*, Durham: Duke University Press, 1995, p. 62.

7 The spelling given is 'Boulainvilliers', though as Renée Simon notes, Boulainviller is actually correct. See 'Avertissement', in Henry de Boulainviller, *Oeuvres Philosophiques*, La Haye: Martinus Nijhoff, 1973.

8 Alessandro Fontana and Mauro Bertrani, SMBD 257/284–5.

9 Thomas Hobbes, *Leviathan*, in *The Collected English Works of Thomas Hobbes*, collected and ed. Sir William Molesworth, London: Routledge/ Thoemmes Press, 1997, vol. III, parts I–II, ch. 17.

10 W. S. Churchill, *Divi Britannici*, 1675, fol. 189–190, quoted in SMBD 91/105.

11 See Richard T. Vann, 'The Free Anglo-Saxons: A Historical Myth', *Journal of the History of Ideas*, 19 (2), April 1958: 259–72.

12 Simon, 'Introduction', in Boulainviller, *Oeuvres Philosophiques*, p. ix. On Boulainviller generally, see Renée Simon, *Henry de Boulainviller:*

Historien, Politique, Philosophe, Astrologue 1658–1722, Paris: Boivie & Cie, n.d.

13 Foucault cites Robert Desnos, 'Description d'une révolte prochaine', *La Révolution surréaliste*, 3, 15 April 1925: 25 to support this (SMBD 190 n. 9/213 n. 9).

14 Emmanuel Sieyès, *Qu'est-ce que le tiers état?* Paris: Société de l'histoire de la Révolution Française, 1888 [1789], p. 27.

15 See Sieyès, *Qu'est-ce que le tiers état?* p. 67: 'The nation exists prior to everything; it is the origin of everything. Its will is always legal, it is the law itself.'

16 Quoted in J. H. Clapham, *The Abbé Sieyès*, Westminster: 1912, p. 199.

17 See DE#192, III 153; EW III, 125; DE#297, IV 193; SKP 161.

18 The literature on the development of statistics and accounting and their political implications is extensive. See, for example, Ian Hacking, *The Emergence of Probability: A Philosophical Study of Early Ideas about Probability, Induction and Statistical Inference*, Cambridge: Cambridge University Press, 1975, and *The Taming of Chance*, Cambridge: Cambridge University Press, 1990, and Theodore Porter, *Trust in Numbers: The Pursuit of Objectivity in Science and Public Life*, Princeton: Princeton University Press, 1996.

19 Alessandro Fontana and Mauro Bertrani, SMBD 251–2/278–9.

20 See Stoler, *Race and the Education of Desire*, p. 87.

3 The Will to Know and the Power of Confession

1 Interview with Daniel Defert on 25 March 1990, cited in Miller, *The Passion of Michel Foucault*, pp. 240–1.

2 Miller, *The Passion of Michel Foucault*, p. 241.

3 The early drafting of the final chapter is perhaps the reason for Stoler's suggestion that Foucault returned to the book's themes in the course; rather than the accurate chronology that the course delivery preceded both the final manuscript and its publication. See *Race and the Education of Desire*, pp. x, xi.

4 Cited in Didier Eribon, *Michel Foucault*, Paris: Flammarion, 3d edn, 2011, p. 428; *Michel Foucault*, trans. Betsy Wing, London: Faber, 1991, p. 270 (hereafter French and English are cited separated by /).

5 See Eribon, *Michel Foucault*, p. 503/311; Keith Gandal and Stephen Kotkin, 'Foucault in Berkeley', *History of the Present*,1, 1985: 6, 15.

6 There is no known French version of this text and the archival traces are incomplete. The published lecture is the Columbia version, now alongside other papers delivered at the event as 'We are Not Repressed' in *Schizo-Culture: The Event 1975*, eds. Sylvère Lotringer and David Morris, Los Angeles: Semiotext(e), 2013, pp. 144–60. The lecture was delivered in English with Foucault in attendance. The typescript is available as 'Michel Foucault on Infantile Sexuality', Sylvère Lotringer Papers

and Semiotext(e) Archive, Fales Library and Special Collections, New York University, MS 211, Series III, Box 24, Folder 19. Two pages were lost and retyped (pp. 21–22). The version in the Berkeley archive is a translation and part summary of the Berkeley lecture, where it is marked as 'transcription and summary by Jacques Favaux; translation by John Leavitt' (BANC 90/136z 1:8, p. 23). Only selections from the penultimate part of the lecture, and only a summary by Favaux of the last pages, are included. The differences between Berkeley and New York are negligible – one translator note is cut; another is typed and crossed out. I am grateful to Sylvère Lotringer for a discussion of how the text came to be published, against Foucault's wishes (personal correspondence, 10 May 2015). The Brazil lectures are BANC CD 964, 967–70.

7   On its contemporary reception, see Jean-François Bert (ed.), *La Volonté de savoir de Michel Foucault: Regards Critiques 1976–1979*, Caen: Presses Universitaires de Caen/IMEC, 2013.

8   Steven Marcus, *The Other Victorians: A Study of Sexuality and Pornography in Mid-Nineteenth-Century England*, New York: Basic Books, 1966.

9   In an interview from around this time, Foucault recognizes that repression was implicitly used in *History of Madness*, and took some time for him to free himself from it (DE#192 III, 148–9; P/K 118–19).

10 Jos van Ussel, *Histoire de la répression sexuelle*, Paris: Laffont, 1972. Foucault mistakenly references him as 'van Hussel'.

11 Anonymous, *My Secret Life*, Grove Press, 2 vols., 1964 [1890].

12 Marcus, *The Other Victorians*, pp. 97, 77; discussed in detail in chs. 3 and 4.

13 For *dispositif*, Hurley has 'layout' here. Foucault deepens his example of schools, and then adds in medicine as another example of 'discourses on sex' (HS I 42–3/30–1).

14 See DE#216 III, 411–12 where there are some brief thoughts on confession in Buddhism and other non-Western traditions.

15 Jacques Ruffié, *De la biologie à la culture*, Paris: Flammarion, 2 vols., 1976.

16 Stoler makes a similar point, see *Race and the Education of Desire*, pp. 91–2.

17 For a helpful clarification of the relation between desire and pleasure, see 'Le gay savoir' in Jean le Bitoux, *Entretiens sur la question gay*, Béziers: H&O, 2005, pp. 45–72.

18 Frank Mort and Roy Peters, 'Foucault Recalled: Interview with Michel Foucault', *New Formations*, pp. 9–22, p. 12.

19 Macey, *Michel Foucault*, p. 116.

20 See Macey, *The Lives of Michel Foucault*, p. 353.

21 Eribon, *Michel Foucault*, pp. 437/274–5.

22 Marchetti and Salomoni, A 317 n. */334 n. *.

23 Interview with Defert, 12 April 2015.

24 Marchetti and Salomoni, A 317/333.

25 Marchetti and Salomoni, A 322/338.

26 Marchetti and Salomoni, A 322/338.
27 Marchetti and Salomoni, A 320–2/336–8
28 Marchetti and Salomoni, A 324/339.
29 Marchetti and Salomoni, A 325/340.
30 The version in DE (#287) is of the later French version, which includes a few extra sentences with some other variants noted.
31 Mort and Peters, 'Foucault Recalled', p. 12.
32 Miller, *The Passion of Michel Foucault*, p. 6. Miller does not recall who told him this (personal correspondence, 12 February 2015).
33 Arnold I. Davidson, *The Emergence of Sexuality: Historical Epistemology and the Formation of Concepts*, Cambridge: Harvard University Press, 2002, p. 57, see p. 218.
34 This is a passage missing from the course summary reprint in the lecture course SMBD.
35 Michel Foucault and Jonathan Simon, discussion 27 October 1983, BANC CD 961.
36 'La vie des hommes infâmes', *Les cahiers du chemin*, 29, 15 January 1977: 12–29, p. 12 n. 1. This note is removed from the reproduction of the text in DE#198 III, 237–53, which has an editorial note that describes how the project changed over time. See also Collectif Maurice Florence, 'La vie poursuivie', in *Archives de l'infamie*, Paris: Les Praries ordinaires, 2009, pp. 34–37.
37 Collectif Maurice Florence, 'La vie poursuivie', p. 45 n. 13.
38 *Le Cercle amoreux d'Henry Legrand*, eds. Jean-Paul and Paul-Ursin Dumont, Paris: Gallimard, 1979.
39 Both the Vincennes course and work with the Groupe Information Santé are discussed in *Foucault: The Birth of Power*.
40 Marchetti and Salomoni, A 317/334.
41 Marchetti and Salomoni, A 319/335–6.
42 Paul Veyne, *Foucault: Sa pensée, sa personne*, Paris: Albin Michel, 2008, pp. 56–7; *Foucault: His Thought, His Character*, trans. Janet Lloyd, Cambridge: Polity, 2010, p. 33 (hereafter French and English are cited separated by /).
43 And yet, some people close to Foucault did perceive something of a crisis. See, for example Gilles Deleuze, *Pourparlers 1972–1990*, Paris: Les Éditions de Minuit, 1986, p. 115; *Negotiations 1972–1990*, trans. Martin Joughlin, New York: Columbia University Press, 1995, p. 83 (and see pp. 143/105, 147–8/108–9); *Foucault*, p. 101/94; and Claude Mauriac, *L'oncel Marcel: Le temps immobile 10*, Paris: Bernard Grasset, 1988, pp./ 221–2.
44 Macey, *Michel Foucault*, pp. 132–3; *The Lives of Michel Foucault*, pp. 423–4. See Nora, 'Il avait un besoin formidable d'être aimé', p. 82.
45 Eribon, *Michel Foucault*, pp. 468–70/292–3.
46 James Bernauer recounts a conversation with Foucault in March 1980 where he said that the topic of confession was suggested to him as an object of inquiry by Ivan Illich. Cited in Bernauer, 'Michel Foucault's Ecstatic Thinking', eds. James Bernauer and David Rasmussen, *The*

Final Foucault, Cambridge: MIT Press, 1987, p. 48. Bernauer says the remark was only made in passing and not followed up (personal correspondence, 3 May 2015).

47 In the Protestant tradition these would be the seventh and tenth commandments. On the Inquisition, see particularly A 198–9/213–14.
48 All these themes are discussed in *Foucault: The Birth of Power*.
49 Veyne, *Foucault*, p. 56/33.
50 Some words or clauses from this crucial passage are omitted in the Hurley translation.
51 Oscar D. Watkins, *A History of Penance*, London: Longman, 2 vols., 1961, Vol. II, p. 748.
52 The Latin text ('Concilium Lateranense IV', XXI) appears in Watkins, *A History of Penance*, pp. 733–4; and in Mary Flowers Braswell, *The Medieval Sinner: Characterization and Confession in the Literature of the English Middle Ages*, East Brunswick: Associated University Presses, 1983, p. 26. Watkins (pp. 748–9) and Braswell (p. 26) both provide translations, which I have followed in places.
53 Tambling, *Confession*, p. 38.
54 See *Canons and Decrees of the Council of Trent*, trans. Rev. H. J. Schroeder, Rockford: Tan, 1978, pp. 92–4.
55 *Catechism of the Council of Trent for Parish Priests, Issued by Order of Pope Pius V*, trans. John A. McHugh and Charles J. Callan, Rockford: Tan, 1982.
56 Matthew, xvi, 19.
57 Haliczer, *Sexuality in the Confessional*, p. 21.
58 Claude Mauriac, *Signes, rencontres et rendez-vous: Le temps immobile 7*, Paris: Bernard Grasset, 1983, pp. 194–8 (quote on p. 195).
59 Haliczer, *Sexuality in the Confessional*, p. 3.
60 Alfonso de' Ligouri, *Préceptes sur le sixième commandment*, 1835, p. 5, cited in HS I 30/21; see A 204/220.
61 Donatien-Alphonse de Sade, *120 Days of Sodom*, ed. I. Pauvert, pp. 139–40, cited in HS I 30–1/21.
62 H. C. Lea, *A History of Auricular Confession and Indulgences in the Latin Church*, Philadelphia, 3 vols., 1896. See the editors' note at A 181 n. 11/195 n. 11and their discussion at A 325–30/340–4.
63 See DE#206 III, 313; P/K 211 for the first reference to Tertullian, though a little later in this interview he is mentioning classical sources including Euripides and the Stoics (DE#206 III, 316; P/K 214). For a discussion, see Jeremy R. Carrette, RC 43; and his *Foucault and Religion: Spiritual Corporality and Political Spirituality*, London: Routledge, 2000.
64 Marchetti and Salomoni, A 325/340.
65 On the 1978 fragment, see Philippe Chevallier, *Michel Foucault et le Christianisme*, Lyon: ENS Éditions, 2011, pp. 149–50. Chevallier also had access to a brief A–Z bibliographical list dating from this time in the late 1970s – he suggests '1975 ? – 1978 ?' as its dating (pp. 8, 77 n. 59).
66 BANC CD 964, 967–70.

67   The topics of the Berkeley and Stanford lectures in May are not known; the March Montreal lecture (IMEC D215) appeared as 'Alternatives à la prison: diffusion ou décroissance du contrôle social? Une entrevue avec Michel Foucault', *Criminologie*, 26 (1), 1993: 13–34; trans. Couze Venn as 'Alternative to the Prison: Dissemination or Decline of Social Control', *Theory, Culture and Society*, 26 (6), 2009: 12–24.
68   On this theme see also DE#186 III, 123–4; DE#200 III, 268; PPC 123; DE#229 III, 515; SKP 145–6; DE#297 IV, 189–90, 191–2; SKP 157, 159–60.
69   The name of the journal derives from a French mnemonic: *Mais où est donc Ornicar?*
70   This opening exchange is omitted from P/K 194–228.
71   This text also appeared in the Italian translation: *La volontà di sapere*, trans. Pasquale Pasquino and Giovanna Procacci, Feltrinelli, Milano 1978, pp. 7–8, in which it is signed, located and dated. A translation of the Italian can be found as 'Preface to the Italian edition of *La volonté de savoir*', trans. Lorenzo Chiesa, *Pli: Warwick Journal of Philosophy*,13, 2002: 11–12.
72   Peter Maass and David Brock, 'The power and politics of Michel Foucault', *Inside (Daily Californian)*, 22 April 1983: 7, 20–22, p. 22.
73   Mort and Peters, 'Foucault Recalled', p. 12.

4   From Infrastructures to Governmentality

1   In SMBD viii/x; see Eribon, *Michel Foucault*, p. 407/258.
2   François Fourquet and Lion Murard, *Les équipments du pouvoir: Villes, territoires et équipements collectifs*, Paris: Union Générale d'Éditions, 1976; originally an issue of *Recherches* in 1973.
3   Anne Querrien, *Généalogie des équipements collectifs: L'école primaire*, Fontenay-sous-Bois: CERFI, 1975; L'enseignement 1. L'école primaire, *Recherches*, 23, 1976. François Fourquet, *Généalogie des équipements collectifs: Histoire des services collectifs dans la comptabilité nationale*, Fontenay-sous-Bois: CERFI, 1976; *Les Comptes de la puissance: histoire de la comptabilité nationale et du plan*, Paris: Recherches, 1980. See also *La programmation des équipements collectifs dans les villes nouvelles (Les équipements d'hygiene mentale)*, Paris: CERFI, 1972.
4   IMEC D.2.4.a/FCL2.A04–03.01, p. 1.
5   IMEC D.2.4.a/FCL2.A04–03.01, p. 2.
6   IMEC D.2.4.b/FCL2.A04–03.02, p. 18.
7   *Résistances à la medicine et démultiplication du concept de santé*, CORDES/Commisariat Général du Plan, November 1980, IMEC D.2.4.d/FCL2.A04–03.04. Donzelot's paper from this is translated as 'Pleasure in Work', in Graham Burchell, Colin Gordon and Peter Miller (eds.) *The Foucault Effect: Studies in Governmentality*, Chicago: University of Chicago Press, 1991, pp. 251–80.

8   IMEC D.2.3/FCL2.A04–04.
9   *Généalogie des équipements de normalisation: Les équipements sanitaires*, sous la direction de Michel Foucault, Fontenay-sous-Bois: CERFI, 1976.
10 The third part appeared in longer form as *Recherches*, 17 in 1975 and in an abridged second edition as François Fourquet and Lion Murard, *Histoire de la psychiatrie de secteur*, Paris: Recherches, 1980.
11 His contribution to the 1976 volume is entitled 'Architecture de l'hôpital'; the 1979 one 'Le camp et la forteresse inversée'.
12 Bruno Fortier (ed.) *La politique de l'espace parisien (à la fin de l'Ancien Régime)*, Paris: CORDA, 1975. The other contributors were Blandine Barret-Kriegel, François Beguin, Daniel Friedmann, and Alain Monchablon.
13 *Naissance de la clinique: Une archéologie du regard médical*, Paris: PUF, 1963, p. 25; trans. Alan Sheridan as *The Birth of the Clinic: An Archaeology of Medical Perception*, London: Routledge, 1973, p. 25.
14 There is now a large literature on the police in this sense. See, for example, Mark Neocleous, *The Fabrication of Social Order: A Critical Theory of Police Power*, London: Pluto, 2000.
15 Michel Foucault (ed.) *Politiques de l'habitat (1800–1850)*, Paris: CORDA, 1977, p. 3.
16 IMEC D.2.2.a/FCL2.A04–02.01, p. 1.
17 IMEC D.2.2.a/FCL2.A04–02.01, p. 1.
18 IMEC D.2.2.b/FCL2.A04–02.02.
19 See IMEC D.2.2.a/FCL2.A04–02.01; IMEC D.2.2.b/FCL2.A04–02.02; and 'Influence des strategies administratives et hygiéniques dans l'histoire des espaces verts à Paris', IMEC D.2.1/FCL2.A04–05, p. 15.
20 'Exposé du sujet', IMEC D.2.2.c/FCL2.A04–02.03, p. 1.
21 IMEC D.2.2.c/FCL2.A04–02.03, p. 2.
22 IMEC D.2.2.c/FCL2.A04–02.03, pp. 3–4.
23 IMEC D.2.2.c/FCL2.A04–02.03, p. 5.
24 IMEC D.2.2.c/FCL2.A04–02.03, p. 7.
25 IMEC D.2.2.c/FCL2.A04–02.03, p. 9.
26 IMEC D.2.2.c/FCL2.A04–02.03, pp. 11, 12.
27 IMEC D.2.2.c/FCL2.A04–02.03, p. 12.
28 Bruno Fortier, Untitled, IMEC D.2.2.d/FCL2.A04–02.04.
29 Fortier, IMEC D.2.2.d/FCL2.A04–02.04, pp. 7–8, 9, 13.
30 Fortier, IMEC D.2.2.d/FCL2.A04–02.04, p. 10.
31 Fortier, IMEC D.2.2.d/FCL2.A04–02.04, pp. 19–20.
32 Fortier, IMEC D.2.2.d/FCL2.A04–02.04, p. 20.
33 See IMEC D.2.1/FCL2.A04–05.
34 IMEC D.2.1/FCL2.A04–05, p. 1.
35 IMEC D.2.1/FCL2.A04–05, pp. 3, 7.
36 Alain Demangeon and Bruno Fortier, *Les vaisseaux et les villes*, Bruxelles: Pierre Mardaga, 1978.
37 IMEC D.2.1/FCL2.A04–05, pp. 1–2.
38 IMEC D.2.1/FCL2.A04–05, p. 4.

39   IMEC D.2.1/FCL2.A04–05, p. 5.
40   IMEC D.2.1/FCL2.A04–05, pp. 16–17.
41   IMEC D.2.1/FCL2.A04–05, pp. 17–22.
42   IMEC D.2.1/FCL2.A04–05, p. 24.
43   Blandine Kriegel, *L'histoire à l'Age classique*, Paris: PUF, 4 vols., 1978.
44   Blandine Kriegel, *L'état et les esclaves: Réflexions pour l'histoire des états*, Paris: Calmann-Lévy, 1979; trans. Marc A. LePain and Jeffrey C. Cohen, *The State and the Rule of Law*, Princeton: Princeton University Press, 1995.
45   See works already cited along with François Ewald, *Histoire de l'état providence: Les origins de la solidarité*, Paris: Éditions Grasset et Fasquelle, 1986.
46   On this shift, see Senellart, STP 381–2/369–70.
47   See Senellart, STP 387 n. 33/394 n. 33 and the discussion in Chapter 7.
48   In a 1975 interview in Brazil, Foucault dates this shift to the seventeenth century, but broadens his analysis to include criminal confession (DE#163, II 809–11).
49   'Governmentality, Calculation, Territory', *Environment and Planning D: Society and Space*, Vol. 25 No. 3, 2007, pp. 562–80; 'How should we do the History of Territory?' *Territory, Politics, Governance*, 1 (1), 2013: 5–20.
50   See *The Birth of Territory*, Chicago: University of Chicago Press, 2013.
51   An earlier English version, a transcript of the texts as delivered, is found as BANC 90/136z 1:9.
52   John Chrysostom, *De Sacerdotio*, VI, 4.
53   Paul Veyne, 'La famille et l'amour sous le Haut-Empire romain', *Annales: Économies, Sociétés, Civilisations*, 33 (1), 1978: 35–63; and *Le Pain et le cirque: sociologie historique d'un pluralisme politique*, Seuil, Paris, 1976; *Bread and Circuses: Historical Sociology and Political Pluralism*, abridged by Oswyn Murray, trans. Brian Pearce, London: Allen Lane, 1990.
54   Gregory Nazianzen, *Oration II*.
55   St Gregory the Great, *Liber regulae pastoralis* (*The Book of Pastoral Rule*), I, 1. In the translation by George E. Demacopoulos, St Vladimir's Seminary Press, Crestwood, NY, 2007 p. 29, this is translated as 'the care of souls is the art of arts'.
56   On shifting meanings of 'government', see STP 124–6/120–2.
57   The PPC reference is to an interview not in DE. See 'Du pouvoir', in Bernard Pivot (ed.), *Ecrire, lire, et en parler: Dix années de littérature mondiale en 55 interviews publiées dans LIRE*, Paris: Robert Laffont, 1985, p. 359. See also A 161–3/174–6.
58   The day before the course finished he took part in an interview about sexuality and children in relation to criminal law (DE#263; PPC 271–85).
59   The most interesting of these is DE#234, which has some fascinating discussion of space, literature, theatre and opera.
60   See Senellart, STP 387/374.

61 This text, along with two responses by Foucault, appeared in Michèle Perrot, *L'impossible prison: Recherches sur le système pénitentiare au XIXe siècle*, Paris: Seuil, 1980.
62 This was initially published as 'Qu'est-ce que la critique? (Critique et *Aufklärung*)', *Bulletin de la Société française de philosophie*, 84 (2), 1990: 25–63; now in QC.
63 An almost complete set of English translations can be found in 'Appendix: Foucault and his Critics, An Annotated Translation', in Janet Afary and Kevin B. Anderson, *Foucault and the Iranian Revolution: Gender and the Seductions of Islamism*, Chicago: University of Chicago Press, 2005, pp. 179–277. With the exception of the first, the French versions (some original, some retranslations), can be found in DE # 241, 243–5, 248–9, 251–3, 259, 261–2, 265, 269, III 662–9, 679–94, 701–6, 708–16, 743–55, 759–62, 780–2, 790–4. A text previously only published in Arabic has recently been discovered: Farès Sassine, 'Il ne peut pas y avoir de sociétés sans soulèvements: Entretien inédit avec Michel Foucault', *Révue Rodeo*, 2, 2013:34–56.
64 For a sample, see Macey, *The Lives of Michel Foucault*, pp. 406–11; Afary and Anderson, *Foucault and the Iranian Revolution*; and Marcelo Hoffmann, *Foucault and Power: The Influence of Political Engagement on Theories of Power*, New York: Bloomsbury, 2014, ch. 4.
65 Afary and Anderson, *Foucault and the Iranian Revolution*, p. 209.
66 Though see C 52/66, which dates the seminar on juridical thought to 1978, along with a 'separate seminar on "The Genealogy of Societies of Security"…led by François Ewald'. Defert suggests that in 1979 there was 'a seminar on "Method in the History of Ideas"', which looks at 'techniques of risk management in modern societies' (C 56/70), but this seems like a conflation of two things: the overall theme of the seminar and the first session.
67 See, among many others, Geoffroy de Lagasnerie, *La dernière leçon de Michel Foucault: Sur le néoliberalisme, la théorie et la politique*, Fayard, 2012. The best overall account remains Thomas Lemke, *Eine Kritik der politischen Vernunft: Foucaults Analyse der modernen Gouvernementalität*, Hamburg/Berlin: Argument Verlag, 1997.
68 Interview with Defert, 12 April 2015.
69 Interview with Defert, 12 April 2015.
70 This distinction is introduced in his discussion with historians in 1978 (DE#278 IV, 22; EW III, 225).
71 Foucault links his previous discussion of crime and penalty to Becker, 'Crime and Punishment: An Economic Approach' (*Journal of Political Economy*, 76 (2), 1968: 196–217), especially in relation to earlier work of Beccaria and Bentham (BB 256/251). Foucault also mentions the hereditary elements of human capital, which provides another link back to earlier work (BB 233–5/227–9).
72 Eribon, *Michel Foucault*, p. 257.
73 See though his later note GL 332 n. 60/350 n. 60 where this manuscript is simply said to be among the materials of the 1979 course.

74 Robert Badinter, *Liberté, libertés: Réflexions du comité pour une charte des libertés*, Paris: Gallimard, 1976. The discussion was only published after Foucault's death: 'Michel Foucault à Goutelas: la redéfinition du 'judiciable', *Justice [Syndicat de la Magistrature]*, 115, June 1984: 36–9.

75 Eribon, *Michel Foucault*, pp. 477–8/297.

76 Reported in Clare O'Farrell, 'Foucault: A View from the Antipode', in Clare O'Farrell (ed.), *Foucault: The Legacy*, Brisbane: Queensland University of Technology, 1997, pp. 1–10, p. 5.

77 Eribon, *Michel Foucault*, pp. 492–5/305–7; see Macey, *The Lives of Michel Foucault*, p. 460. For a discussion, see Marcelo Hoffman, 'Beyond Foucault on the Political Party', unpublished manuscript.

78 Interview with Defert, 12 April 2015; see DE 357 IV, 734 n. * where it is referred to as the 'white book'; Miller, *The Passion of Michel Foucault*, p. 454 n. 28; Rosa Rodríguez, 'The Female Subject after the Death of Man', in Ricardo Miguel-Alfonso and Silvia Caporale-Bizzini (eds.), *Reconstructing Foucault: Essays in the Wake of the 80s*, Amsterdam: Rodopi, 1994, p. 257.

79 Jamin Raskin, 'A last interview with French philosopher Michel Foucault', *City Paper*, Vol. 8 No. 3, 27 July–2 August 1984, p. 18. There is a very interesting discussion of Foucault's relation to socialism in an interview conducted on 21 April 1983 at Berkeley, BANC CD 843 pt 1–2.

5 Return to Confession

1 Claude Mauriac, *Mauriac et fils: Le temps immobile 9*, Paris: Bernard Grasset, 1986, p. 328; Macey, *Lives of Michael Foucault*, pp. 370–1.

2 Senellart, GL 332/334.

3 See Philippe Ariès, 'Saint Paul et la chair', *Communications*, Vol. 35, 1982, p. 34.

4 Michael Meranze, personal correspondence, 10 July 2015, recalls how important Peter Brown, *Augustine of Hippo: A Biography*, Berkeley: University of California Press, 1967, was for Foucault.

5 See BNF NAF28284 (3), Folder J, p. 10. On this transition, see Macey, *The Lives of Michel Foucault*, pp. 415–6; Eribon, *Michel Foucault*, pp. 467–8/291–2; Senellart, GL 335/336.

6 Dio Cassius, *Roman History*, 77, 11

7 Senellart notes that Foucault worked very thoroughly on Cajetan, referencing a 62-page set of notes (GL 88–9 n. 8/90–1 n. 8).

8 *Dictionnaire des philosophes*, ed. Denis Huisman, Paris: PUF, 2 vols., 1984, Vol. I, pp. 941–4. The opening paragraph of the text by Ewald, which precedes the sentence by him in brackets, is not included in the reprint in DE#345, 631–6; EW II 459–63.

9 Defert and Ewald, DE#345 IV, 631. Little of this explanatory note appears in EW II, 459 n. *

10 Conversation with Arpád Szakolczai, in *Max Weber and Michel Foucault: Parallel Life-Works*, London: Routledge, 1988, p. 270 n. 4.
11 This is relegated to a note in SV 299 n. 1.
12 On 6 May 1980, Foucault met with theologians, mainly Jesuits, organized by James Bernauer (see Bernauer, RC xvii; Carrette, RC 2).
13 A typescript exists as 'Howison Lectures at Berkeley', BANC 90/136z 1:11.
14 I am grateful to Peter Brown for sharing his memories of their conversations.
15 One of these was previously published as 'Power, Moral Values, and the Intellectual', trans. Michael Bess, *History of the Present*, 4, 1988: 1–2, 11–13. The other is previously unpublished. English edition forthcoming as *About the Beginning of the Hermeneutics of the Subject: Lectures at Dartmouth College, 1980*, trans. Graham Burchell, Chicago: University of Chicago Press, 2015.
16 Michel Foucault and Richard Sennett, 'Sexuality and Solitude', *London Review of Books*, 3 (9), 21 May 1981: 3–7. The original publication bookends Foucault's lecture with an introduction and a short conclusion by Sennett. These are not included in most reprints (i.e. EW I 175–84), nor in the French translation (DE#295, IV 168–78).
17 BANC CD 971. I am grateful to Mark Blasius for discussions of this lecture and providing me with a better recording.
18 For a sequence of references tracing the use of this phrase see OHS 54 n. 4.
19 See also: 'I had to reject *a priori* theories of the subject in order to analyse the relationships that may exist between the constitution of the subject or different forms of the subject and games of truth, practices of power, etc.' (DE#356 IV, 718; EW I, 290; see DE#295 IV, 169–70; EW I, 176–7).
20 Unpublished manuscript from September 1980, cited by Gros, HSu 508/526.
21 Foucault used this same story in his 1963 essay 'L'eau et la folie' (DE#16 I, 270–1).
22 In the 'Sexuality and Solitude' introduction, Sennett that says they used the phrase 'the technology of the self" in the seminar; Foucault also uses 'technologies of the self' in his lecture (EW I 177; DE#295 IV, 171).
23 The passage in brackets was only said at Berkeley.
24 This may have been anticipated by a comment in GL 301/307, though Senellart notes that the unpaginated manuscript does not provide a definitive answer (GL 312 n. 55/319 n. 55).
25 Saint Francis de Sales, *Introduction to the Devout Life*, Book III, 39 – trans. John K. Ryan, London: Longmans, Green and Co., 1953, p. 248. This reappears in SV.
26 Foucault suggests that he had drafted a discussion of Augustine, and especially the *Confessions*, for the Berkeley lectures, but had not had time to deliver it (OHS 107).

27 'Sexuality and Solitude', in Marshall Blonsky, *On Signs*, Oxford: Blackwell, 1985, p. 371. Unlike the LRB version, this is based on the written text, not the transcript. For a comparison of the second half of the lecture see RC 182–7.

28 For an analysis of *The Abnormals* in relation to the destroyed *La Chair et le corps*, see Marchetti and Salomoni, A 325–30/340–4; and Marchetti, 'La chair et les corps', *Critique*, 660, May 2002: 354–67.

29 Henry Charles Lea, *A History of Auricular Confession and Indulgences in the Latin Church*, Philadelphia: Lea Brothers and Co., 3 vols., 1896.

30 Marchetti and Salomoni, A 324/340–1.

31 According to the editors (A 184 n. 38/197–8 n. 38), Foucault's source may be Lea, *A History of Auricular Confession*, Vol. I, p. 395, although his reference to the first confessional dates from 1516, while Lea's reference is to 1565. The editors were unable to validate Foucault's earlier reference.

32 See Chapter 1. Interestingly, Jean Gerson, who occupies a central place in the history of the confession of masturbation, is only mentioned briefly in the course summary rather than the course itself (A 309/326). For a detailed discussion see Tentler, *Sin and Confession*, especially pp. 91–3.

33 Chevallier, *Michel Foucault et le Christianisme*, pp. 149–50, 152 n. 70.

34 Senellart, GL 345 n. 127/354 n. 127; see Chapter 7.

35 Lea, *A History of Auricular Confession*, I, p. 230.

36 Pierre J. Payer, 'Foucault on Penance and the Shaping of Sexuality', *Studies in Religion*, 14 (3), 1985: 313–20.

37 Payer, 'Foucault on Penance', p. 315; see also Tentler, *Sin and Confession*, p. 223.

38 Payer, 'Foucault on Penance', p. 317.

39 The version in DE#349 IV, 658 differs in small respects.

40 For a contemporary summary of these lectures by one of the auditors, see Jean François, 'Aveu, Vérité, Subjectivité: Autour d'un enseignement de Michel Foucault', *Revue interdisciplinaire d'études juridiques*, 7, 1981: 163–82.

41 Françoise Tulkens (eds.), *Généalogie de la défense sociale en Belgique (1880–1914): Travaux du séminaire qui s'est tenu à l'Université Catholique de Louvain sous la direction de Michel Foucault*, Bruxelles: E. Story-Scientia, 1988. On this seminar see also Tulkens, 'Contributions au séminaire "Généalogie de la défense sociale en Belgique (1880–1914)"', *CRID&P*, 5 (1), 1985: 1–12. Foucault briefly comments on the purpose of the seminar in a contemporaneous interview (WDTT 248–9/255).

42 Brion and Harcourt, WDTT v/3.

43 Brion and Harcourt, WDTT -/271–2.

44 Brion and Harcourt, WDTT -/272.

45 Brion and Harcourt, WDTT 294/300.

46 See Francesco Paulo Adorno, *Le style du philosophe: Foucault et le dire vrai*, Éditions Kimé, Paris. 1986, pp. 86–7.

6 The Pleasures of Antiquity

1 See also Eribon, *Michel Foucault*, pp. 517/318. If the 'Maurice Florence' text is indeed a fragment of this introduction, there is no trace of it there. Based no doubt on conversations with Foucault, Dreyfus and Rabinow suggest that 'Volume 2 of *The History of Sexuality* was to have begun with an analysis of the early Christian confessional practices which constituted a hermeneutics of desire. This was to include an introductory chapter on the relation of sexuality and self-mastery in ancient culture. The chapter soon became problematic for two reasons.' One was historical, the other was the focus on self-care. 'Foucault thus had to modify his original hypothesis that elaboration of techniques of self-analysis and control was a Christian invention' ('Foucault's Interpretative Analytic of Ethics: Afterword (1983)', in *Michel Foucault*, p. 254).

2 See Discussion with Dreyfus and Rabinow, 21 April 1983, IMEC D250(6), p. 5.

3 Foucault reuses this phrase at the end of 'The Battle for Chastity' (DE#313 IV, 308; EW I, 196). See Peter Brown, *The Making of Late Antiquity*, Cambridge, MA: Harvard University Press, 1978, p. 2, where he talks a 'watershed', taking the phrase from W. H. C. Frend, *Martyrdom and Persecution in the Early Church: A Study of a Conflict from the Maccabees to Donatus*, Oxford: Basil Blackwell, 1965, p. 389. The division is not quite the same in all three authors: for Frend it is between antiquity and the Middle Ages; for Brown between 'the pagan, classical world and the Christian Late Roman Empire'; and for Foucault the difficulty of establishing a clear break between paganism and Christianity.

4 Foucault uses Artémidore, *La Clef des songes: Onirocriticon*, trans. A. J. Festugière, Paris: J. Vrin, 1975; though also makes reference to *The Interpretation of Dreams: Oneirocritica by Artemidorus*, trans. Robert J. White, Park Ridge: Noyes Press, 1975 (HS III, 17 n. 3/9 n. *). I have consulted both editions, and also the bi-lingual Daniel E. Harris-McCoy, *Artemidorus' Oneirocritica: Text, Translation, and Commentary*, Oxford: Oxford University Press, 2012.

5 Foucault actually says four chapters. They are Book I, Chapters 78, 79, 80.

6 The Festugière edition entitles this chapter '*Du rêve d'Œdipe*', but this does not appear in the Greek text or other editions.

7 Some years later (HS II 33 n. 1/255 n. 16), Foucault would reference Georges Duby's *Le chevalier, la femme et le prêtre: Le mariage dans la France féodale*, Paris: Hachette, 1981 as significant. Defert told me it was crucial to Foucault's understanding of medieval love and marriage (interview with Defert, 12 April 2015).

8 The source of Foucault's quote from Augustine is not clear, but these questions are explored in the *Confessions*, especially Book X.

9   Veyne, 'La Famille et l'amour à Rome sous le haut-empire romain'; Claude Vatin, *Recherches sur le mariage et la condition de la femme mariée à l'époque hellénistique*, Paris: de Boccard, 1970.

10 See HS II, 25–6/17.

11 Gros suggests (SV 271 n. 4, 318) that this is a likely allusion to Heidegger.

12 As Gros notes (SV 315–16) this is not a theme developed in Foucault's other writings of this period.

13 Otto Friedrich with Sandra Burton, 'France's Philosopher of Power', *Time*, 16 November 1981: 58–9.

14 Luther H. Martin, Huck Gutman and Patrick H. Hutton (eds.), *Technologies of the Self: A Seminar with Michel Foucault*, London: Tavistock, 1988, p. 8. n. 3. On this event, see William R. Hackman, 'The Foucault Conference', *Telos*, No 51, Spring 1982, pp. 191–6; Friedrich with Burton, 'France's Philosopher of Power'.

15 Dreyfus and Rabinow, *Michel Foucault*, p. 208. The French original is found as 'Le pouvoir, comment s'exerce t'il?' BANC 90/136z 1:14.

16 Paul Rabinow, personal correspondence, 20 May 2015.

17 See Chapter 4 for a brief mention of the 1978 lecture; and the longer discussion in Chapter 7.

18 Gros, SV 320.

19 Keith Gandal says he was the treasurer of the French branch of Solidarity. 'Intellectual Work and Politics', *Telos*, 67, 1986: 121–34, p. 125.

20 Eribon, *Michel Foucault*, pp. 478–87/297–302.

21 Michel Foucault, Henry Juramy, Christian Revon, Jacques Vergès, Jean Lapeyrie, Dominique Nocaudie, 'Se défendre', *Pour la défense libre*, supplement to *Actes*, 24–5, 1979: 5–6. See C 57/73.

22 This draft is available in Paris: *Histoire de la sexualité*, BNF NAF28284 (2–5).

23 Discussion with Dreyfus and Rabinow, 19 April 1983, IMEC D250(5), p. 2; see Macey, *The Lives of Michel Foucault*, p. 425. Eribon, *Michel Foucault*, pp. 519–20/319, recounts the same story but suggests this refers to the promised *Le Gouvernement de soi et des autres*. (Eribon's account is amended between the two editions to reference the archived interview.)

24 Plutarch, *Sayings of Spartans*, in *Moralia*, vol. III, 217a.

25 On attribution and dating, see the introduction to Plato, *Alcibiades*, ed. Nicholas Denyer, Cambridge: Cambridge University Press, 2001.

26 On *parrēsia* see HSu 132–3/137, 158/164, 231–2/242, 348–9/366–7, and especially the lectures of 10 March 1982.

27 See Gros, HSu 195 n. 17/203 n. 17.

28 See also 'Plonger sur place ou plonger du sommet chez Marcus Aurèle: deux exercises spirituels' (extract from manuscript of 24 February 1982 lecture), in Philippe Artières, Jean-François Bert, Frédéric Gros and Judith Revel (eds.), *Cahier de L'Herne 95: Michel Foucault*, Paris: Éditions de L'Herne, 2011, pp. 105–6.

29 The reference is to Pierre Hadot, *Exercices spirituels et philosophie antique*, Paris: Albin Michel, 2002, pp. 145–64. For his discussion of Foucault's use of his work, which can be quite critical, see pp. 305–11 and 'Réflexions sur la notion de "culture de soi" ' in *Michel Foucault philosophe: Rencontre international, Paris 9, 10, 11* January 1988, Paris: Seuil, 1989, pp. 261–70.

30 See also 'Le gay savoir'; Thierry Voeltzel, *Vingt ans et après*, pp. 11–40; and EW I, 163–73; DE#358 IV, 735–46.

31 See Gros, HSu 41 n. 7/40 n. 7.

32 See Gros, HSu 416 n. 14/434 n. 14, who lists the key locations.

33 In September 1981, in discussion with Didier Eribon, Foucault related the influences he thought Lacan shared with Sartre: Hegel, Hypollite and Heidegger. Eribon's notes clarify: 'Heidegger put in question the entire philosophy of the subject from Descartes to Husserl, which Sartre took up again or it was thought he took it up again'. 'Appendice', in Didier Eribon, *Michel Foucault et ses contemporains*, 1994, Paris: Fayard, pp. 261–3, p. 262.

34 Gros, HSu 505/523–4.

35 On this relation more generally, see my *Mapping the Present*.

36 'Conferences on Semiotics, University of Toronto, Summer 1980 [*sic*]', BANC 90/136z, 1:10.

37 The first few pages are different (EW III, 403–7; DE#364 IV, 813–16), and close to the 1980 Princeton lecture, and then it is an expanded and amended version.

38 I have referenced the texts as they appear in EW I and III, which accord with the editorial notes in DE.

39 See Eribon, *Michel Foucault*, pp. 470–1/293, which reproduces the series' announcement, written by Foucault.

40 Unpublished manuscript in 'Culture de soi' dossier, cited by Gros, HSu 514/532.

7 The Two Historical Plans of the *History of Sexuality*

1 Foucault may have read Philippe Ariès, *L'enfant et la vie famille sous l'ancien régime*, Paris: Plon, 1960 when published, since they shared a publisher and Ariès was one of the readers of *Histoire de la folie* (DE#348 IV, 649). Part I, ch. 5 is entitled 'From Immodesty to Innocence', and shares some thematic relations with the material in the 1974–75 course, but he is not mentioned in either the lectures or the editors' notes. He is mentioned in DP. Foucault reviewed Ariès's *L'homme devant la mort*, Paris: Seuil, 1977 in 1978 (DE#225 III, 503–5), and briefly referred to him in a 1977 interview (DE#195 III, 192; P/K 148–9). He then wrote an obituary of him in 1984 (DE#347 IV, 646–9), and participated in an interview about his work alongside Arlette Farge for *Le matin* (DE#348 IV, 649–55).

2   Fragments of this manuscript are archived in Paris: *Histoire de la sexualité*, BNF NAF28284 (2–5). But rather than the files containing an entire manuscript of the earlier draft, they contain multiple versions of some sections, notably the introduction and the opening chapter of HS II; along with other material which has been reworked for the actually published Volumes II and III.

3   BNF NAF28284 (2), Folder 2, pp. 1–5. This is summarized in C 61/78–9, and see also Philippe Artières and Mathieu Potte-Bonville, *D'après Foucault: Gestes, luttes, programmes*, Paris: Points, 2012, pp. 173–4.

4   *The Foucault Reader* version (EW I, 199–205) later appeared in French as DE#340 IV, 578–84. But this was *not* a translation, even though that is the norm for texts first published in another language. The complete text of this fragment can be found in BNF NAF28284 (2), Folder 10; and BANC 90/136z 1:13. Only the 'Preface' was published; the 'Introduction' itself, divided into 'Question' and 'Method', was not.

5   BANC 90/136z 1:13, p. 48.

6   'The Culture of the Self', 12 April 1983, BANC CD 839 (lecture), 840–2 (discussions); in QC.

7   Phillip Horwitz, 'Don't Cry for Me Academia', *Jimmy and Lucy's House of K*, 2 August 1984, pp. 78–80.

8   Maass and Brock, 'The power and politics of Michel Foucault', p. 22. Defert told Mauriac how when he expressed his admiration of the finished book, Foucault replied that it had not given him much pleasure in the writing. Mauriac, *Le Temps accompli*, p. 32.

9   See BNF NAF28284 (3).

10 Gros, HSu 63 n. 36/63 n. 36.

11 See also Gros, HSu 493–4/513–14.

12 My interpretation thus differs from, for example, Eribon, *Michel Foucault*, pp. 520–1/310–1, who suggests the projects are integrated and merged.

13 Gros, HSu 496–7/514–15.

14 There is quite a lengthy discussion of writing in EW I, 272–77; DE#326 IV, 403–8.

15 See Gros, LHS 489/507–8, 496/514–15.

16 Gros, HSu 497–8/516–17.

17 Gros, HSu 499/517.

18 *Recherches sur la philosophie et le langage*, 3, 1983: 54–78.

19 A recently published lecture from Grenoble ('La Parrêsia', *Anabases*, 16, 2012: 157–88; trans. Graham Burchell as 'Parrēsia', *Critical Inquiry*, 41 (2), 2015: 219–53) is dated 18 May 1982. The manuscript has the date in Foucault's handwriting (Arnold I. Davidson, personal correspondence, 24 January 2015). It is not clear that two lectures were given on the same day, so it may be that Foucault gave the text on Artemidorus to the Grenoble House Journal instead. The difference in style shows the contrast between a lecture and a text for publication very clearly.

20   The reprint of this text in DE IV contains several editors' notes. There
     are no notes in the original.
21   The English translation sometimes uses 'ethics' and sometimes 'moral-
     ity' to translate la morale, even though those words are used to render
     other French words. I have translated as 'moral'. Foucault defines it as
     'an ensemble of values and rules of action that are recommended to
     individual through the intermediary of various prescriptive agencies
     such as the family, educational institutions, churches, and so forth',
     sometimes in a clear, codified way, and sometimes in a 'complex inter-
     play of elements' (HS II 36/25).
22   Eribon, Michel Foucault, pp. 520–1/319–20; Macey, The Lives of
     Michel Foucault, p. 466; Nora, 'Il avait un besoin formidable d'être
     aimé', p. 82; Defert, 'Je crois au temps...', p. 4.
23   Hubert Dreyfus and Paul Rabinow, Michel Foucault: Un parcours phi-
     losophique, trans. Fabienne Durand-Bogaert, Paris: Gallimard, 1984,
     pp. 322–46. This 1984 version appears as DE#344; a translation of the
     1983 English text appears as DE#326. There are several substantial
     changes.
24   See also DE#338 IV, 546; HS II, 20/12.
25   Michel Foucault, insert in L'Usage des plaisirs and Le Souci de soi,
     p. 2. The complete text is reproduced in Eribon, Michel Foucault,
     pp. 521–3/320–1.
26   Insert, p. 1.
27   Insert, p. 1.
28   The numbering does not appear in the French.
29   A passage in early drafts (see DE#338, IV 549 n. 2) which discusses the
     texts used, Foucault's use of Greek and Latin terms interpolated in
     translations, and his thanks to the Bibliothèque du Saulchoir is missing
     from HS 26 n. 2/255 n. 4.
30   'The Culture of the Self: Discussion with Department of History', 19
     April 1983, BANC CD 842; QC 132.
31   The importance of this term, and its plural nature, makes it surprising
     Robert Hurley chose The Use of Pleasure to translate L'Usage des
     plaisirs, though the plural appears at many other points in the English.
32   Helen North, Sophrosyne: Self-Knowledge and Self-Restraint in Greek
     Literature, Ithaca: Cornell University Press, 1966, pp. 202–3; Aristotle,
     Nicomachean Ethics, 1118b–1119a, 1150a–1152a.
33   The English translation is missing a clause of the French here.
34   Foucault's reference is to Plato, Protagoras, 309a, which validates the
     first half of the claim.
35   Preparatory material for 'Politics and Ethics', April 1983, BANC
     90/136z 1:4, pp. 2–3.
36   Sarah B. Pomeroy, Goddesses, Whores, Wives and Slaves: Women in
     Classical Antiquity, London: Robert Hale and Co., 1975; Veyne and
     Vatin are referenced above.
37   Foucault does note, though, that the texts he focuses on here are limited
     compared to work of this time on diet (HS III 189/140).

38 On their contemporary reception, see Luca Paltrinieri (ed.), *L'Usage des plaisirs et Le Souci de soi de Michel Foucault: Regards Critiques 1976–1979*, Caen: Presses Universitaires de Caen/IMEC, 2014.
39 'The Culture of the Self: Discussion with Department of History', 19 April 1983, BANC CD 842; QC 144.
40 The quote is from Cassian, *Institutiones*, Book VI, 6; *The Institutes*, trans. Boniface Ramsey, New York: The Newman Press, 2000, p. 155.
41 Interview with Defert, 12 April 2015; see Defert, 'Je crois au temps...', pp. 4–5.
42 Miller, *The Passion of Michel Foucault*, p. 465–6 n. 53, notes that the interview was conducted at Foucault's bedside. Foucault left it to Defert to correct the final version.
43 Eribon, *Michel Foucault*, pp. 521/319–20.
44 Interview with Defert, 12 April 2015; see Nora, 'Il avait un besoin formidable d'être aimé', p. 83. For a discussion of the uses of Foucault's apartment see Mathieu Lindon, *Ce qu'aimer veut dire*, Paris: POL, 2011.

8 Speaking Truth to Power

1 Defert and Ewald, DE#329 IV, 415. The English translation (EW I, 207) omits this editorial note. On this link, see also Gros, GSO 348/377.
2 Discussion with Dreyfus and Rabinow, 15 April 1983, IMEC D250(3), p. 10. For a detailed discussion of this period, see Pierre Payer, *Sex and the Penitentials: The Development of a Sexual Code 550–1150*, Toronto: University of Toronto Press, 1984.
3 Discussion with Dreyfus and Rabinow, 15 April 1983, IMEC D250(3), p. 3. The remark is cut from EW I 253; DE#326 IV, 384.
4 Jerry Wakefield recalls spending time with Foucault looking at medieval penitential texts at the Boalt Hall Law library at Berkeley in late 1983 (personal correspondence, 5 June 2015).
5 Before Foucault and Farge's work, the standard study was Frantz Funck-Brentano, *Les lettres de cachet*, Paris: Librarie Hachette, 1926.
6 C 43/53; Nora, 'Il avait un besoin formidable d'être aimé', p. 82; Macey, *Michel Foucault*, pp. 135–7; Eribon, *Michel Foucault*, p. 442/277. See Macey, *The Lives of Michel Foucault*, p. 453 where the planned book has a different title.
7 Marchetti and Salomoni, A 49 n. 6/53 n. 6.
8 DF 8; Eribon, *Michel Foucault*, p. 258. While cut from the 3rd edn, this can be found in *Michel Foucault*, Paris: Flammarion, 1991, p. 273.
9 Arlette Farge, *Delinquance et criminalité: Le vol d'aliments a Paris au XVIIIe siècle*, Paris, Plon, 1974, cited in DP 91 n. 4/311 n. 2, 92 n. 3/77.
10 Arlette Farge, *Vivre dans la rue à Paris au XVIIIe siècle*, Paris: Julliard/Gallimard, 1979, p. 10. See Defert and Ewald's note, DE#198 III, 237.

11 Arlette Farge, 'Travailler avec Michel Foucault', *Le Débat*, 41, 1986: 164–7; see Macey, *The Lives of Michel Foucault*, pp. 453–4; *Michel Foucault*, pp. 136–7. See also Keith Gandal and Paul Simmons, 'La vie fragile: An Interview with Arlette Farge', *History of the Present*, 2, 1986: 23–4.

12 Funck-Brentano, *Les Lettres de cachet*, p. 49.

13 Farge, 'Familles: L'honneur et le secret', p. 610.

14 This was long known. Funck-Brentano, *Les Lettres de cachet*, p. 249, argues that they were not 'a means of oppression at the hands of a royal power, he enforced a limitation on their use'. Instead, they were more of a 'spontaneous outburst from the underbelly of the people'.

15 Arlette Farge, 'Familles: L'honneur et le secret', in Philippe Ariès et Georges Duby (ed.) *Histoire de la vie privée Tome 3: De la Renaissance aux Lumières*, Paris: Seuil, 1986, pp. 581–619, p. 601.

16 Farge, 'Travailler avec Michel Foucault', p. 165; see Macey, *The Lives of Michel Foucault*, p. 455.

17 Farge, 'Familles: L'honneur et le secret'.

18 'La Parrêsia', 'Parrēsia'.

19 For a longer discussion, see my *Mapping the Present*, pp. 113–14.

20 Georges Dumézil, *Apollon sonore et autres essais: Vingt-cinq esquisses de mythologie*, Paris: Gallimard, 1982.

21 As Gros notes (GSO 155–6 n. 6/169 n. 6), this recalls the project of a 'dynastics of knowledge' proposed in 1972 (DE#119 II, 406).

22 Gros, GSO 356/384.

23 See also Gros, GSO 355/383.

24 See Gros, GSO 351–2/380.

25 In an undated manuscript page, c. 1983, Foucault uses 'historical ontology' as one of the ways to describe genealogy. BANC 90/136z, 1:13, n.p.

26 Joseph Pearson (ed.), *Discourse and Truth: The Problematization of ΠΑΡΡΗΣΙΑ – Notes to the Seminar given by Foucault at the University of California at Berkeley*, 1985, iii +121 pp.; *Fearless Speech*, ed. Joseph Pearson, Los Angeles: Semiotext(e), 2001. I am grateful to Pearson for confirming the subtitle was a later addition (personal correspondence, 26 July 2015). A critical edition of this text is forthcoming from Vrin.

27 A photo of this group with Foucault, who is wearing the cowboy hat they gave him, can be found in Eribon, *Michel Foucault*. I am grateful to Dario Biocca, Arturo Escobar, Keith Gandal, David Horn, David Levin, Mark Maslan, Jonathan Simon and Jerome Wakefield for sharing their memories of this time.

28 See Keith Gandal and Stephen Kotkin, 'Governing Work and Social Life in the USA and the USSR', *History of the Present*, 1, 1985: 4–14.

29 Keith Gandal, 'New Arts of Government in the Great War and Post-War Period', IMEC E.1.29/FCL2.A04–06, pp. 1, 3.

30 See Stephen Kotkin, *Magnetic Mountain: Stalinism as a Civilization*, Berkeley: University of California Press, 1995, p. xviii; David Horn, *Social Bodies: Science, Reproduction, and Italian Modernity*, Princeton:

Princeton University Press, 1994, p. ix; and Keith Gandal, *The Gun and the Pen: Hemingway, Fitzgerald, Faulkner, and the Fiction of Mobilization*, Oxford: Oxford University Press, 2008, p. vi.

31 Paul Rabinow, personal correspondence, 20 May 2015.

32 Quoted in Gandal, 'Intellectual Work and Politics', p. 134 n. 34.

33 See also Gros, CT 315–16/344–5.

34 Georges Dumézil, 'Nous devons un coq à Asklépios' in *Le Moyne noir en gris dedans Varennes'*, Paris: Gallimard, 1984, pp. 129–70.

35 Plato, *Phaedo*, 118a.

36 Peter Sloterdijk, *Kritik der zynischen Vernunft*, Frankfurt: Suhrkamp, 1983, trans. Michael Eldred as *Critique of Cynical Reason*, Minneapolis: University of Minnesota Press, 1987.

37 There were interviews conducted after this date, but no lectures.

38 On Foucault's illness and the aftermath, the best accounts are in Mauriac, *Le temps accompli*; Lindon, *Ce qu'aimer veut dire* and Daniel Defert, *Une vie politique: Entretiens avec Philippe Artières et Éric Favereau*, Paris: Seuil, 2014, ch. 6. A semi-fictionalized version can be found in Hervé Guibert, *À l'ami qui ne m'a pas sauvé la vie*, Paris: Gallimard, 1990.

39 On the very late Foucault, one of the best accounts in English is the first part of Edward McGuishin, *Foucault's Askēsis: An Introduction to the Philosophical Life*, Evanston, IL: Northwestern University Press, 2007.

40 The full manuscript of this draft of *L'Archéologie du savoir* is available as BNF NAF28284 (1).

41 The *Cahier L'Herne* contains these for a first draft of the introduction of the early draft of *L'Archéologie du savoir* and lectures on Picasso and Manet. His reading notes for *Les Mots et les choses* are available at http://lbf-ehess.ens-lyon.fr/ead.html?c=FRENS_00002_ref1475.

42 'Politics and Ethics: An Interview', *The Foucault Reader*, ed. Paul Rabinow, London: Penguin, 1991, p. 380; DE#341 IV, 590. The first remark is cut from a much longer passage of the original transcript: 'Power is not discipline, it is not violence and it is not domination . . . The relation of violence is a relation of force; the relation of power is something else' (BANC 90/136z 1:4, p. 27).

43 Daniel Defert, 'Les archives de Foucault ont une histoire politique', *Le Nouvel Observateur*, 26 November 2012.

Index